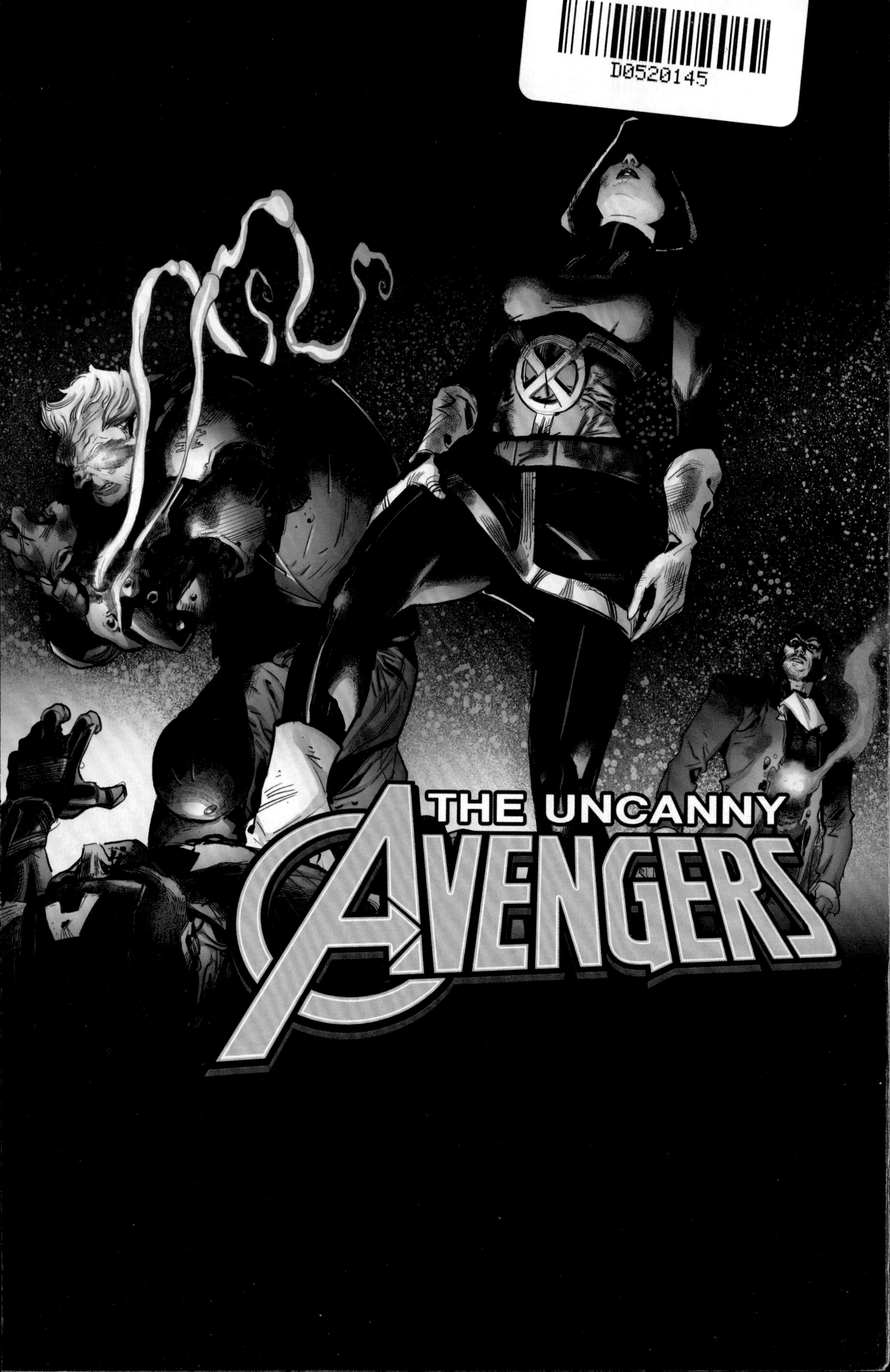
THE UNCANNY
AVENGERS

WHEN ULTRON MERGED WITH HANK PYM AND RETURNED TO EARTH, THE UNITY SQUAD TEAMED UP WITH OTHER AVENGERS TO DRIVE HIM INTO THE SUN. BUT THEIR MOMENT OF TRIUMPHANT COOPERATION WAS SHORT-LIVED. A NEW INHUMAN NAMED ULYSSES WITH THE ABILITY TO PREDICT THE FUTURE HAS DIVIDED THE SUPER HERO COMMUNITY, AND WITH NO CURE IN SIGHT FOR MUTANTS NEGATIVELY AFFECTED BY THE INHUMAN TERRIGEN MISTS, TENSIONS ARE RISING...

COLLECTION EDITOR: **JENNIFER GRÜNWALD**
ASSISTANT EDITOR: **CAITLIN O'CONNELL**
ASSOCIATE MANAGING EDITOR: **KATERI WOODY**
EDITOR, SPECIAL PROJECTS: **MARK D. BEAZLEY**
VP PRODUCTION & SPECIAL PROJECTS: **JEFF YOUNGQUIST**
SVP PRINT, SALES & MARKETING: **DAVID GABRIEL**
BOOK DESIGNER: **JAY BOWEN**

EDITOR IN CHIEF: **AXEL ALONSO**
CHIEF CREATIVE OFFICER: **JOE QUESADA**
PUBLISHER: **DAN BUCKLEY**
EXECUTIVE PRODUCER: **ALAN FINE**

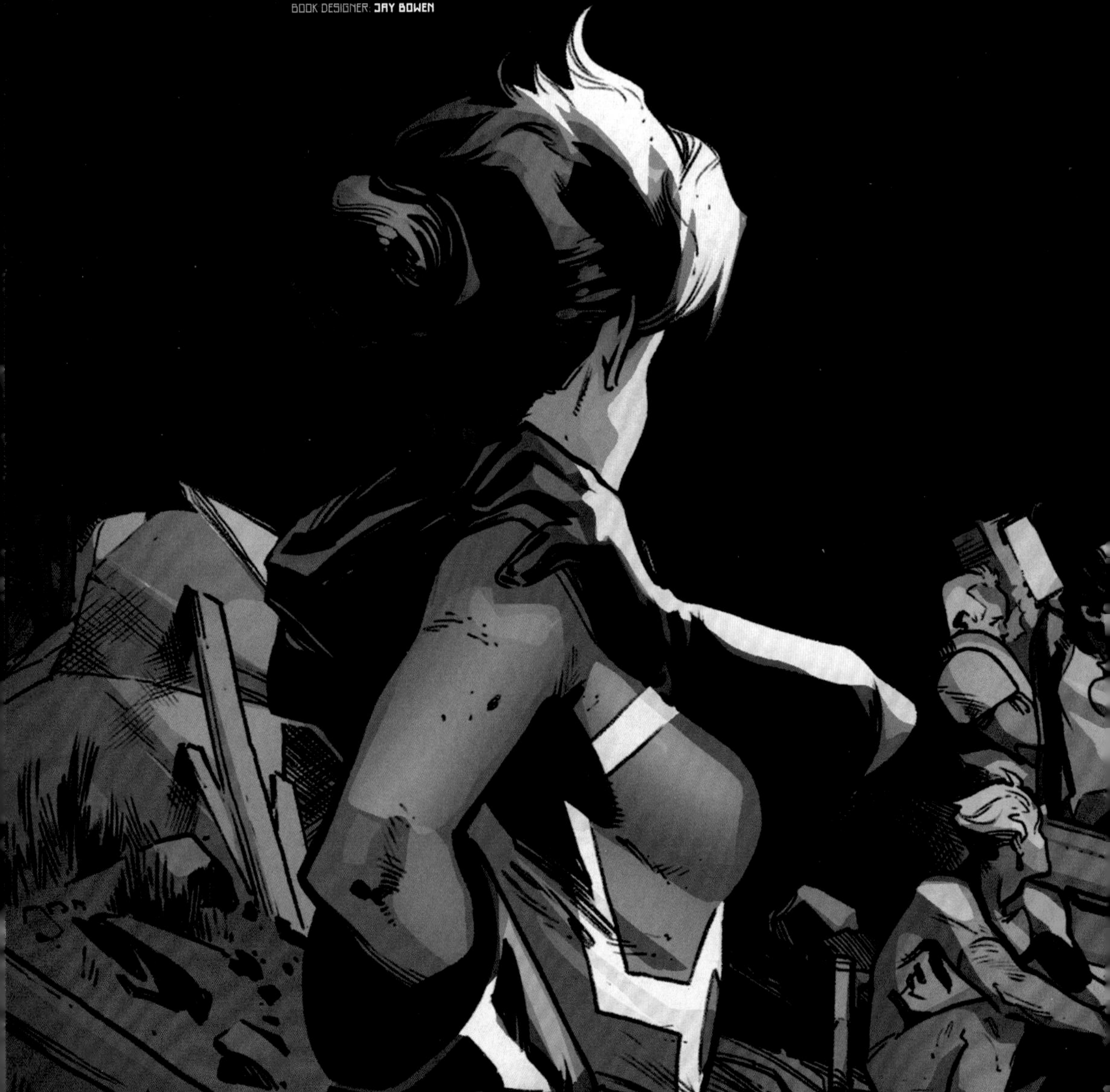

UNCANNY AVENGERS: UNITY VOL. 3 — CIVIL WAR II. Contains material originally published in magazine form as UNCANNY AVENGERS #13-17. First printing 2017. ISBN# 978-1-302-90234-6. Published by MARVEL WORLDWIDE, INC., a subsidiary of MARVEL ENTERTAINMENT, LLC. OFFICE OF PUBLICATION: 135 West 50th Street, New York, NY 10020.

Printed in Canada. ALAN FINE, President, Marvel Entertainment; DAN BUCKLEY, President, TV, Publishing & Brand Management; JOE QUESADA, Chief Creative Officer; TOM BREVOORT, SVP of Publishing; DAVID BOGART, SVP of Business Affairs & Operations, Publishing & Partnership; C.B. CEBULSKI, VP of Brand Management & Development, Asia; DAVID GABRIEL, SVP of Sales & Marketing, Publishing; JEFF YOUNGQUIST, VP of Production & Special Projects; DAN CARR, Executive Director of Publishing Technology; ALEX MORALES, Director of Publishing Operations; SUSAN CRESPI, Production Manager; STAN LEE, Chairman Emeritus. For information regarding advertising in Marvel Comics or on Marvel.com, please contact Vit DeBellis, Integrated Sales Manager, at vdebellis@marvel.com. For Marvel subscription inquiries, please call 888-511-5480. **Manufactured between 1/27/2017 and 2/28/2017 by SOLISCO PRINTERS, SCOTT, QC, CANADA.**

10 9 8 7 6 5 4 3 2 1

THE UNCANNY
AVENGERS
CIVIL WAR II

GERRY DUGGAN
WRITER

RYAN STEGMAN (#13-14)
& PEPE LARRAZ (#15-17)
ARTISTS

RICHARD ISANOVE (#13-14)
& DAVID CURIEL (#15-17)
COLOR ARTISTS

VC's CLAYTON COWLES
LETTERER

**RYAN STEGMAN &
RICHARD ISANOVE** (#13-14),
MEGHAN HETRICK (#15) AND
**STEVE McNIVEN, JAY LEISTEN
& DAVID CURIEL** (#16-17)
COVER ART

ALANNA SMITH
ASSISTANT EDITOR

TOM BREVOORT WITH
DANIEL KETCHUM
EDITORS

AVENGERS CREATED BY **STAN LEE** & **JACK KIRBY**

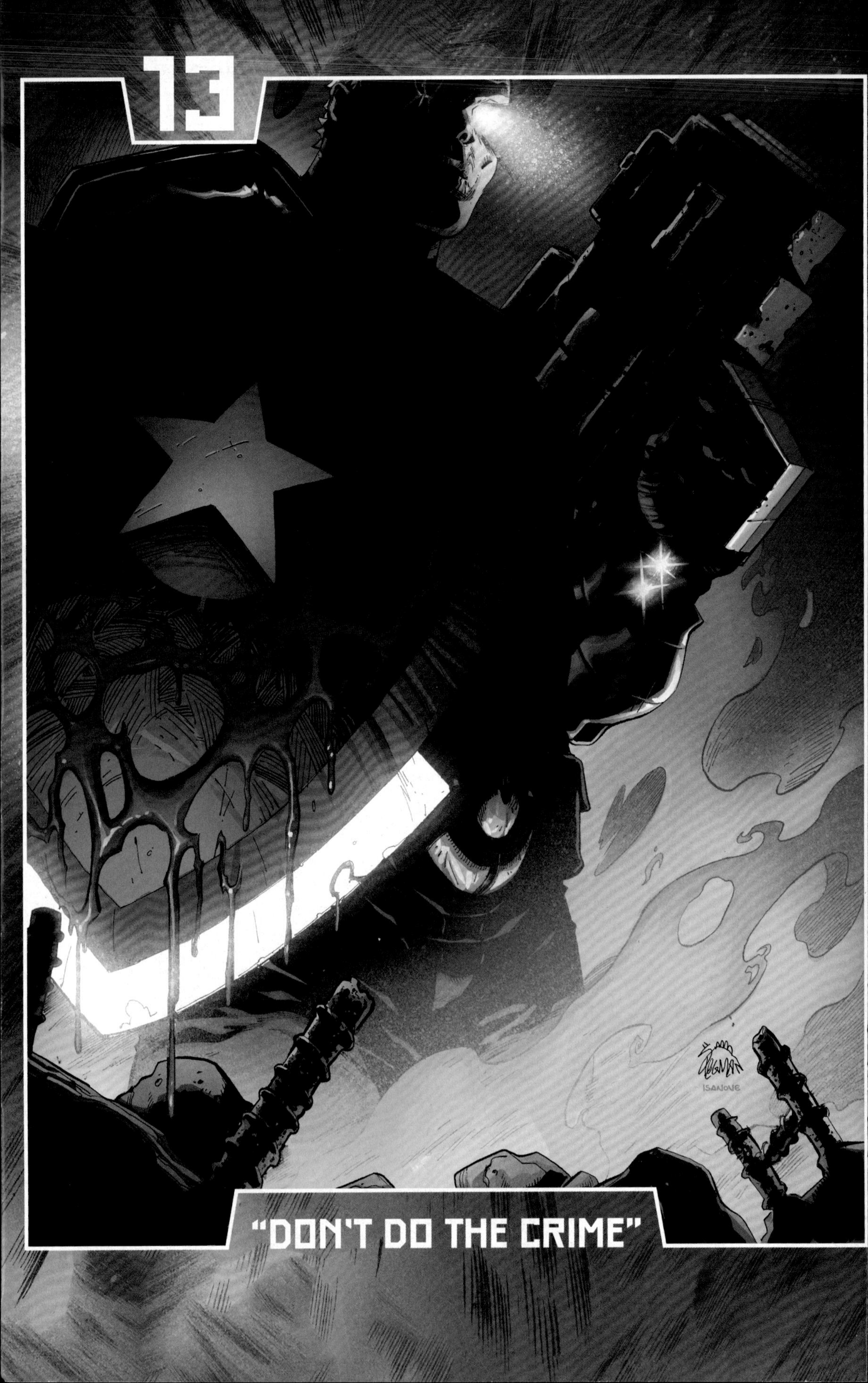
13
"DON'T DO THE CRIME"

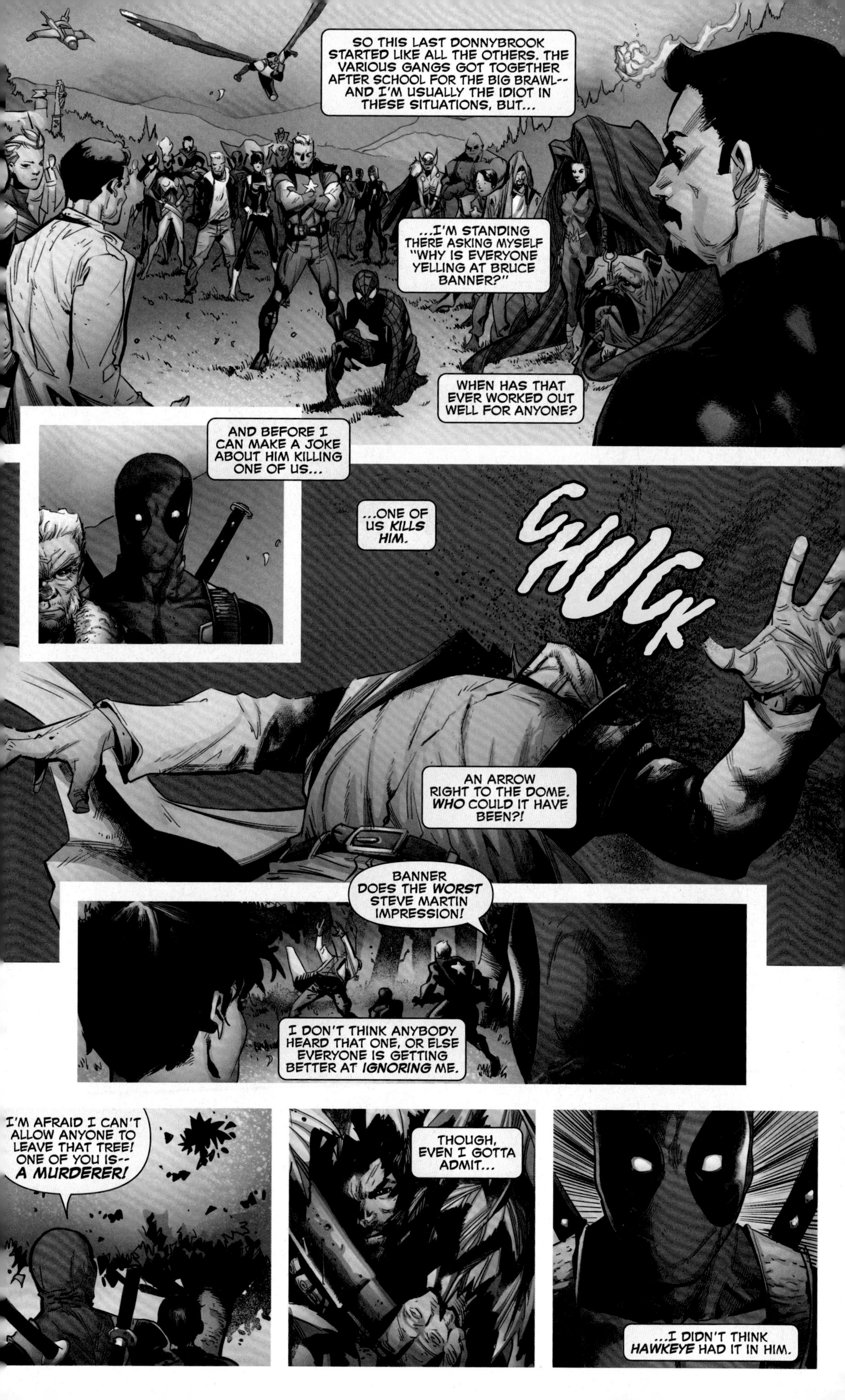
SO THIS LAST DONNYBROOK STARTED LIKE ALL THE OTHERS. THE VARIOUS GANGS GOT TOGETHER AFTER SCHOOL FOR THE BIG BRAWL--AND I'M USUALLY THE IDIOT IN THESE SITUATIONS, BUT...
...I'M STANDING THERE ASKING MYSELF "WHY IS EVERYONE YELLING AT BRUCE BANNER?"
WHEN HAS THAT EVER WORKED OUT WELL FOR ANYONE?
AND BEFORE I CAN MAKE A JOKE ABOUT HIM KILLING ONE OF US...
...ONE OF US KILLS HIM.
CHUCK
AN ARROW RIGHT TO THE DOME. WHO COULD IT HAVE BEEN?!
BANNER DOES THE WORST STEVE MARTIN IMPRESSION!
I DON'T THINK ANYBODY HEARD THAT ONE, OR ELSE EVERYONE IS GETTING BETTER AT IGNORING ME.
I'M AFRAID I CAN'T ALLOW ANYONE TO LEAVE THAT TREE! ONE OF YOU IS-- A MURDERER!
THOUGH, EVEN I GOTTA ADMIT...
...I DIDN'T THINK HAWKEYE HAD IT IN HIM.

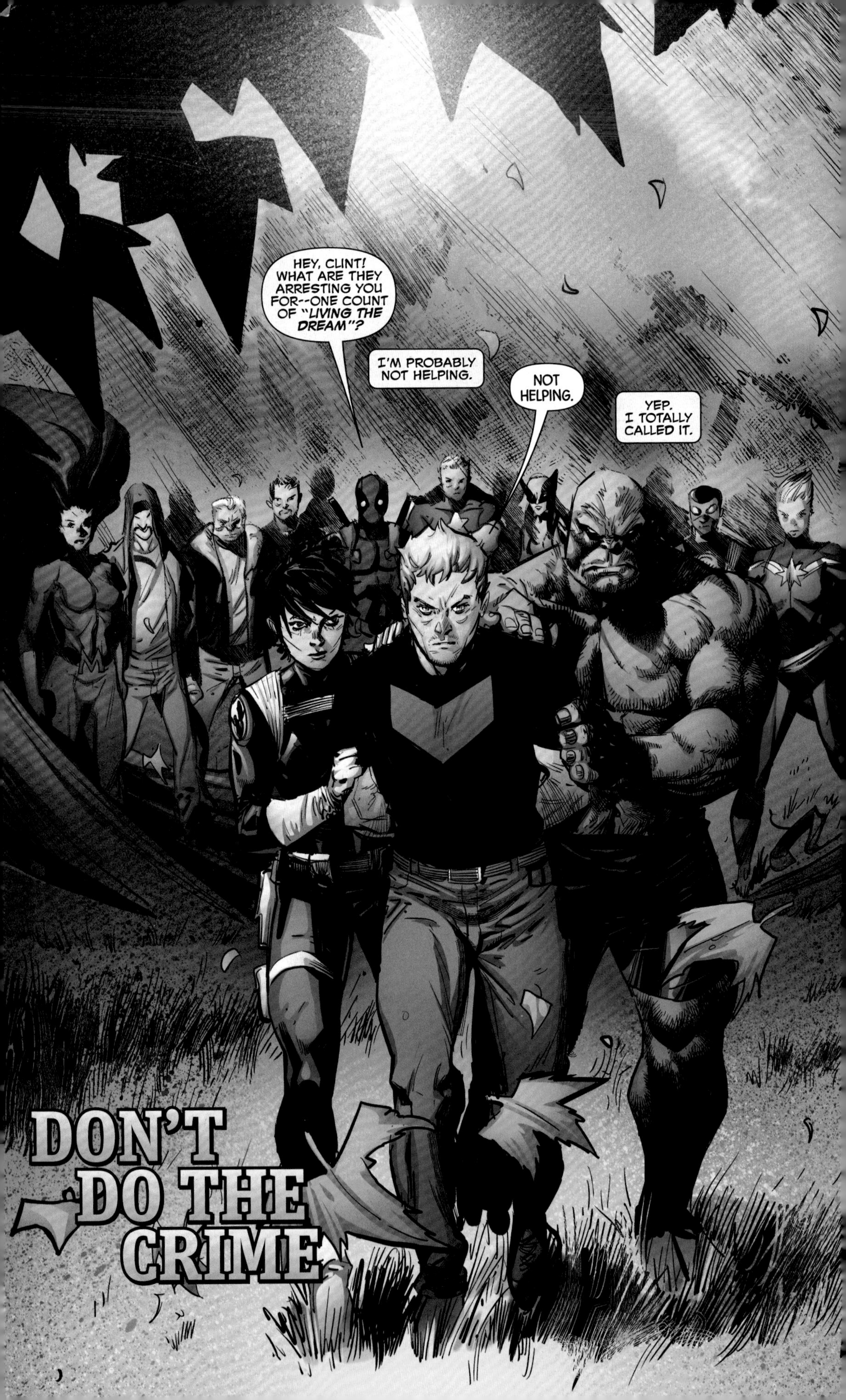
HEY, CLINT! WHAT ARE THEY ARRESTING YOU FOR--ONE COUNT OF "LIVING THE DREAM"?
I'M PROBABLY NOT HELPING.
NOT HELPING.
YEP. I TOTALLY CALLED IT.
DON'T DO THE CRIME

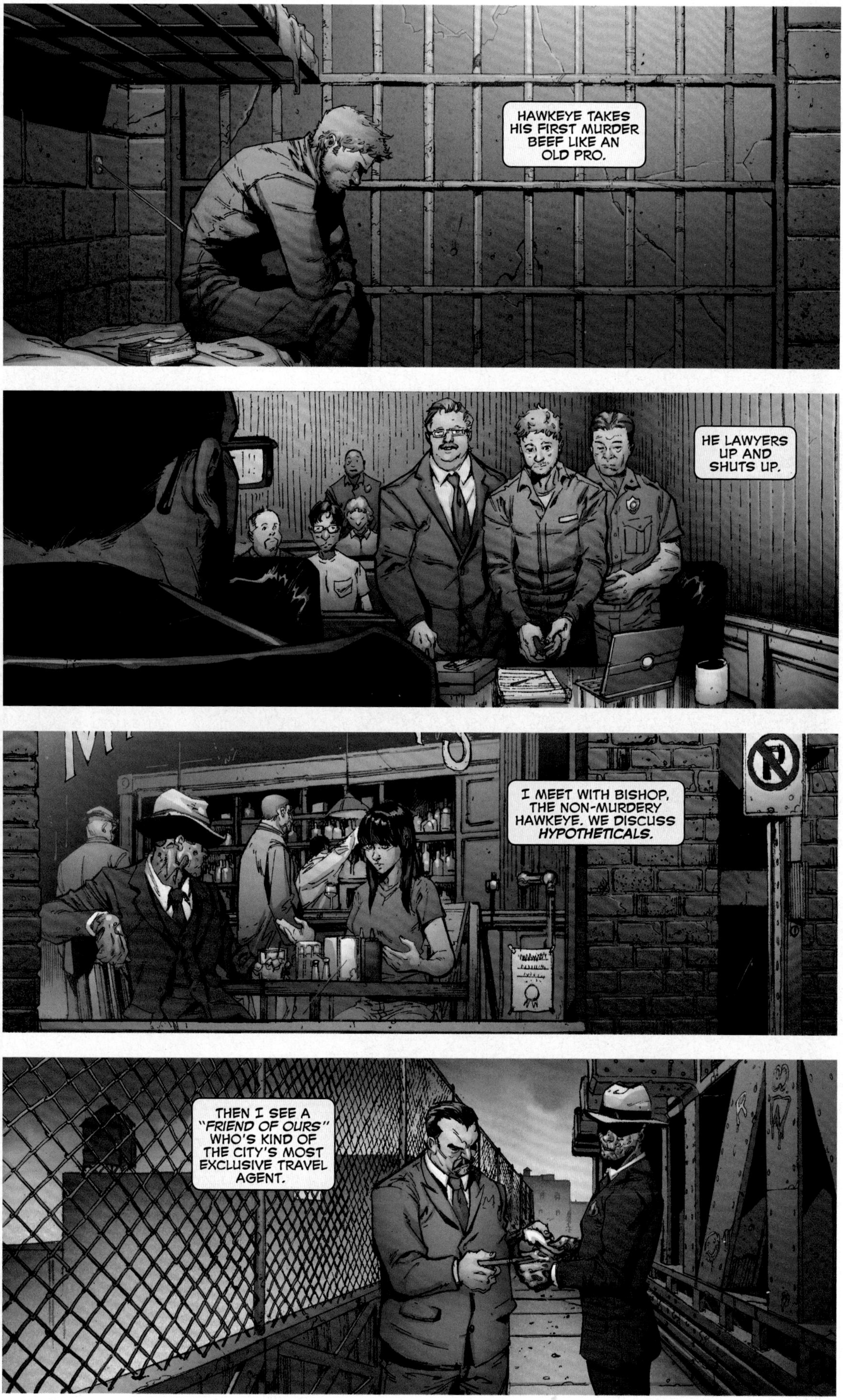
HAWKEYE TAKES HIS FIRST MURDER BEEF LIKE AN OLD PRO.
HE LAWYERS UP AND SHUTS UP.
I MEET WITH BISHOP, THE NON-MURDERY HAWKEYE. WE DISCUSS *HYPOTHETICALS.*
THEN I SEE A "*FRIEND OF OURS*" WHO'S KIND OF THE CITY'S MOST EXCLUSIVE TRAVEL AGENT.

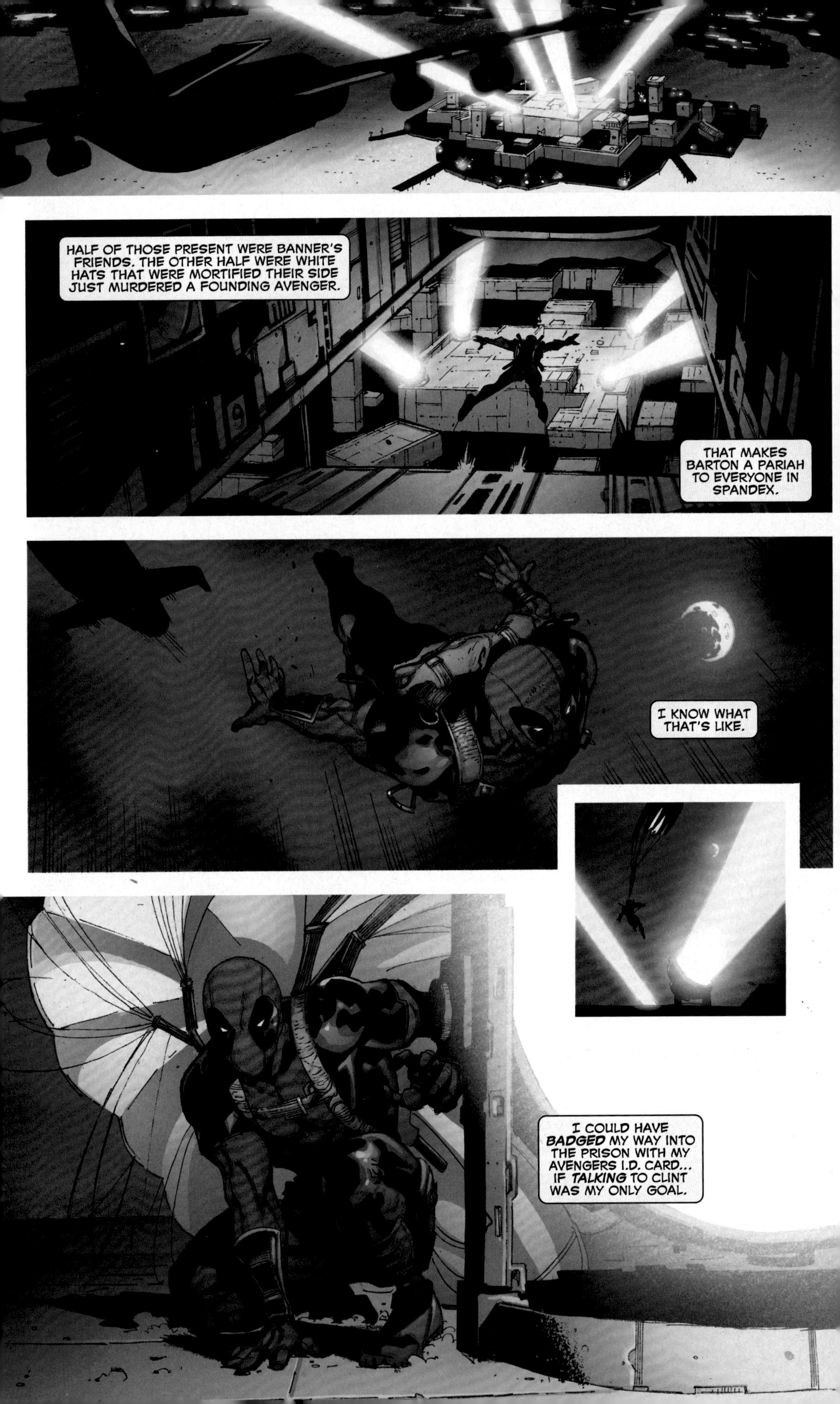
HALF OF THOSE PRESENT WERE BANNER'S FRIENDS. THE OTHER HALF WERE WHITE HATS THAT WERE MORTIFIED THEIR SIDE JUST MURDERED A FOUNDING AVENGER.
THAT MAKES BARTON A PARIAH TO EVERYONE IN SPANDEX.
I KNOW WHAT THAT'S LIKE.
I COULD HAVE BADGED MY WAY INTO THE PRISON WITH MY AVENGERS I.D. CARD... IF TALKING TO CLINT WAS MY ONLY GOAL.

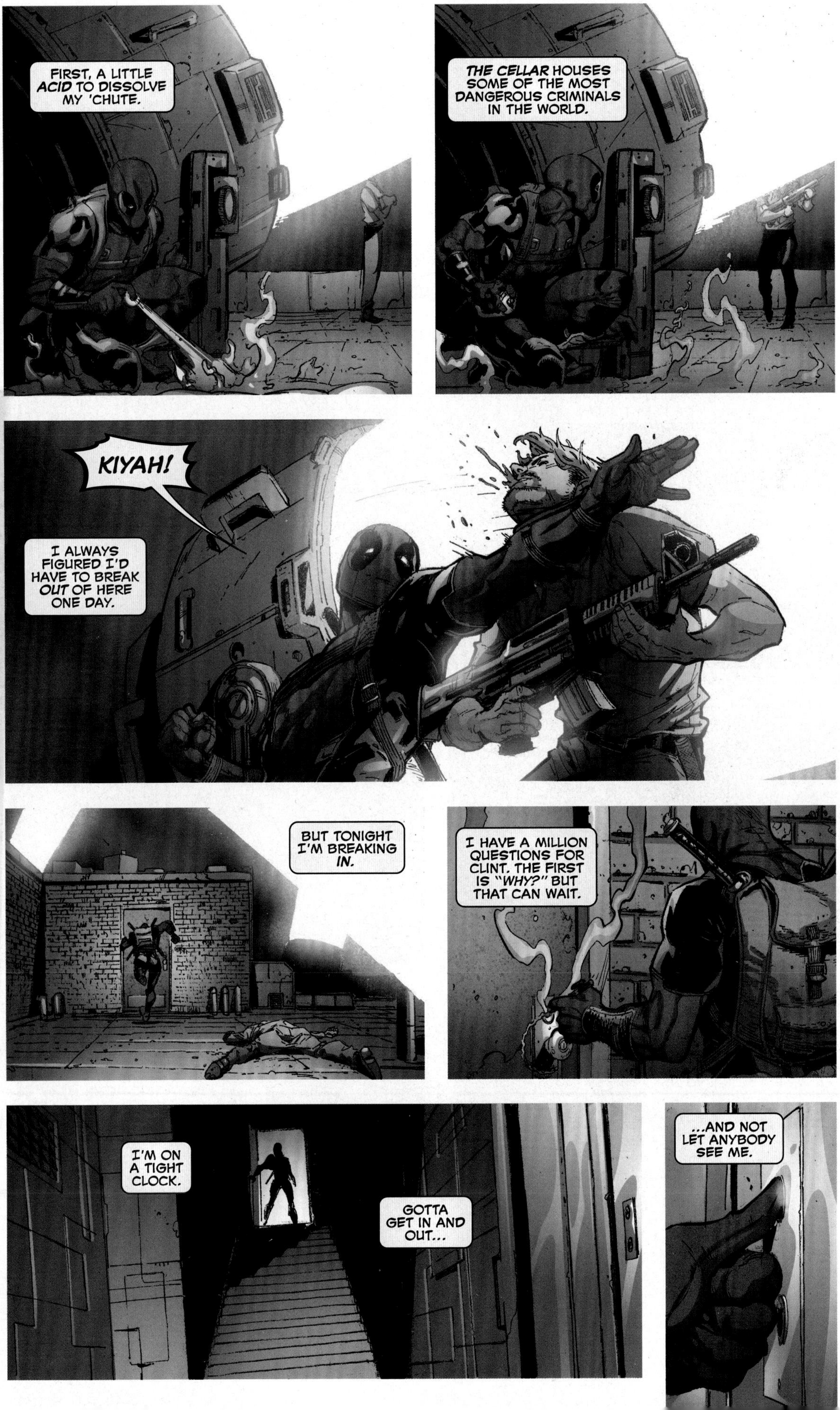
FIRST, A LITTLE ACID TO DISSOLVE MY 'CHUTE.
THE CELLAR HOUSES SOME OF THE MOST DANGEROUS CRIMINALS IN THE WORLD.
KIYAH!
I ALWAYS FIGURED I'D HAVE TO BREAK OUT OF HERE ONE DAY.
BUT TONIGHT I'M BREAKING IN.
I HAVE A MILLION QUESTIONS FOR CLINT. THE FIRST IS "WHY?" BUT THAT CAN WAIT.
I'M ON A TIGHT CLOCK.
GOTTA GET IN AND OUT...
...AND NOT LET ANYBODY SEE ME.

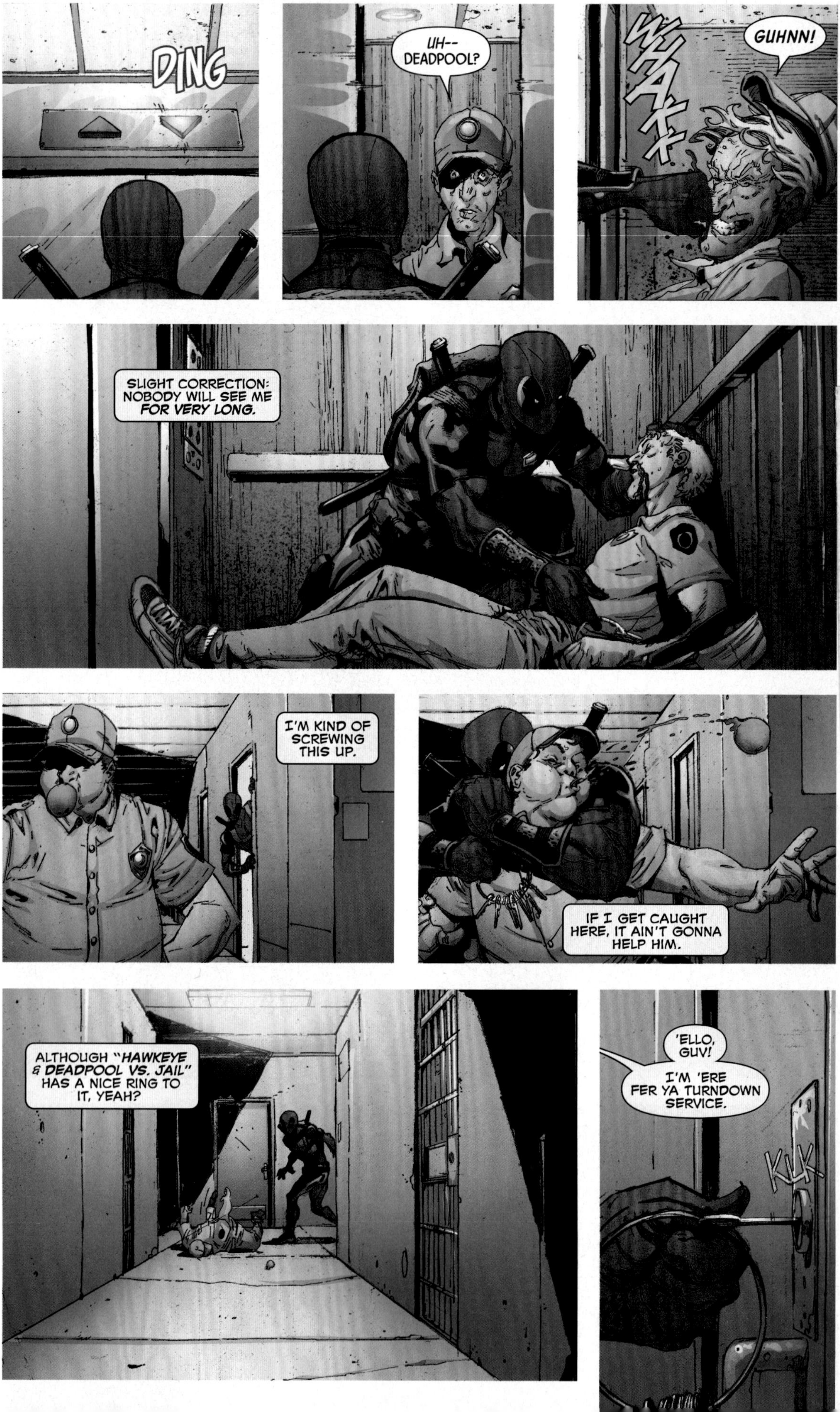
DING
UH-- DEADPOOL?
WHAKK
GUHNN!
SLIGHT CORRECTION: NOBODY WILL SEE ME FOR VERY LONG.
I'M KIND OF SCREWING THIS UP.
IF I GET CAUGHT HERE, IT AIN'T GONNA HELP HIM.
ALTHOUGH "HAWKEYE & DEADPOOL VS. JAIL" HAS A NICE RING TO IT, YEAH?
'ELLO, GUV!
I'M 'ERE FER YA TURNDOWN SERVICE.
KLIK

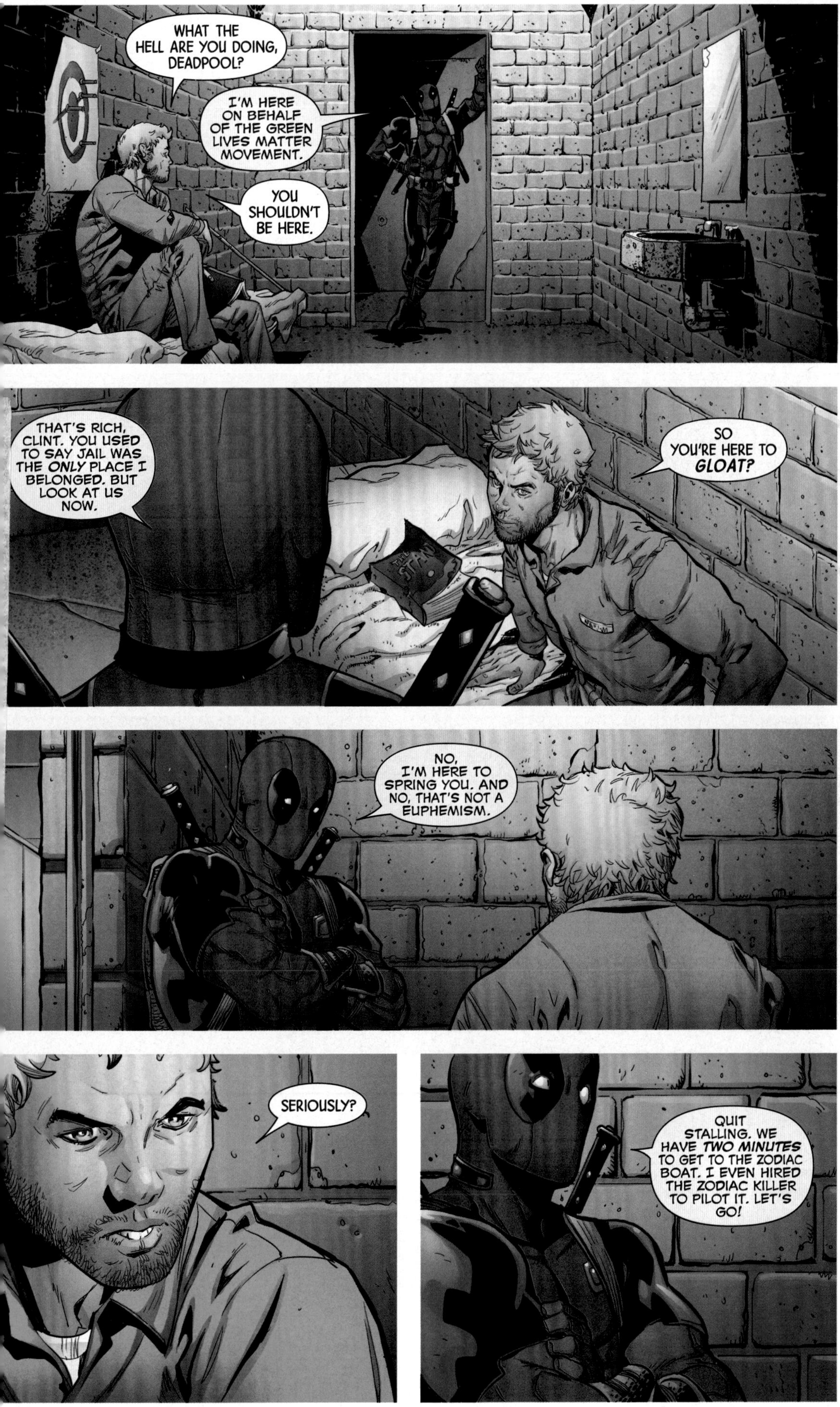
WHAT THE HELL ARE YOU DOING, DEADPOOL?
I'M HERE ON BEHALF OF THE GREEN LIVES MATTER MOVEMENT.
YOU SHOULDN'T BE HERE.
THAT'S RICH, CLINT. YOU USED TO SAY JAIL WAS THE ONLY PLACE I BELONGED. BUT LOOK AT US NOW.
SO YOU'RE HERE TO GLOAT?
NO, I'M HERE TO SPRING YOU. AND NO, THAT'S NOT A EUPHEMISM.
SERIOUSLY?
QUIT STALLING. WE HAVE TWO MINUTES TO GET TO THE ZODIAC BOAT. I EVEN HIRED THE ZODIAC KILLER TO PILOT IT. LET'S GO!

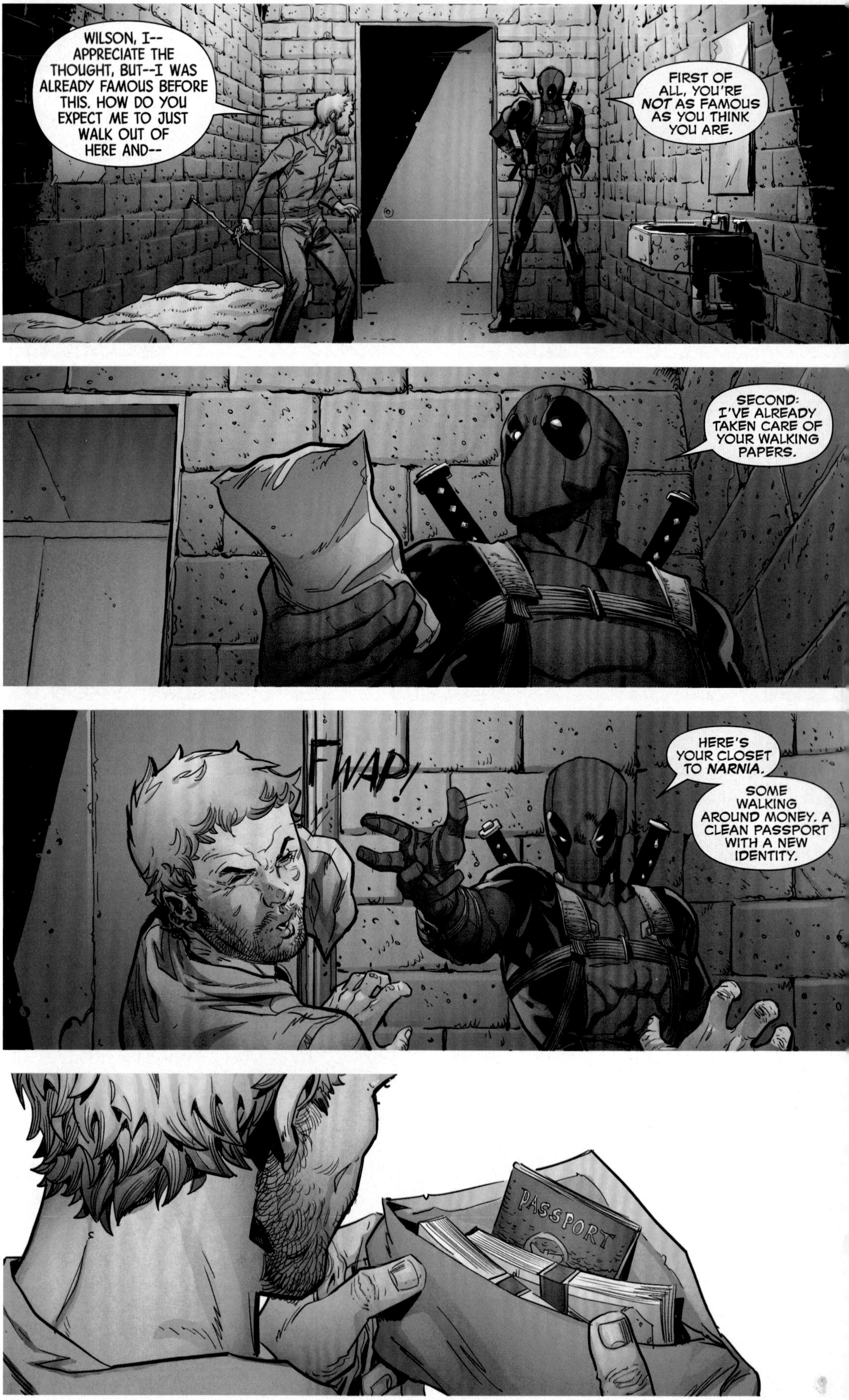
WILSON, I--APPRECIATE THE THOUGHT, BUT--I WAS ALREADY FAMOUS BEFORE THIS. HOW DO YOU EXPECT ME TO JUST WALK OUT OF HERE AND--
FIRST OF ALL, YOU'RE NOT AS FAMOUS AS YOU THINK YOU ARE.
SECOND: I'VE ALREADY TAKEN CARE OF YOUR WALKING PAPERS.
FWAP!
HERE'S YOUR CLOSET TO NARNIA.
SOME WALKING AROUND MONEY. A CLEAN PASSPORT WITH A NEW IDENTITY.
PASSPORT

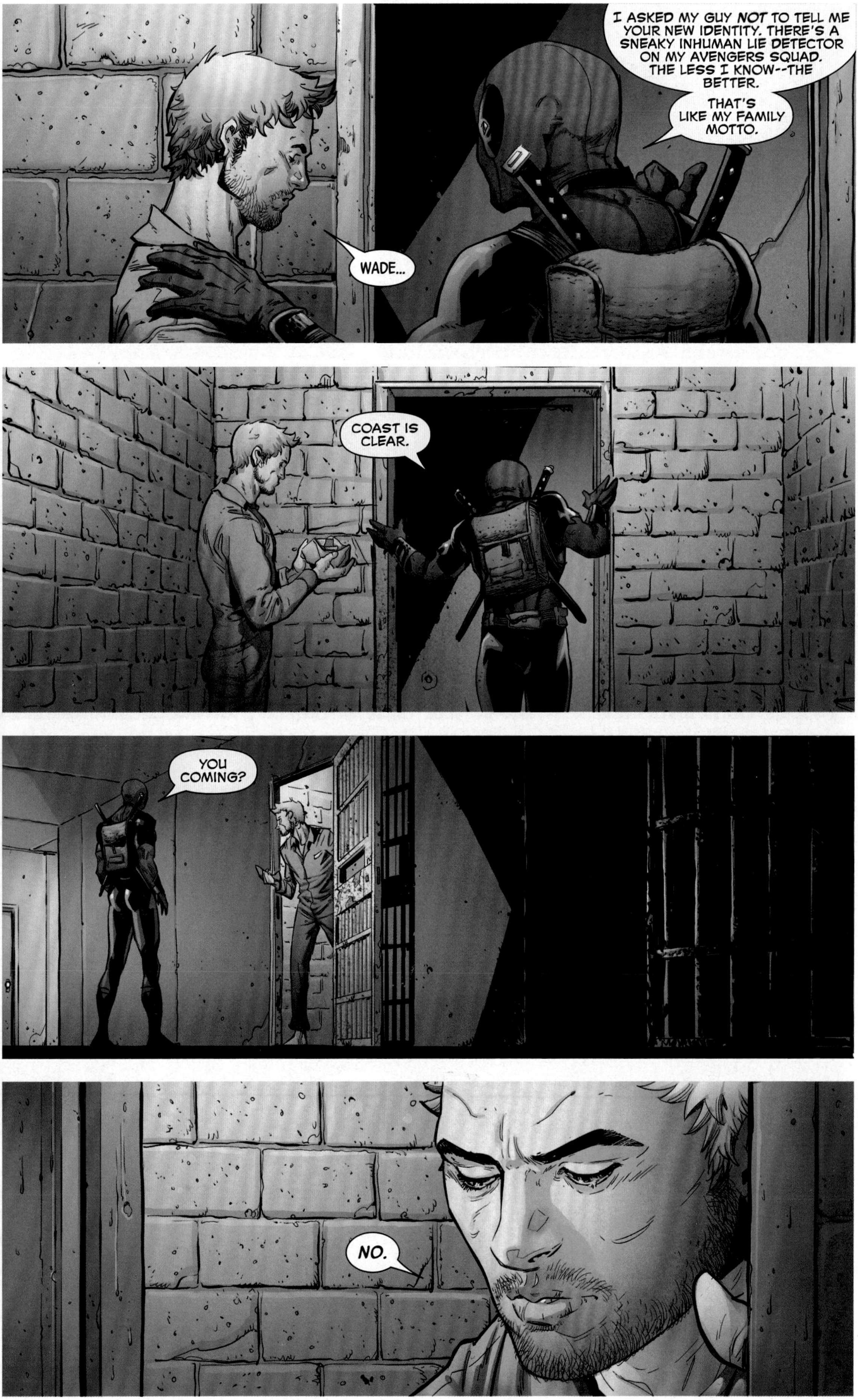
I ASKED MY GUY NOT TO TELL ME YOUR NEW IDENTITY. THERE'S A SNEAKY INHUMAN LIE DETECTOR ON MY AVENGERS SQUAD. THE LESS I KNOW--THE BETTER.
THAT'S LIKE MY FAMILY MOTTO.
WADE...
COAST IS CLEAR.
YOU COMING?
NO.

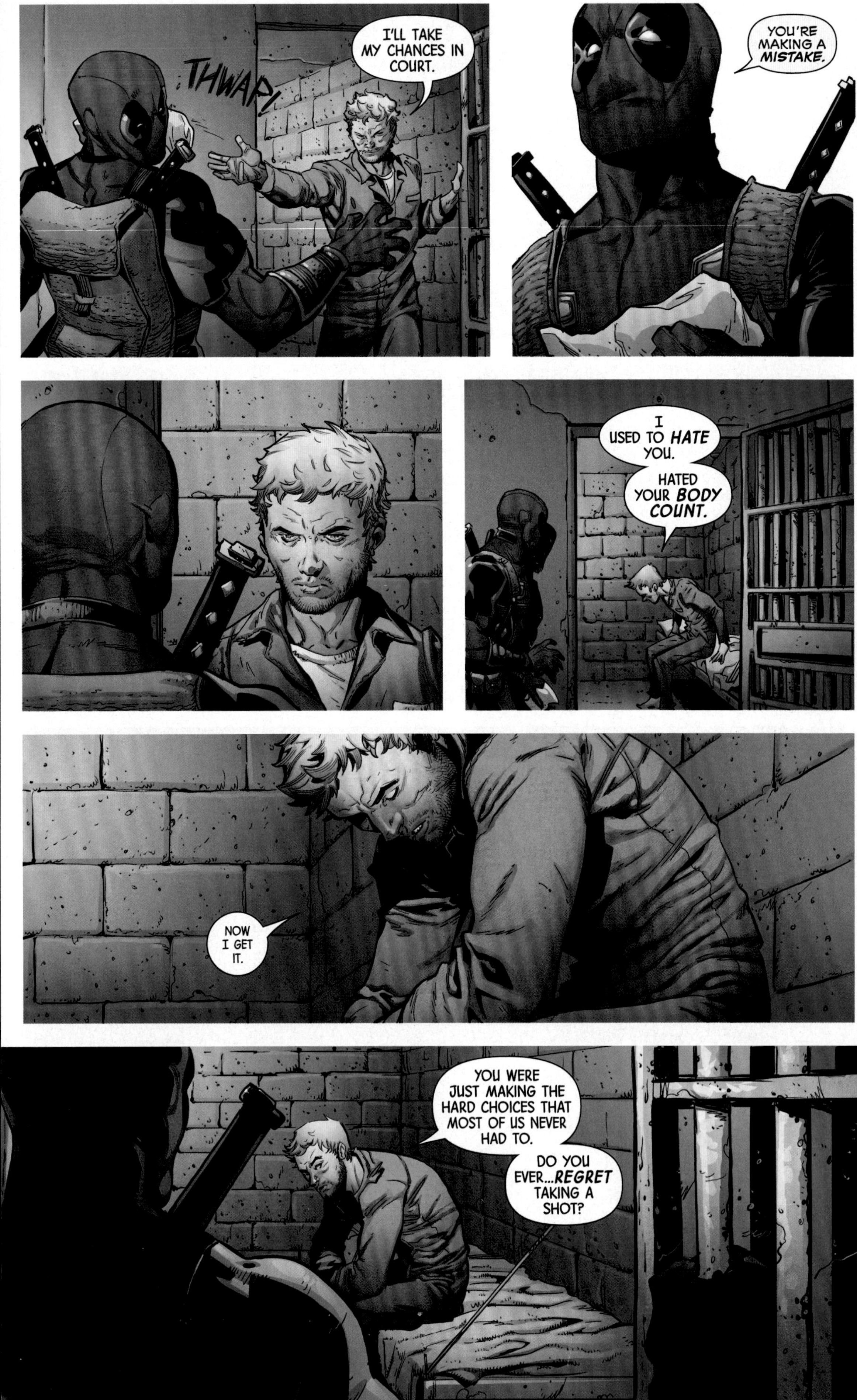
THWAP!
I'LL TAKE MY CHANCES IN COURT.
YOU'RE MAKING A MISTAKE.
I USED TO HATE YOU.
HATED YOUR BODY COUNT.
NOW I GET IT.
YOU WERE JUST MAKING THE HARD CHOICES THAT MOST OF US NEVER HAD TO.
DO YOU EVER...REGRET TAKING A SHOT?

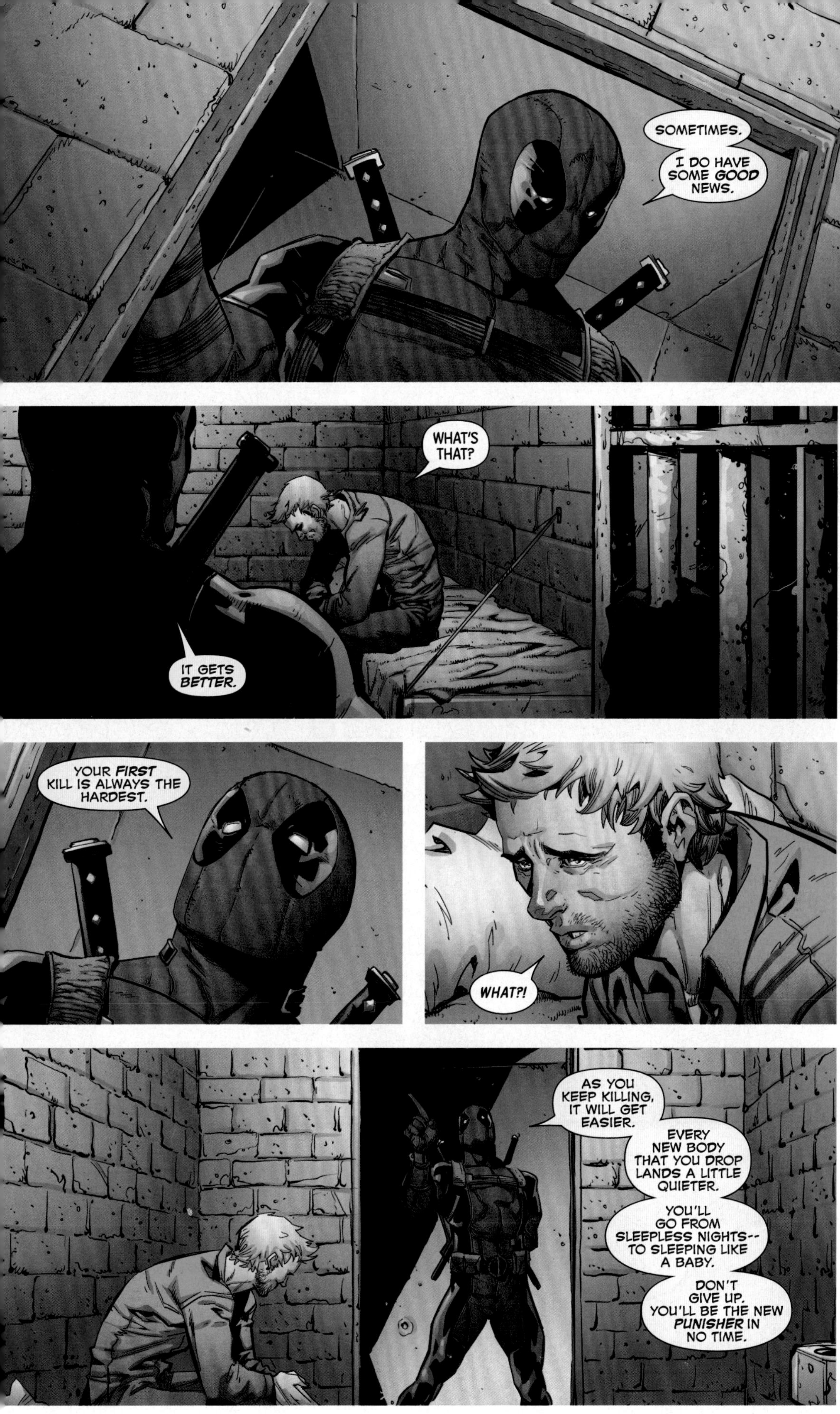
SOMETIMES.
I DO HAVE SOME GOOD NEWS.
WHAT'S THAT?
IT GETS BETTER.
YOUR FIRST KILL IS ALWAYS THE HARDEST.
WHAT?!
AS YOU KEEP KILLING, IT WILL GET EASIER.
EVERY NEW BODY THAT YOU DROP LANDS A LITTLE QUIETER.
YOU'LL GO FROM SLEEPLESS NIGHTS-- TO SLEEPING LIKE A BABY.
DON'T GIVE UP. YOU'LL BE THE NEW PUNISHER IN NO TIME.

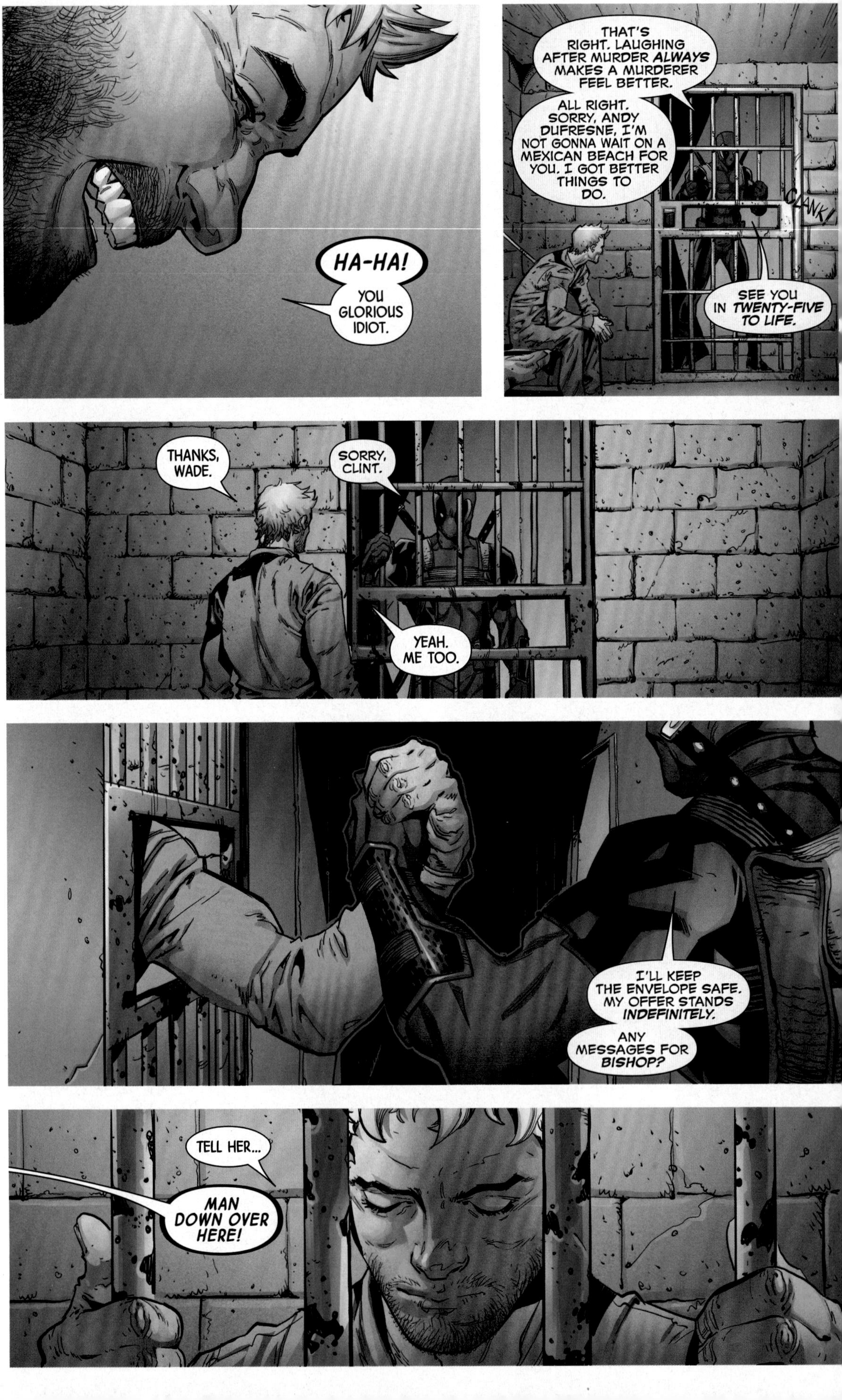
HA-HA!
YOU GLORIOUS IDIOT.
THAT'S RIGHT. LAUGHING AFTER MURDER *ALWAYS* MAKES A MURDERER FEEL BETTER.
ALL RIGHT. SORRY, ANDY DUFRESNE, I'M NOT GONNA WAIT ON A MEXICAN BEACH FOR YOU. I GOT BETTER THINGS TO DO.
CLANK!
SEE YOU IN *TWENTY-FIVE TO LIFE.*
THANKS, WADE.
SORRY, CLINT.
YEAH. ME TOO.
I'LL KEEP THE ENVELOPE SAFE. MY OFFER STANDS *INDEFINITELY.*
ANY MESSAGES FOR *BISHOP?*
TELL HER...
MAN DOWN OVER HERE!

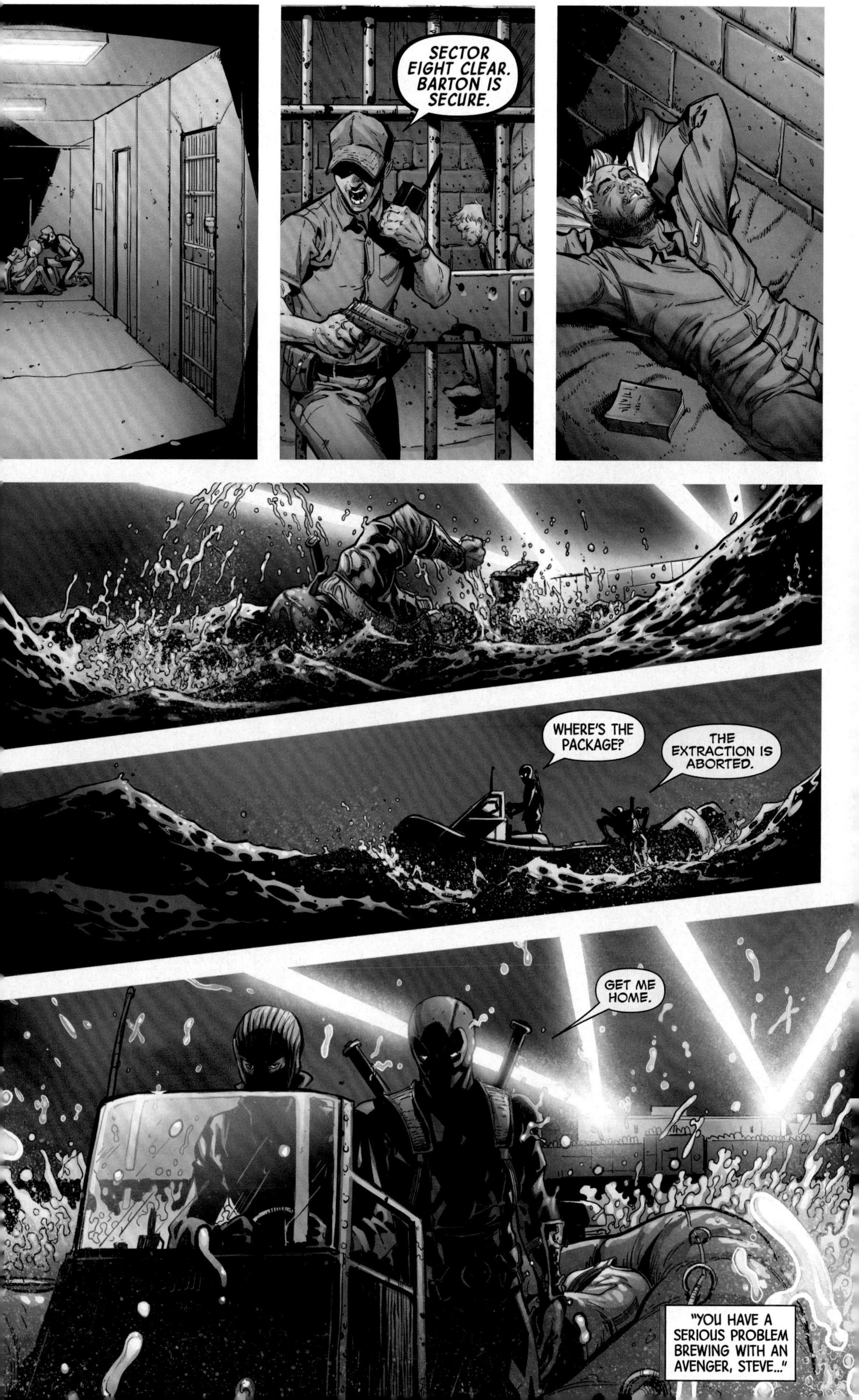
SECTOR EIGHT CLEAR. BARTON IS SECURE.
WHERE'S THE PACKAGE?
THE EXTRACTION IS ABORTED.
GET ME HOME.
"YOU HAVE A SERIOUS PROBLEM BREWING WITH AN AVENGER, STEVE..."

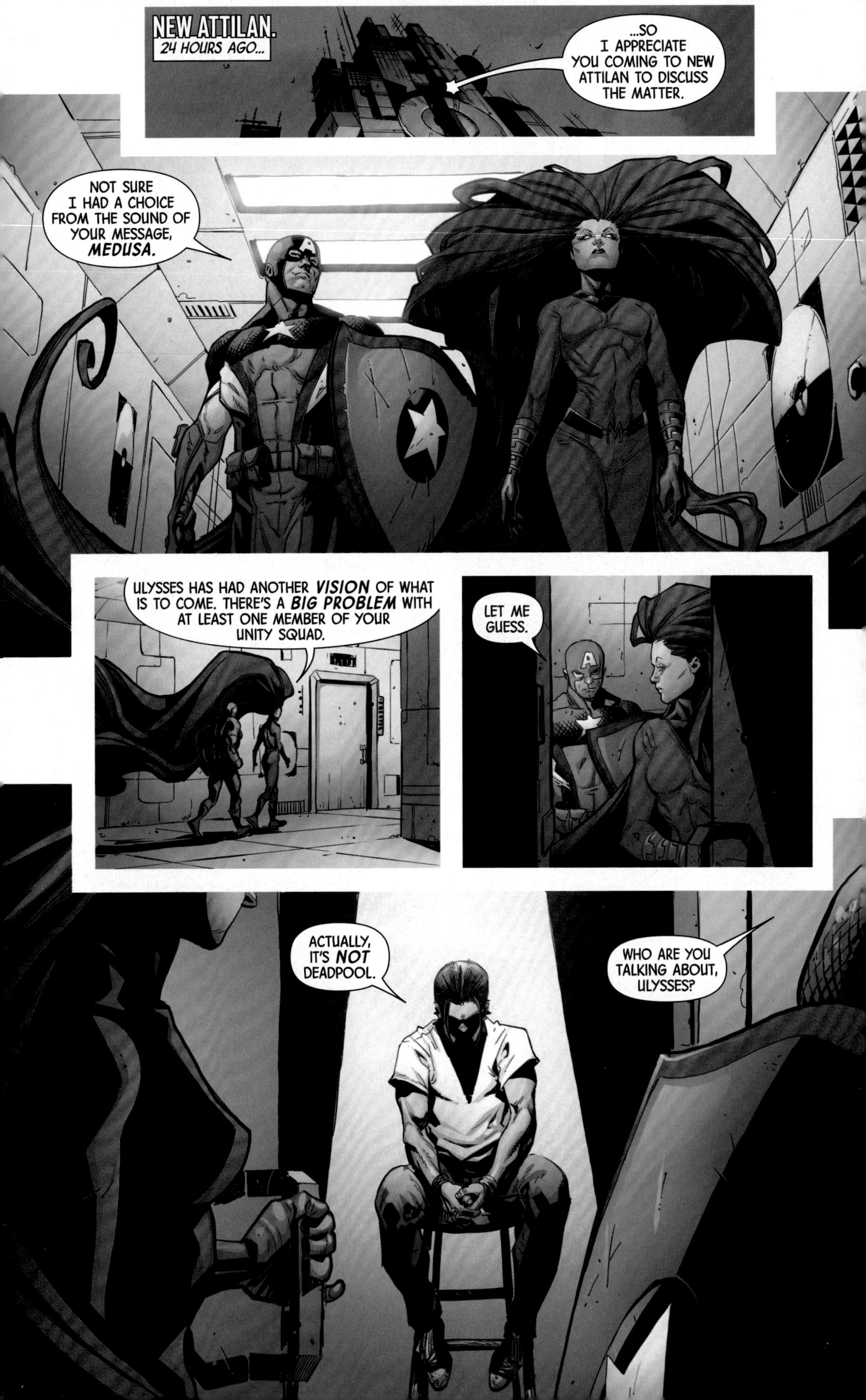
NEW ATTILAN.
24 HOURS AGO...
...SO I APPRECIATE YOU COMING TO NEW ATTILAN TO DISCUSS THE MATTER.
NOT SURE I HAD A CHOICE FROM THE SOUND OF YOUR MESSAGE, MEDUSA.
ULYSSES HAS HAD ANOTHER VISION OF WHAT IS TO COME. THERE'S A BIG PROBLEM WITH AT LEAST ONE MEMBER OF YOUR UNITY SQUAD.
LET ME GUESS.
ACTUALLY, IT'S NOT DEADPOOL.
WHO ARE YOU TALKING ABOUT, ULYSSES?

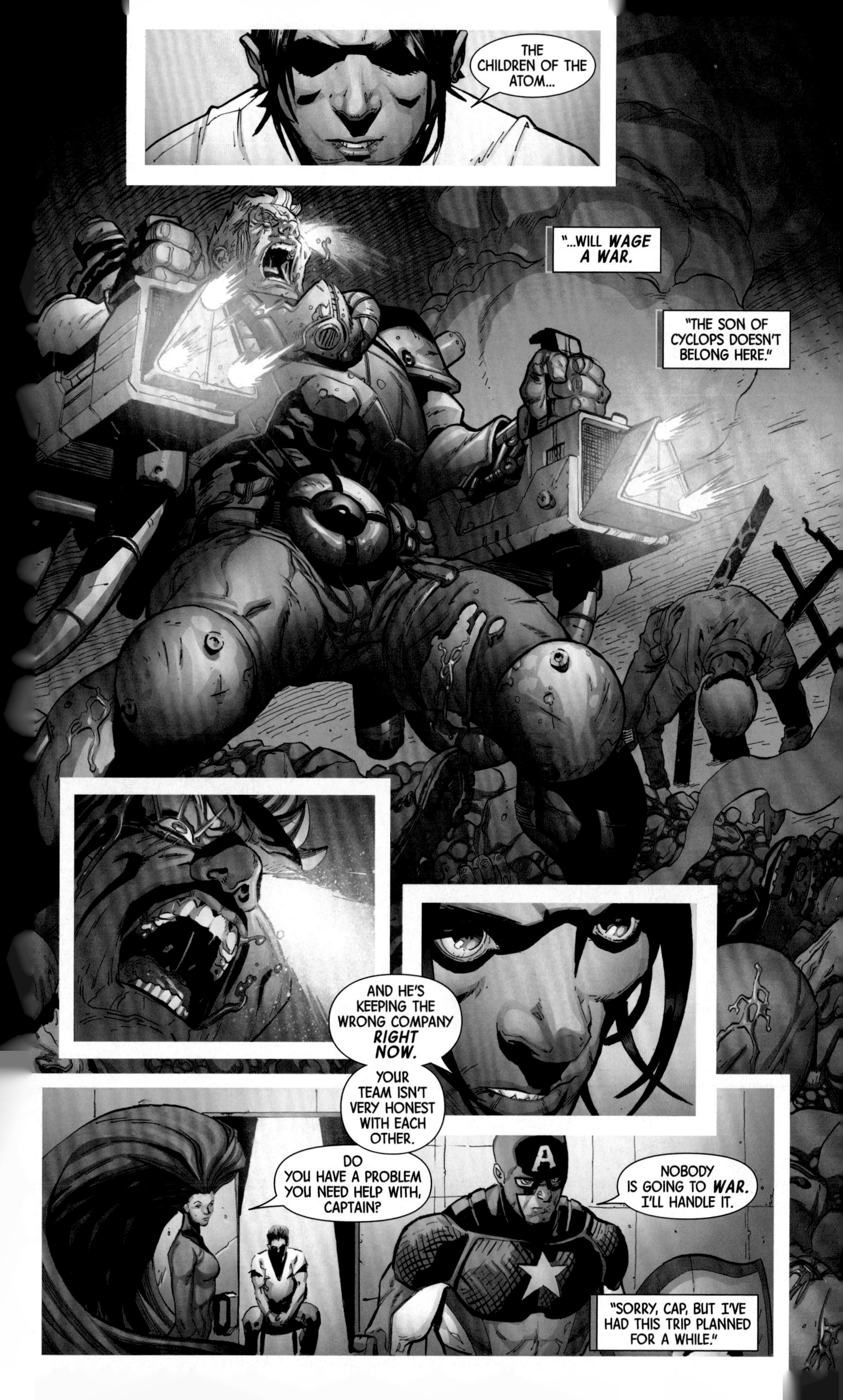
THE CHILDREN OF THE ATOM...
"...WILL WAGE A WAR.
"THE SON OF CYCLOPS DOESN'T BELONG HERE."
AND HE'S KEEPING THE WRONG COMPANY RIGHT NOW.
YOUR TEAM ISN'T VERY HONEST WITH EACH OTHER.
DO YOU HAVE A PROBLEM YOU NEED HELP WITH, CAPTAIN?
NOBODY IS GOING TO WAR. I'LL HANDLE IT.
"SORRY, CAP, BUT I'VE HAD THIS TRIP PLANNED FOR A WHILE."

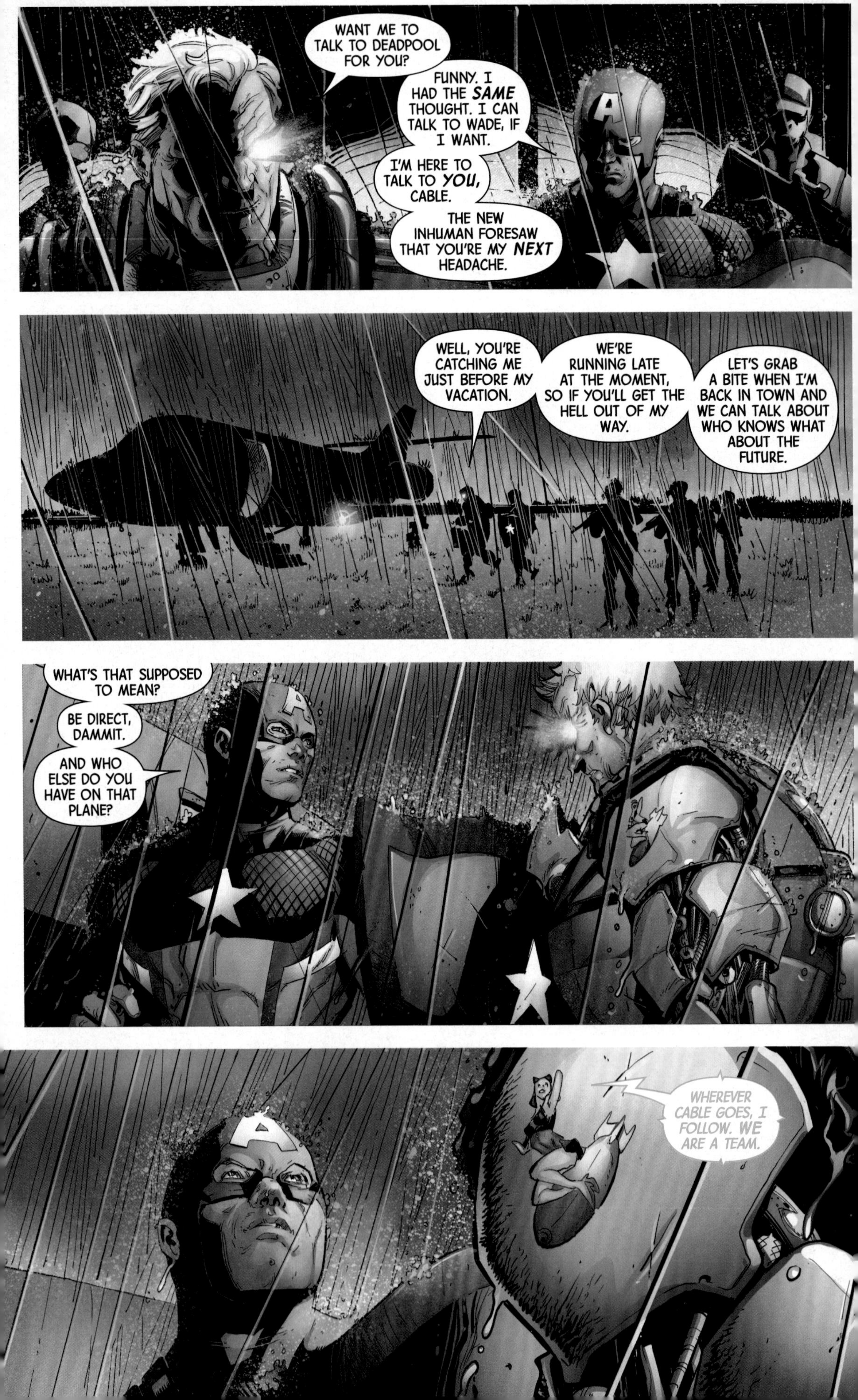
WANT ME TO TALK TO DEADPOOL FOR YOU?
FUNNY. I HAD THE SAME THOUGHT. I CAN TALK TO WADE, IF I WANT.
I'M HERE TO TALK TO YOU, CABLE.
THE NEW INHUMAN FORESAW THAT YOU'RE MY NEXT HEADACHE.
WELL, YOU'RE CATCHING ME JUST BEFORE MY VACATION.
WE'RE RUNNING LATE AT THE MOMENT, SO IF YOU'LL GET THE HELL OUT OF MY WAY.
LET'S GRAB A BITE WHEN I'M BACK IN TOWN AND WE CAN TALK ABOUT WHO KNOWS WHAT ABOUT THE FUTURE.
WHAT'S THAT SUPPOSED TO MEAN?
BE DIRECT, DAMMIT.
AND WHO ELSE DO YOU HAVE ON THAT PLANE?
WHEREVER CABLE GOES, I FOLLOW. WE ARE A TEAM.

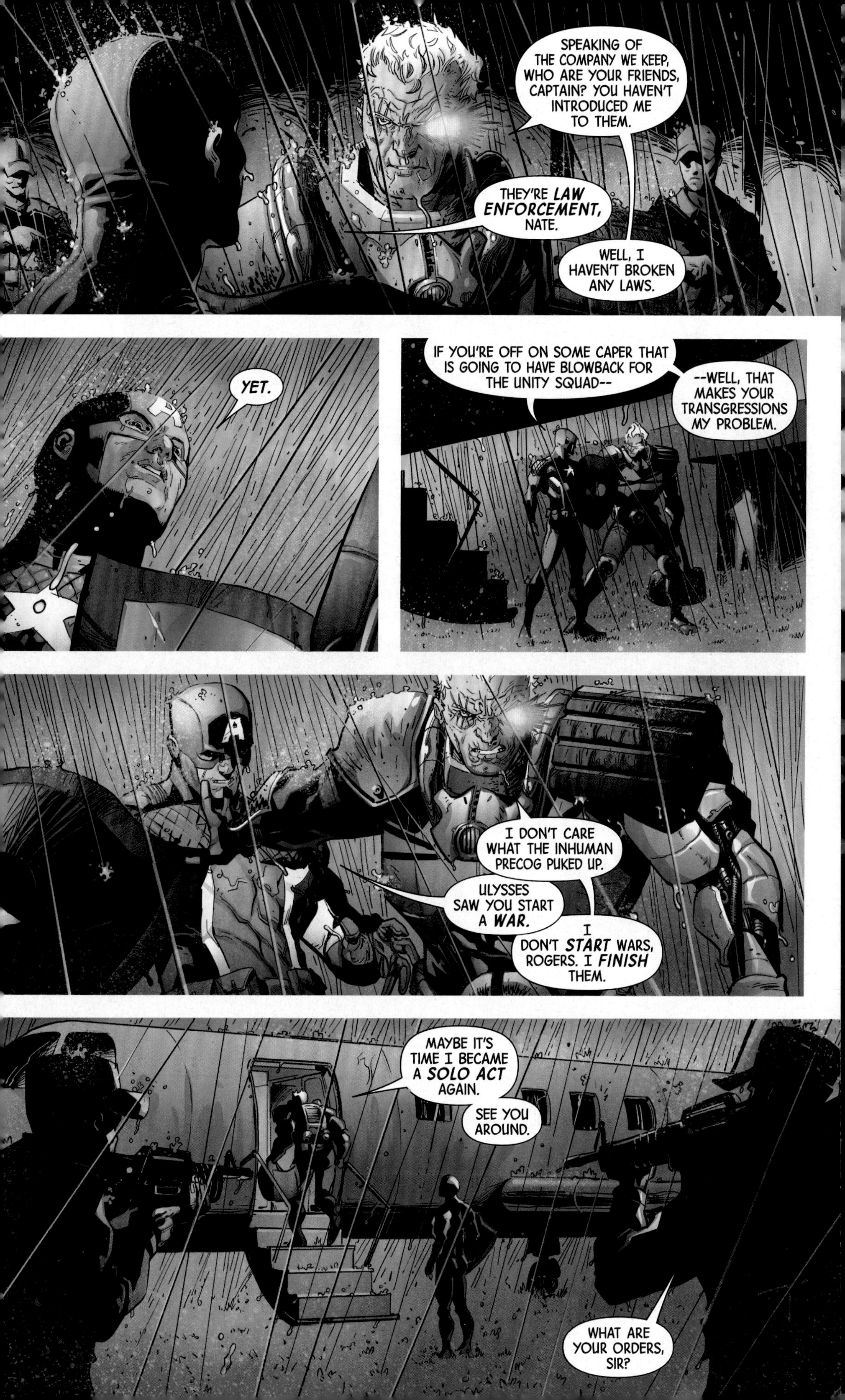
SPEAKING OF THE COMPANY WE KEEP, WHO ARE YOUR FRIENDS, CAPTAIN? YOU HAVEN'T INTRODUCED ME TO THEM.
THEY'RE *LAW ENFORCEMENT,* NATE.
WELL, I HAVEN'T BROKEN ANY LAWS.
YET.
IF YOU'RE OFF ON SOME CAPER THAT IS GOING TO HAVE BLOWBACK FOR THE UNITY SQUAD--
--WELL, THAT MAKES YOUR TRANSGRESSIONS MY PROBLEM.
I DON'T CARE WHAT THE INHUMAN PRECOG PUKED UP.
ULYSSES SAW YOU START A *WAR.*
I DON'T *START* WARS, ROGERS. I *FINISH* THEM.
MAYBE IT'S TIME I BECAME A *SOLO ACT* AGAIN.
SEE YOU AROUND.
WHAT ARE YOUR ORDERS, SIR?

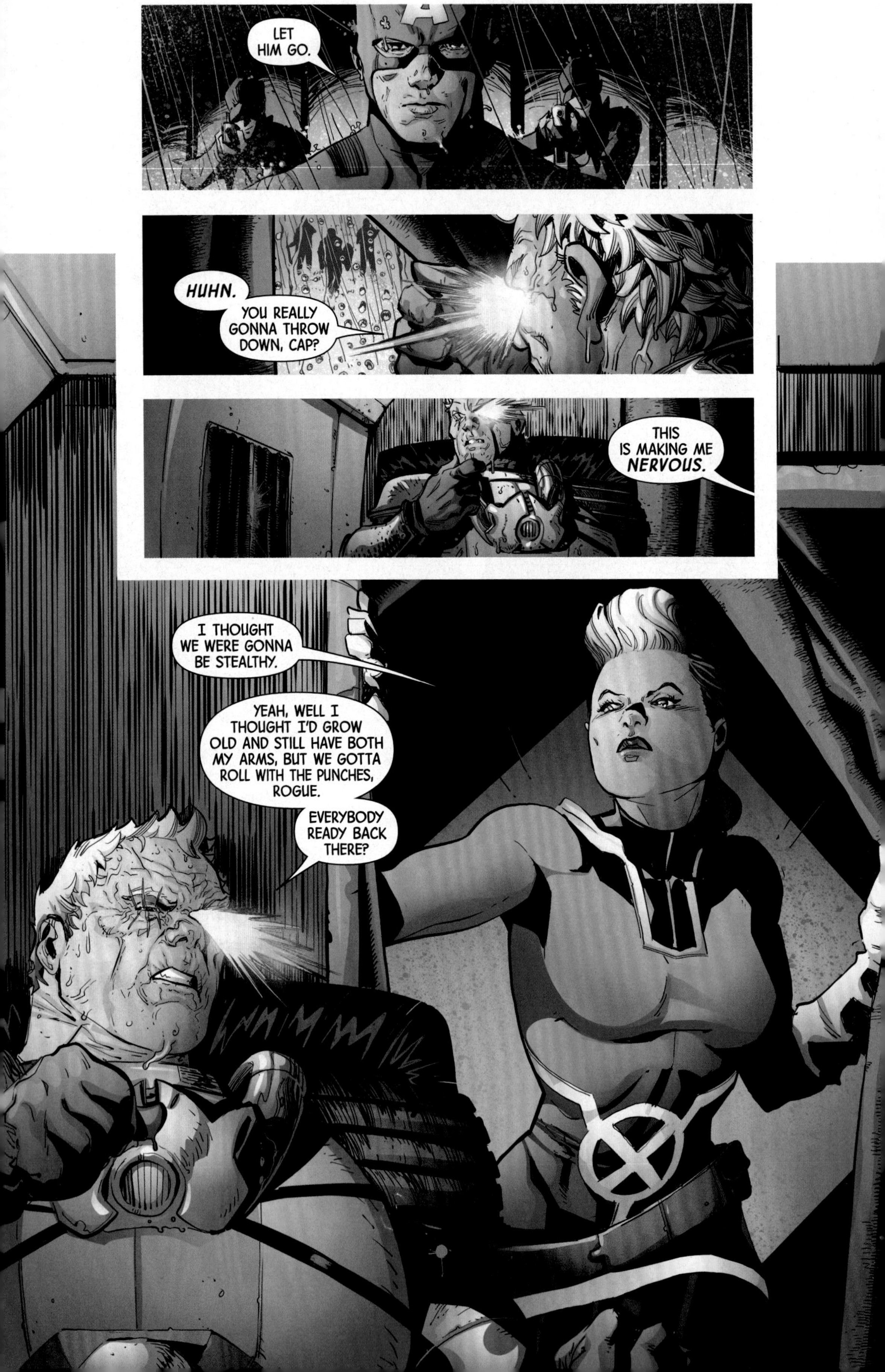
LET HIM GO.
HUHN.
YOU REALLY GONNA THROW DOWN, CAP?
THIS IS MAKING ME NERVOUS.
I THOUGHT WE WERE GONNA BE STEALTHY.
YEAH, WELL I THOUGHT I'D GROW OLD AND STILL HAVE BOTH MY ARMS, BUT WE GOTTA ROLL WITH THE PUNCHES, ROGUE.
EVERYBODY READY BACK THERE?

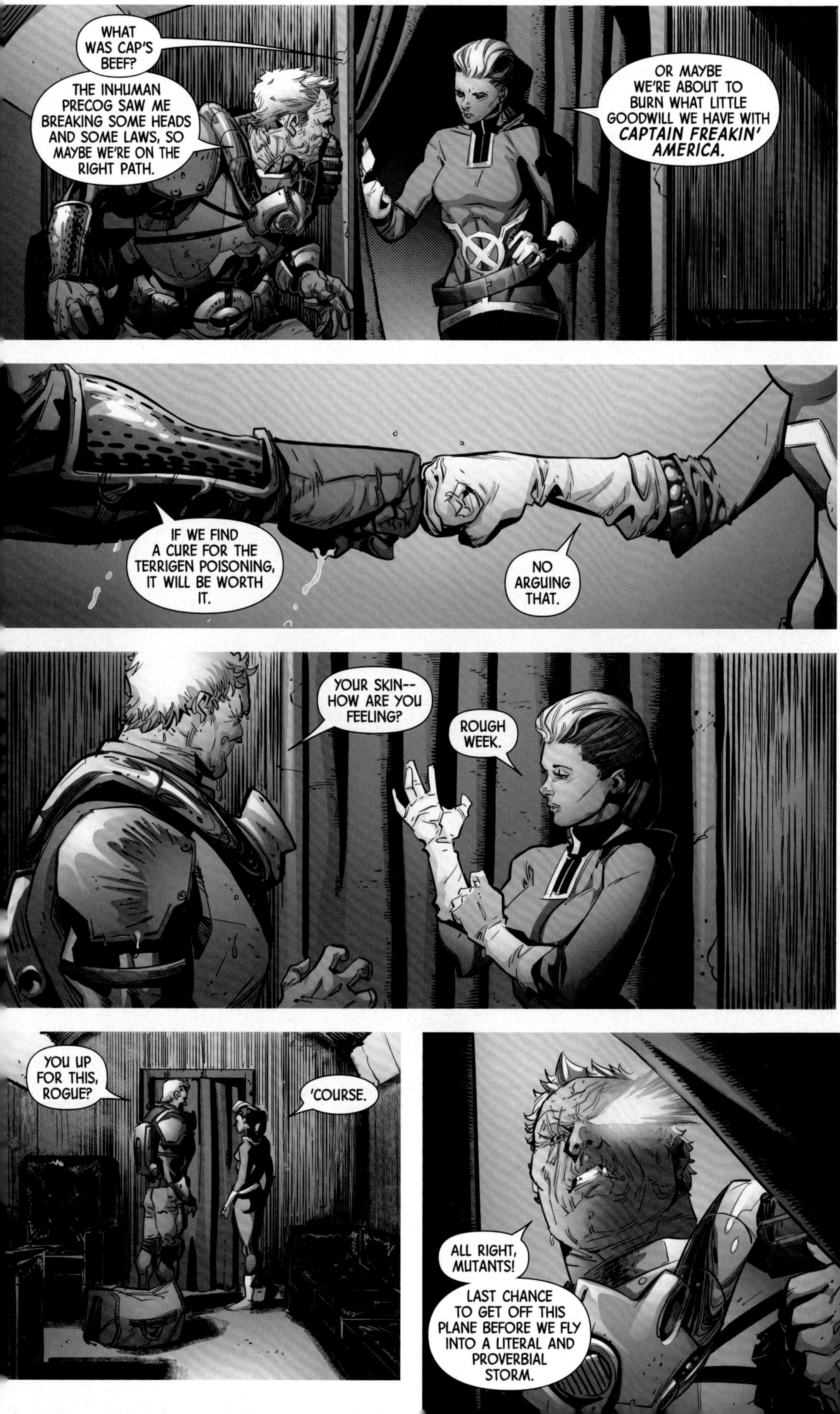
WHAT WAS CAP'S BEEF?
THE INHUMAN PRECOG SAW ME BREAKING SOME HEADS AND SOME LAWS, SO MAYBE WE'RE ON THE RIGHT PATH.
OR MAYBE WE'RE ABOUT TO BURN WHAT LITTLE GOODWILL WE HAVE WITH *CAPTAIN FREAKIN' AMERICA.*
IF WE FIND A CURE FOR THE TERRIGEN POISONING, IT WILL BE WORTH IT.
NO ARGUING THAT.
YOUR SKIN-- HOW ARE YOU FEELING?
ROUGH WEEK.
YOU UP FOR THIS, ROGUE?
'COURSE.
ALL RIGHT, MUTANTS!
LAST CHANCE TO GET OFF THIS PLANE BEFORE WE FLY INTO A LITERAL AND PROVERBIAL STORM.

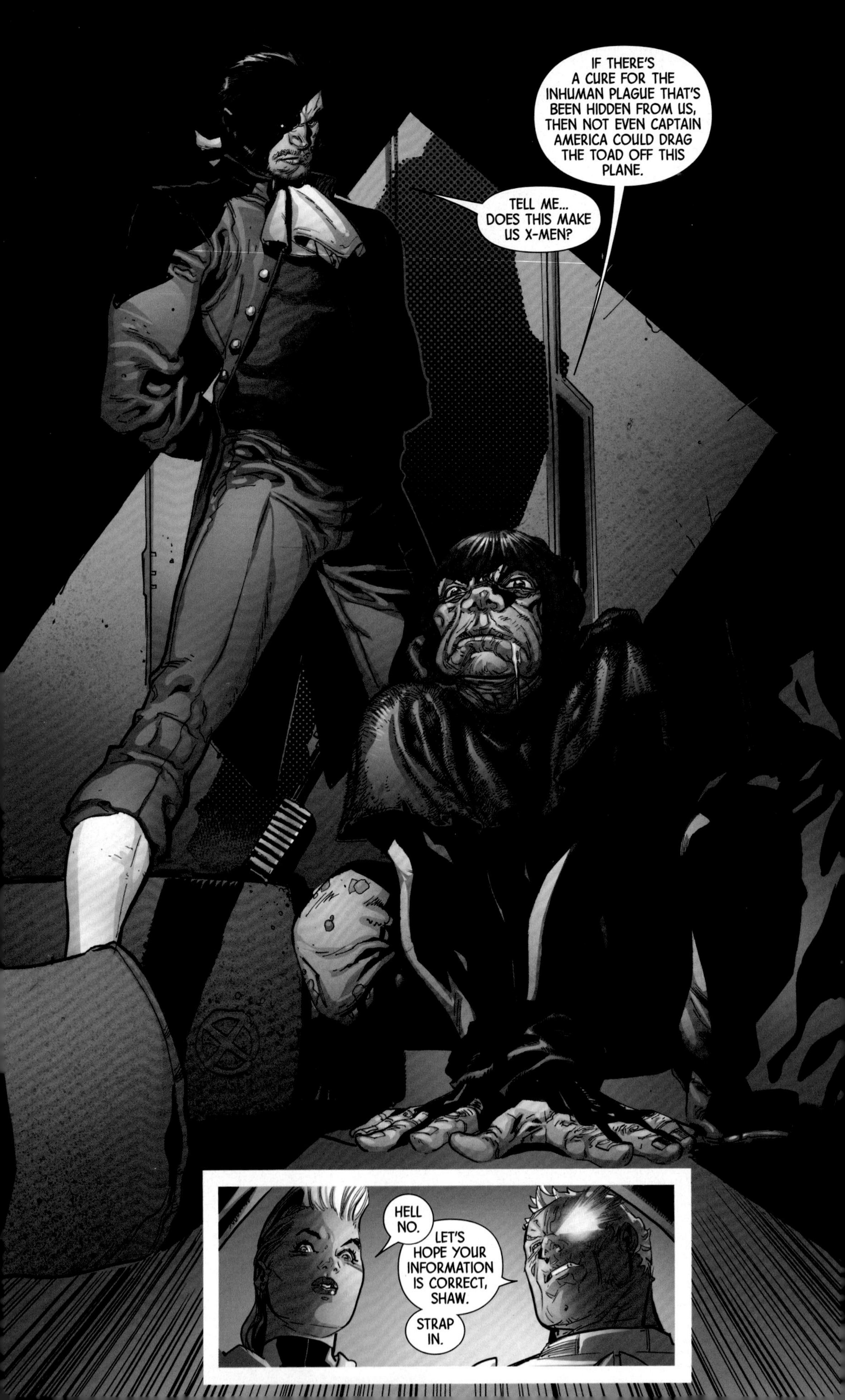
TELL ME... DOES THIS MAKE US X-MEN?
IF THERE'S A CURE FOR THE INHUMAN PLAGUE THAT'S BEEN HIDDEN FROM US, THEN NOT EVEN CAPTAIN AMERICA COULD DRAG THE TOAD OFF THIS PLANE.
HELL NO.
LET'S HOPE YOUR INFORMATION IS CORRECT, SHAW.
STRAP IN.

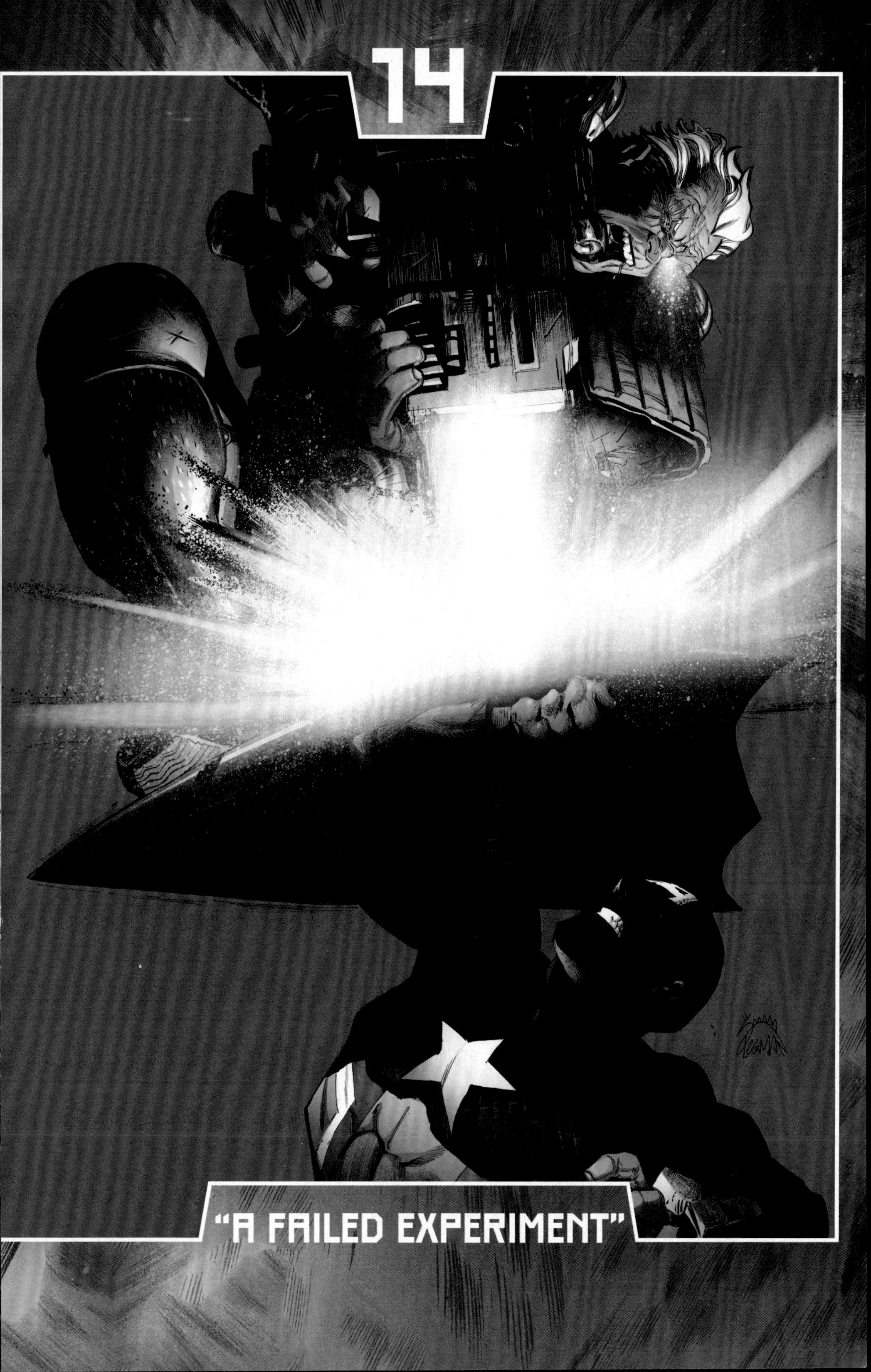
14
“A FAILED EXPERIMENT”

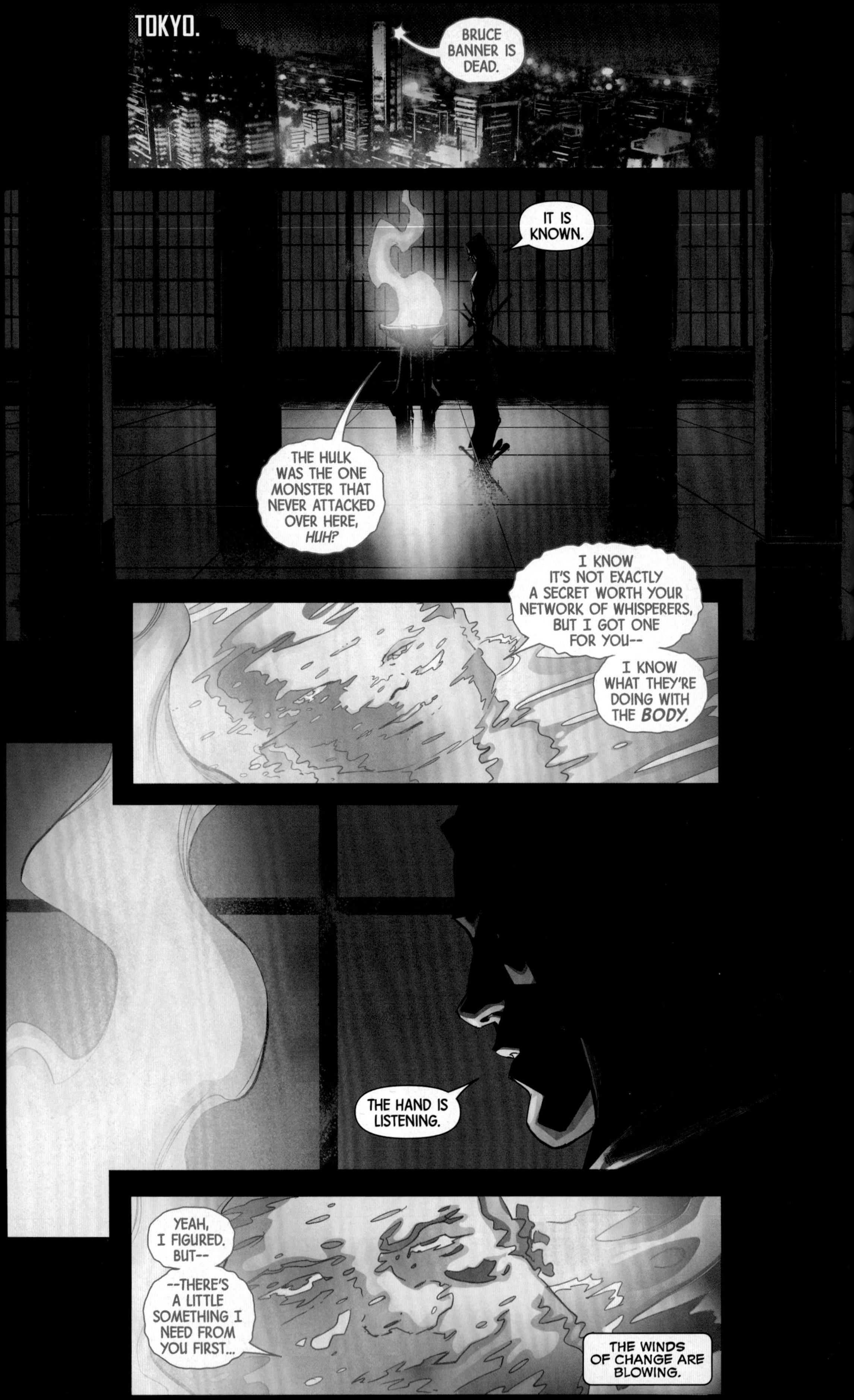
TOKYO.
BRUCE BANNER IS DEAD.
IT IS KNOWN.
THE HULK WAS THE ONE MONSTER THAT NEVER ATTACKED OVER HERE, HUH?
I KNOW IT'S NOT EXACTLY A SECRET WORTH YOUR NETWORK OF WHISPERERS, BUT I GOT ONE FOR YOU--
I KNOW WHAT THEY'RE DOING WITH THE BODY.
THE HAND IS LISTENING.
YEAH, I FIGURED. BUT--
--THERE'S A LITTLE SOMETHING I NEED FROM YOU FIRST...
THE WINDS OF CHANGE ARE BLOWING.

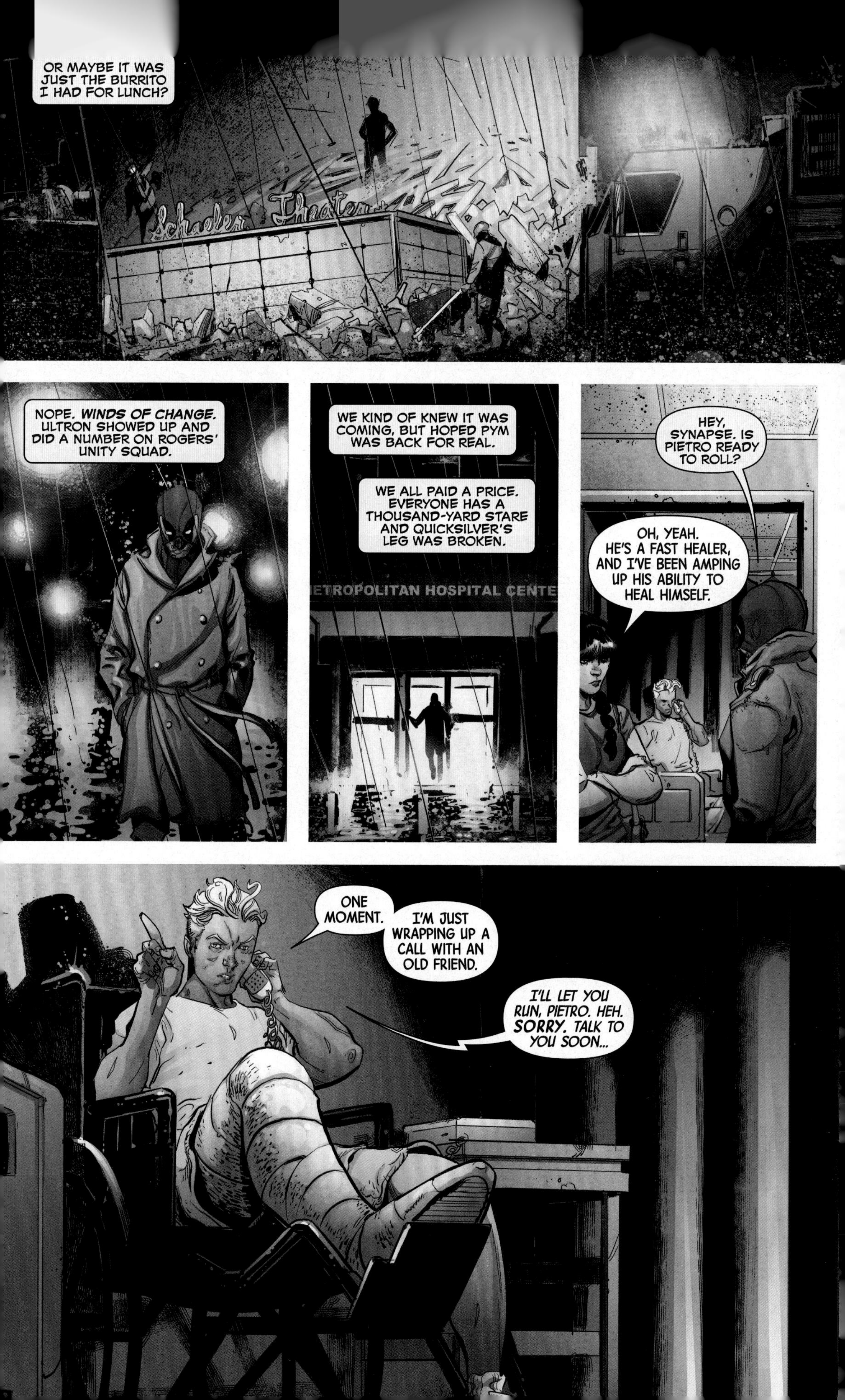

OR MAYBE IT WAS JUST THE BURRITO I HAD FOR LUNCH?
Schaeler Theater
NOPE. WINDS OF CHANGE. ULTRON SHOWED UP AND DID A NUMBER ON ROGERS' UNITY SQUAD.
WE KIND OF KNEW IT WAS COMING, BUT HOPED PYM WAS BACK FOR REAL.
WE ALL PAID A PRICE. EVERYONE HAS A THOUSAND-YARD STARE AND QUICKSILVER'S LEG WAS BROKEN.
METROPOLITAN HOSPITAL CENTE
HEY, SYNAPSE. IS PIETRO READY TO ROLL?
OH, YEAH. HE'S A FAST HEALER, AND I'VE BEEN AMPING UP HIS ABILITY TO HEAL HIMSELF.
ONE MOMENT.
I'M JUST WRAPPING UP A CALL WITH AN OLD FRIEND.
I'LL LET YOU RUN, PIETRO. HEH. SORRY. TALK TO YOU SOON...

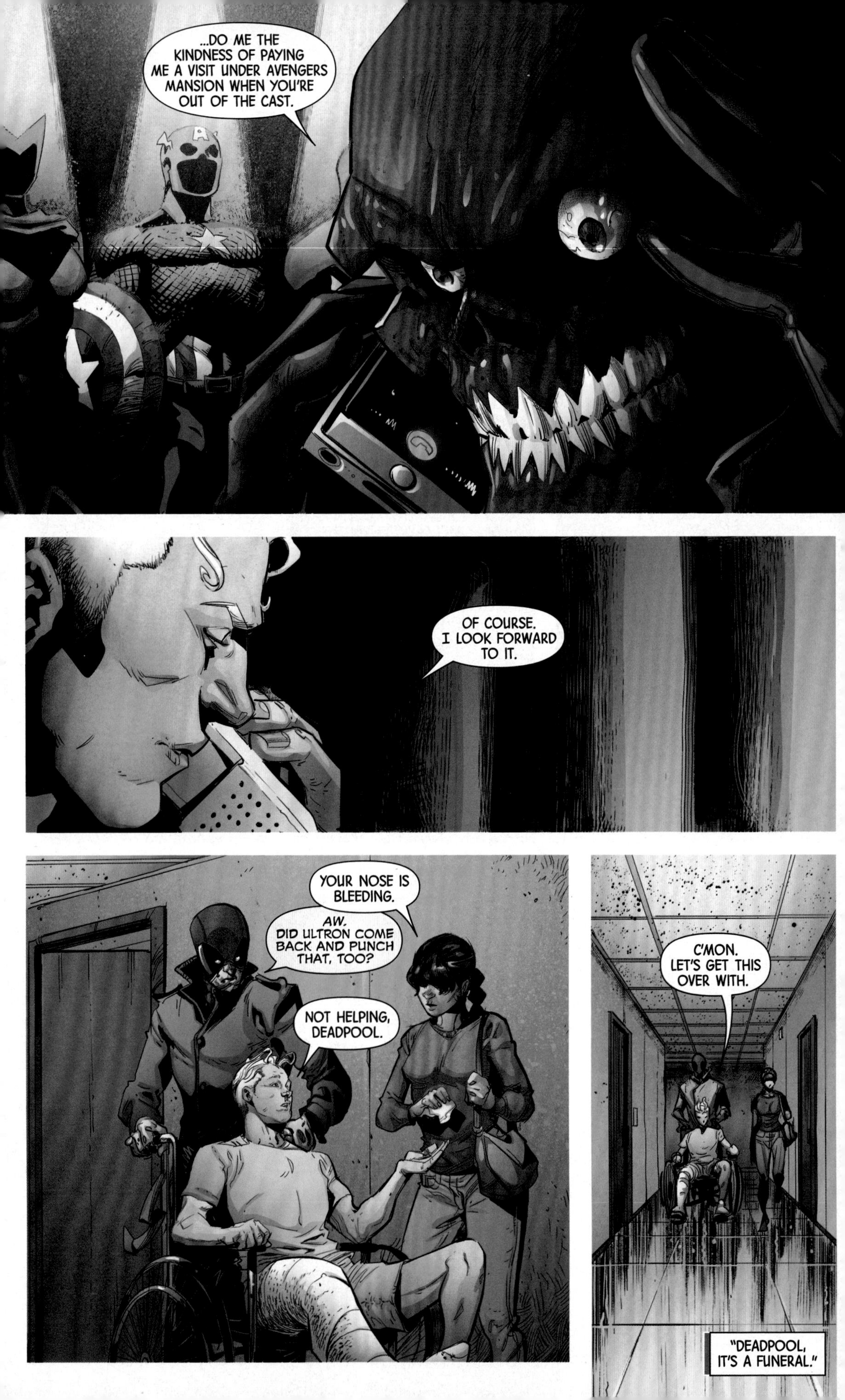
...DO ME THE KINDNESS OF PAYING ME A VISIT UNDER AVENGERS MANSION WHEN YOU'RE OUT OF THE CAST.
OF COURSE. I LOOK FORWARD TO IT.
YOUR NOSE IS BLEEDING.
AW. DID ULTRON COME BACK AND PUNCH THAT, TOO?
NOT HELPING, DEADPOOL.
C'MON. LET'S GET THIS OVER WITH.
"DEADPOOL, IT'S A FUNERAL."

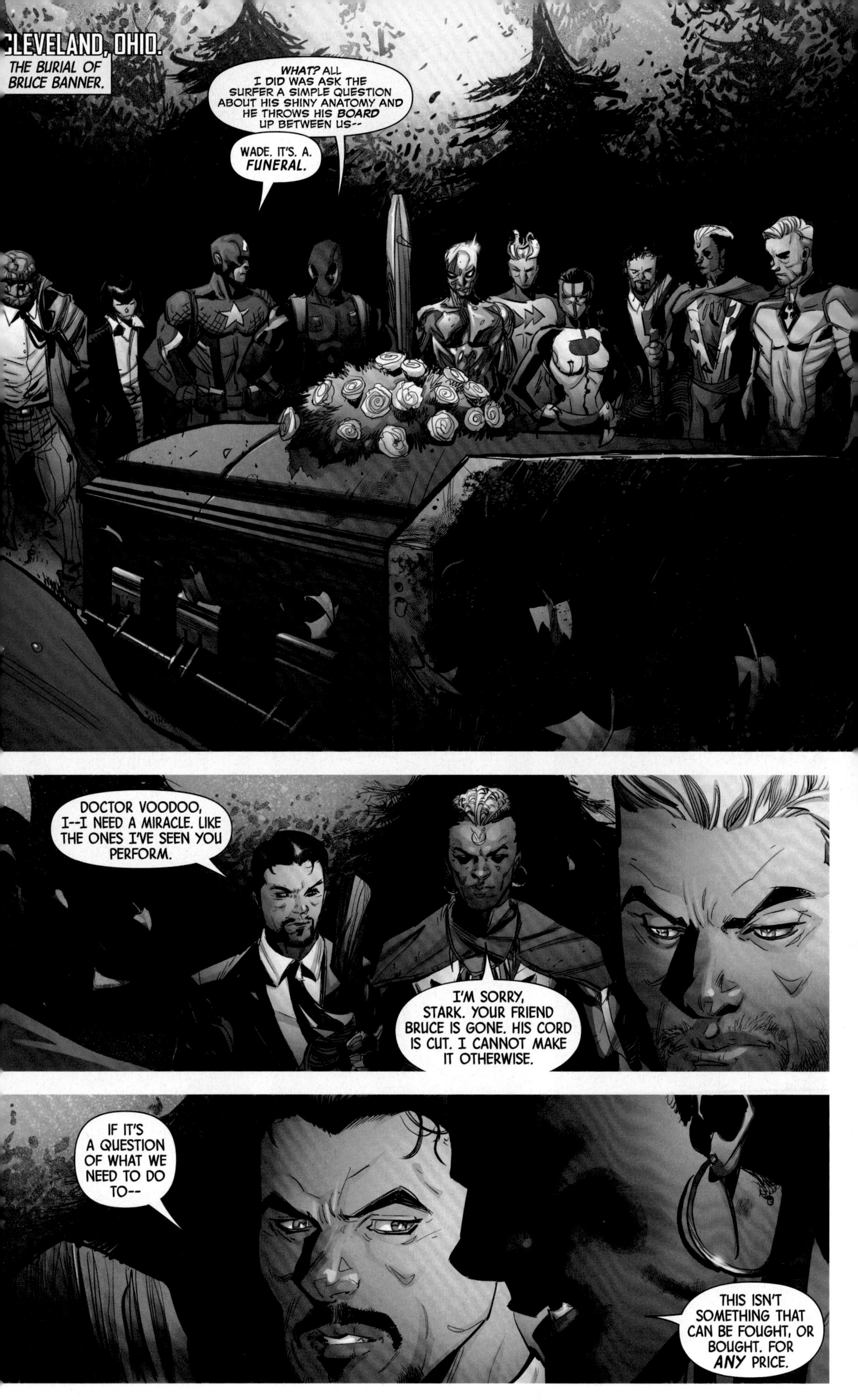
CLEVELAND, OHIO.
THE BURIAL OF BRUCE BANNER.
WHAT? ALL I DID WAS ASK THE SURFER A SIMPLE QUESTION ABOUT HIS SHINY ANATOMY AND HE THROWS HIS BOARD UP BETWEEN US--
WADE. IT'S. A. FUNERAL.
DOCTOR VOODOO, I--I NEED A MIRACLE. LIKE THE ONES I'VE SEEN YOU PERFORM.
I'M SORRY, STARK. YOUR FRIEND BRUCE IS GONE. HIS CORD IS CUT. I CANNOT MAKE IT OTHERWISE.
IF IT'S A QUESTION OF WHAT WE NEED TO DO TO--
THIS ISN'T SOMETHING THAT CAN BE FOUGHT, OR BOUGHT. FOR ANY PRICE.

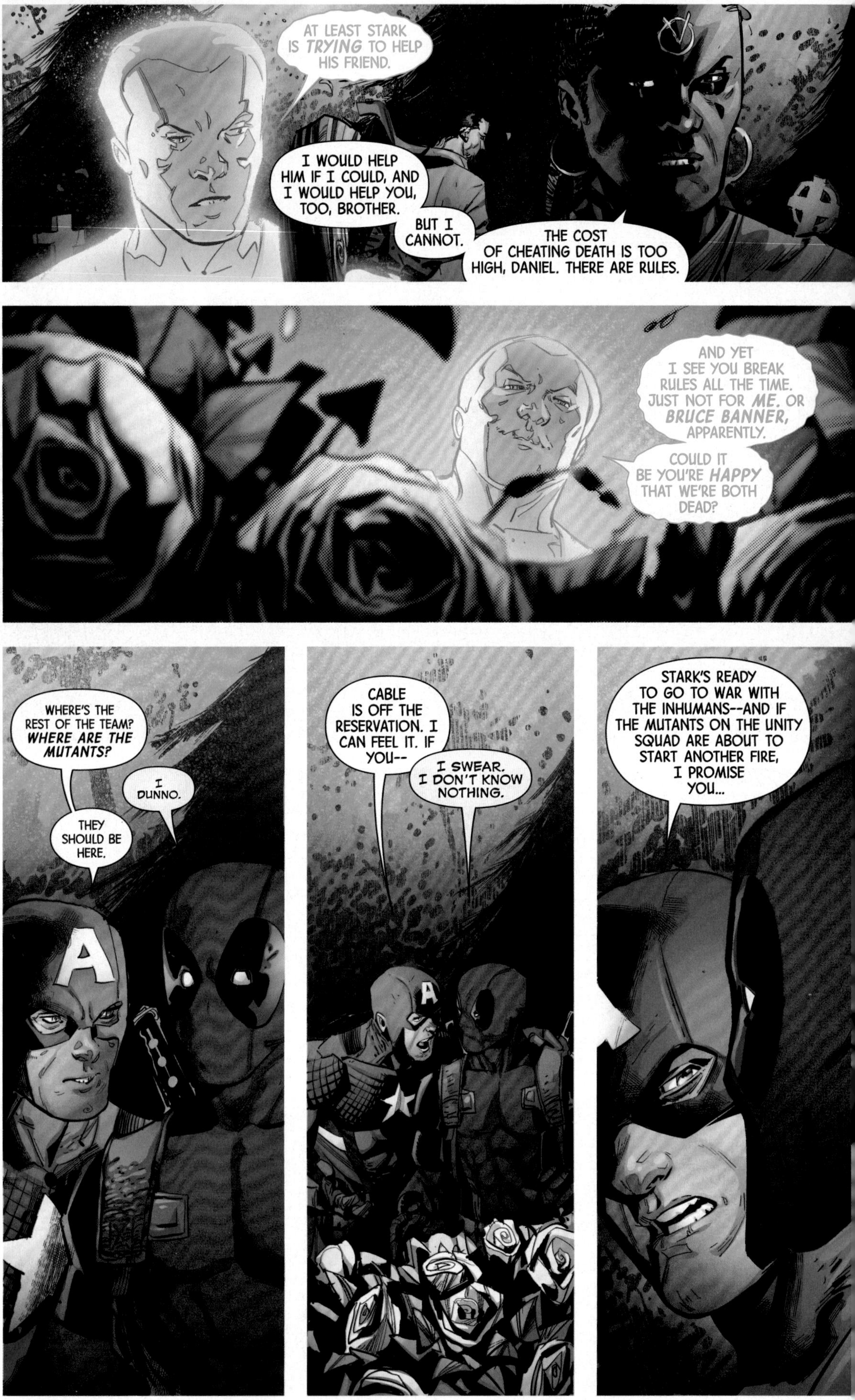
AT LEAST STARK IS *TRYING* TO HELP HIS FRIEND.
I WOULD HELP HIM IF I COULD, AND I WOULD HELP YOU, TOO, BROTHER.
BUT I CANNOT.
THE COST OF CHEATING DEATH IS TOO HIGH, DANIEL. THERE ARE RULES.
AND YET I SEE YOU BREAK RULES ALL THE TIME. JUST NOT FOR *ME.* OR *BRUCE BANNER,* APPARENTLY.
COULD IT BE YOU'RE *HAPPY* THAT WE'RE BOTH DEAD?
WHERE'S THE REST OF THE TEAM? *WHERE ARE THE MUTANTS?*
THEY SHOULD BE HERE.
I DUNNO.
CABLE IS OFF THE RESERVATION. I CAN FEEL IT. IF YOU--
I SWEAR. I DON'T KNOW NOTHING.
STARK'S READY TO GO TO WAR WITH THE INHUMANS--AND IF THE MUTANTS ON THE UNITY SQUAD ARE ABOUT TO START ANOTHER FIRE, I PROMISE YOU...

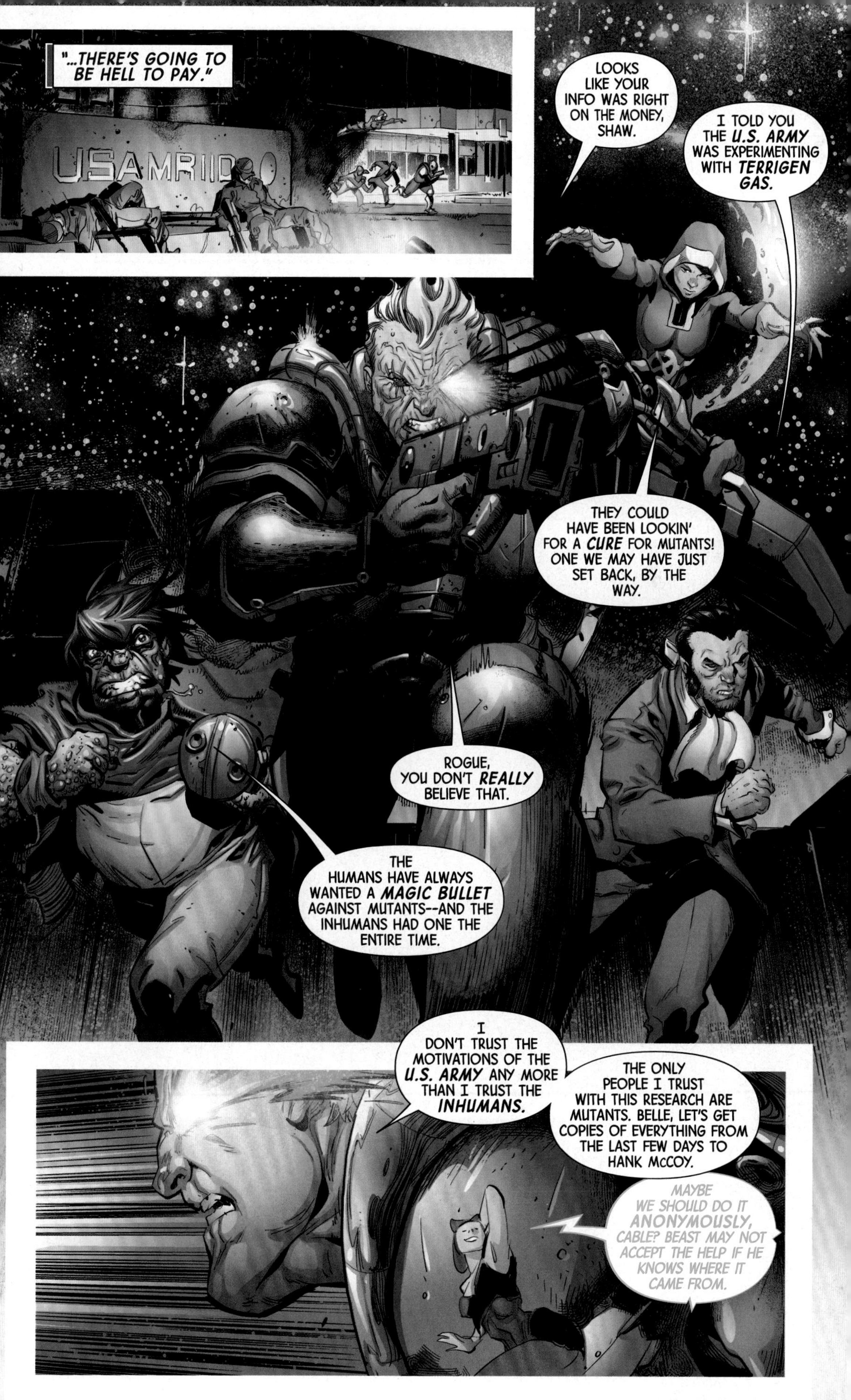
"...THERE'S GOING TO BE HELL TO PAY."
USAMRIID
LOOKS LIKE YOUR INFO WAS RIGHT ON THE MONEY, SHAW.
I TOLD YOU THE U.S. ARMY WAS EXPERIMENTING WITH TERRIGEN GAS.
THEY COULD HAVE BEEN LOOKIN' FOR A CURE FOR MUTANTS! ONE WE MAY HAVE JUST SET BACK, BY THE WAY.
ROGUE, YOU DON'T REALLY BELIEVE THAT.
THE HUMANS HAVE ALWAYS WANTED A MAGIC BULLET AGAINST MUTANTS--AND THE INHUMANS HAD ONE THE ENTIRE TIME.
I DON'T TRUST THE MOTIVATIONS OF THE U.S. ARMY ANY MORE THAN I TRUST THE INHUMANS.
THE ONLY PEOPLE I TRUST WITH THIS RESEARCH ARE MUTANTS. BELLE, LET'S GET COPIES OF EVERYTHING FROM THE LAST FEW DAYS TO HANK McCOY.
MAYBE WE SHOULD DO IT ANONYMOUSLY, CABLE? BEAST MAY NOT ACCEPT THE HELP IF HE KNOWS WHERE IT CAME FROM.

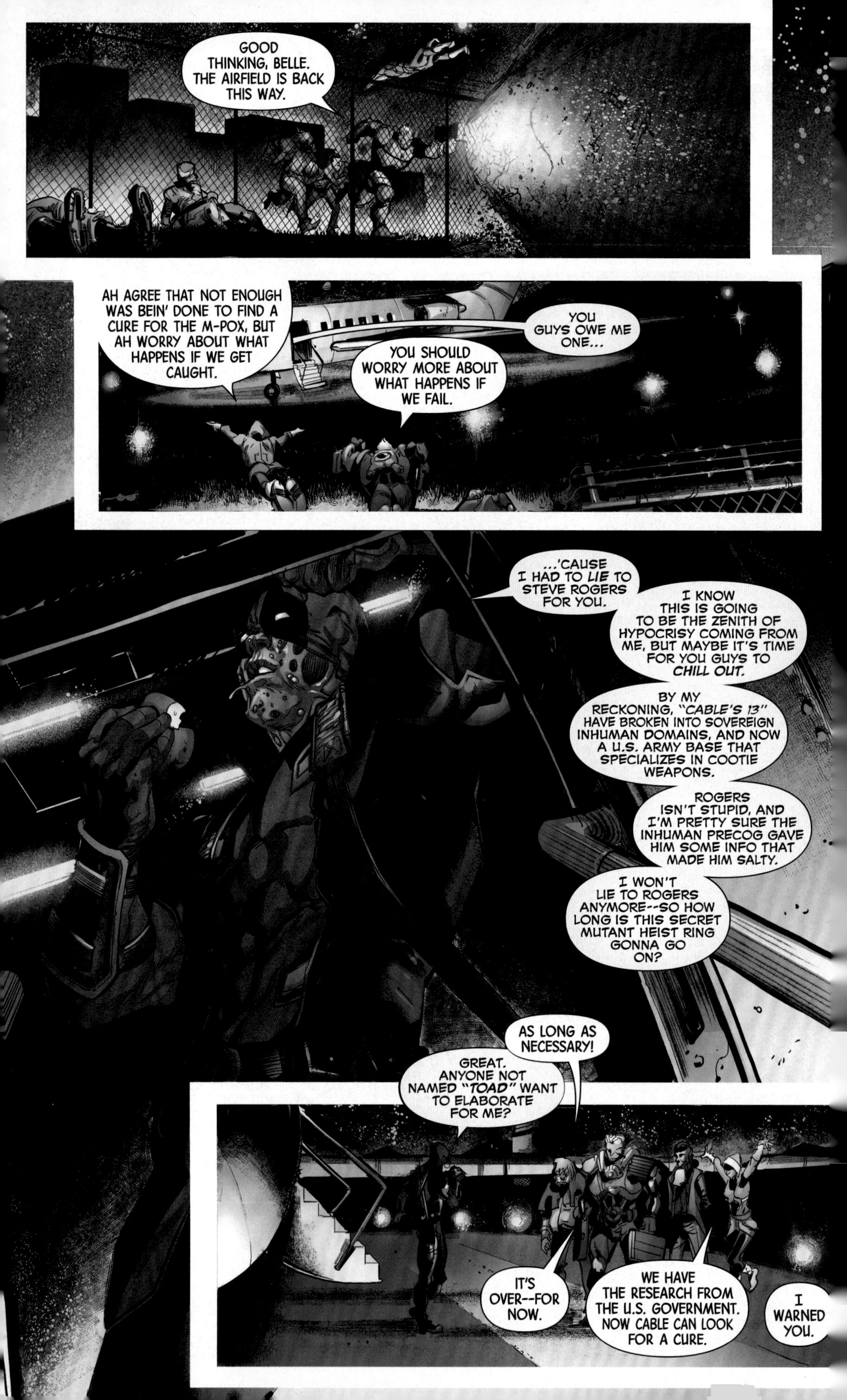
GOOD THINKING, BELLE. THE AIRFIELD IS BACK THIS WAY.
AH AGREE THAT NOT ENOUGH WAS BEIN' DONE TO FIND A CURE FOR THE M-POX, BUT AH WORRY ABOUT WHAT HAPPENS IF WE GET CAUGHT.
YOU SHOULD WORRY MORE ABOUT WHAT HAPPENS IF WE FAIL.
YOU GUYS OWE ME ONE...
...'CAUSE I HAD TO *LIE* TO STEVE ROGERS FOR YOU.
I KNOW THIS IS GOING TO BE THE ZENITH OF HYPOCRISY COMING FROM ME, BUT MAYBE IT'S TIME FOR YOU GUYS TO *CHILL OUT.*
BY MY RECKONING, "*CABLE'S 13*" HAVE BROKEN INTO SOVEREIGN INHUMAN DOMAINS, AND NOW A U.S. ARMY BASE THAT SPECIALIZES IN COOTIE WEAPONS.
ROGERS ISN'T STUPID, AND I'M PRETTY SURE THE INHUMAN PRECOG GAVE HIM SOME INFO THAT MADE HIM SALTY.
I WON'T LIE TO ROGERS ANYMORE--SO HOW LONG IS THIS SECRET MUTANT HEIST RING GONNA GO ON?
AS LONG AS NECESSARY!
GREAT. ANYONE NOT NAMED "*TOAD*" WANT TO ELABORATE FOR ME?
IT'S OVER--FOR NOW.
WE HAVE THE RESEARCH FROM THE U.S. GOVERNMENT. NOW CABLE CAN LOOK FOR A CURE.
I WARNED YOU.

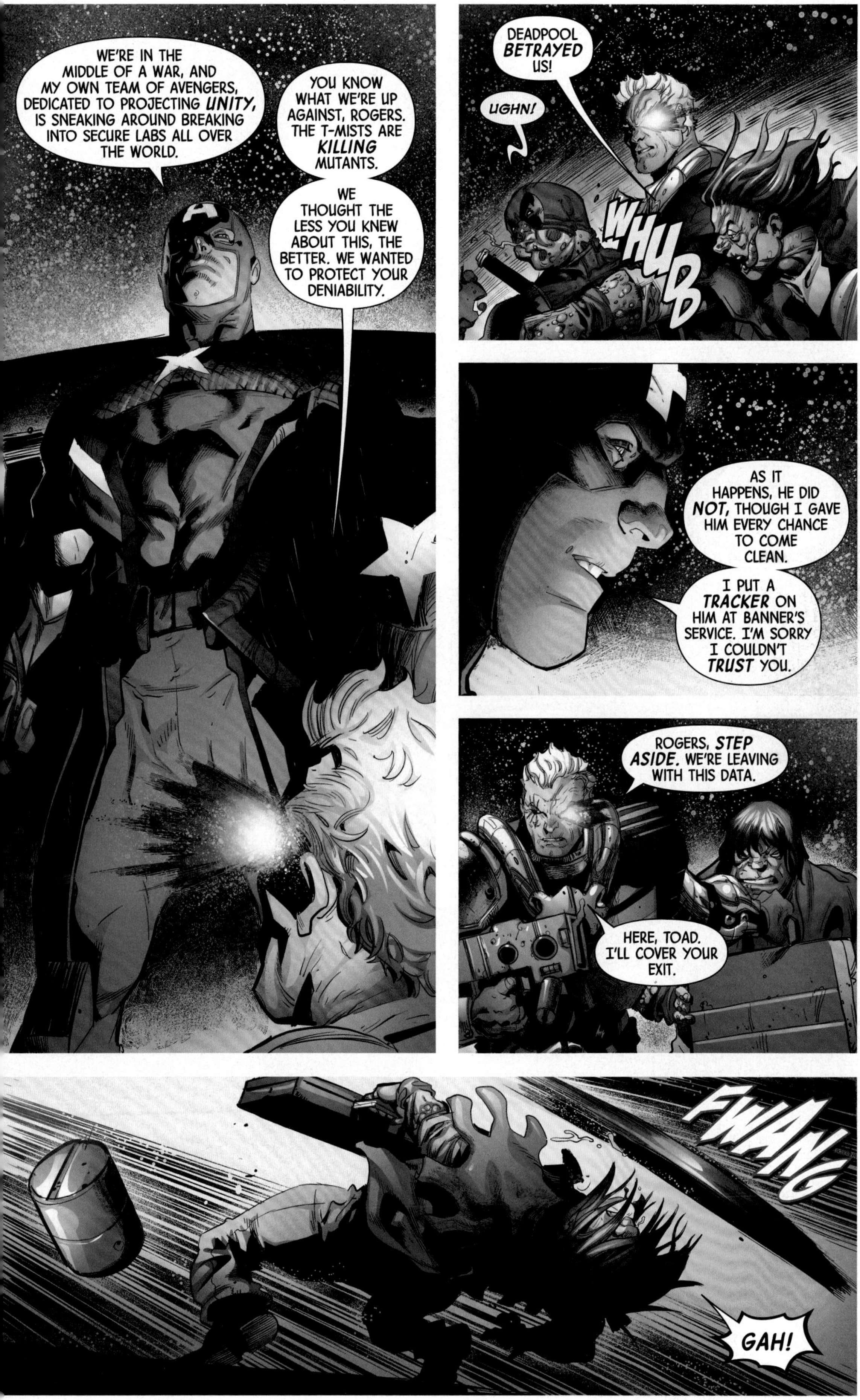
WE'RE IN THE MIDDLE OF A WAR, AND MY OWN TEAM OF AVENGERS, DEDICATED TO PROJECTING UNITY, IS SNEAKING AROUND BREAKING INTO SECURE LABS ALL OVER THE WORLD.
YOU KNOW WHAT WE'RE UP AGAINST, ROGERS. THE T-MISTS ARE KILLING MUTANTS.
WE THOUGHT THE LESS YOU KNEW ABOUT THIS, THE BETTER. WE WANTED TO PROTECT YOUR DENIABILITY.
DEADPOOL BETRAYED US!
UGHN!
WHUB
AS IT HAPPENS, HE DID NOT, THOUGH I GAVE HIM EVERY CHANCE TO COME CLEAN.
I PUT A TRACKER ON HIM AT BANNER'S SERVICE. I'M SORRY I COULDN'T TRUST YOU.
ROGERS, STEP ASIDE. WE'RE LEAVING WITH THIS DATA.
HERE, TOAD. I'LL COVER YOUR EXIT.
FWANG
GAH!

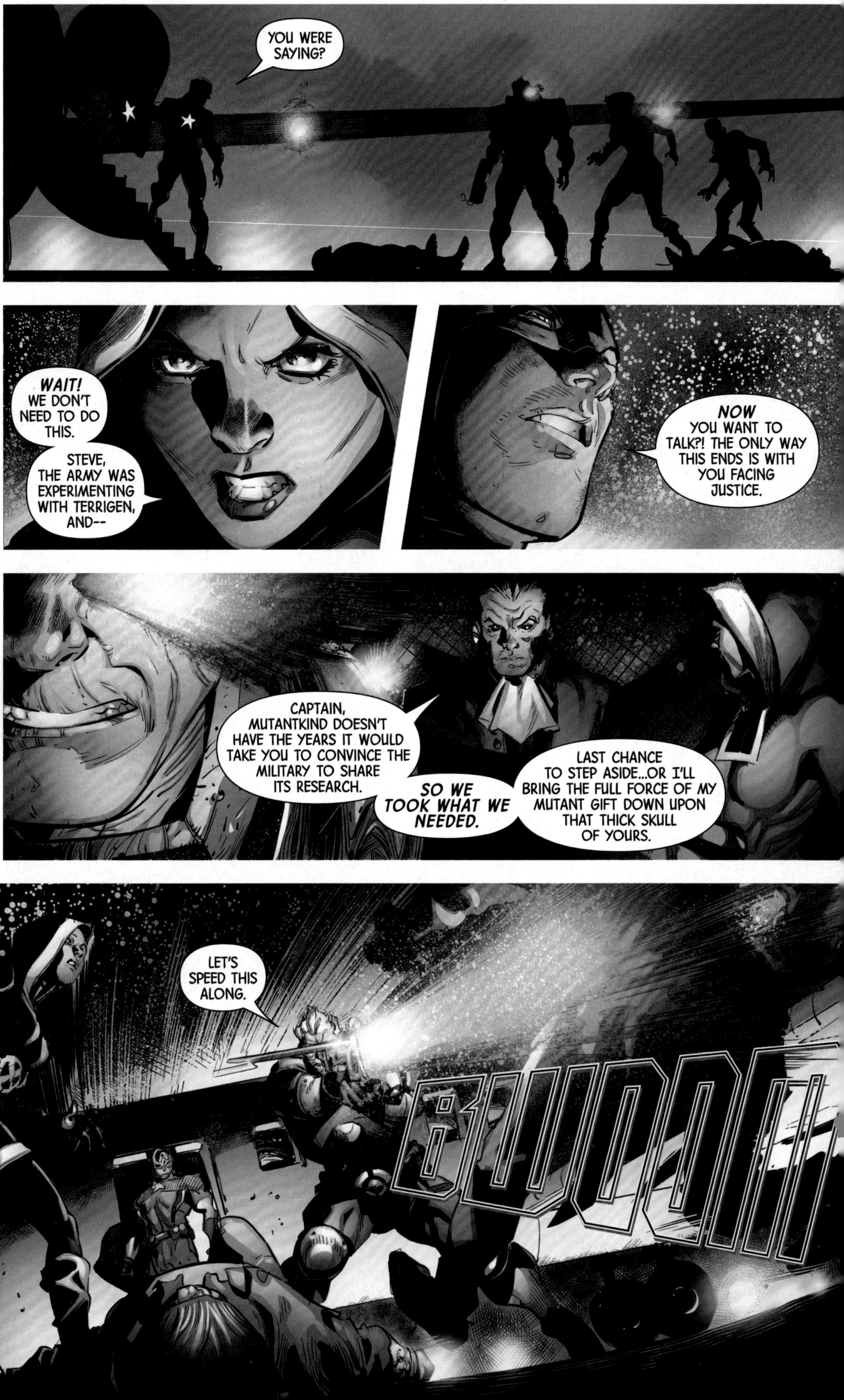
YOU WERE SAYING?
WAIT! WE DON'T NEED TO DO THIS.
STEVE, THE ARMY WAS EXPERIMENTING WITH TERRIGEN, AND--
NOW YOU WANT TO TALK?! THE ONLY WAY THIS ENDS IS WITH YOU FACING JUSTICE.
CAPTAIN, MUTANTKIND DOESN'T HAVE THE YEARS IT WOULD TAKE YOU TO CONVINCE THE MILITARY TO SHARE ITS RESEARCH.
SO WE TOOK WHAT WE NEEDED.
LAST CHANCE TO STEP ASIDE...OR I'LL BRING THE FULL FORCE OF MY MUTANT GIFT DOWN UPON THAT THICK SKULL OF YOURS.
LET'S SPEED THIS ALONG.

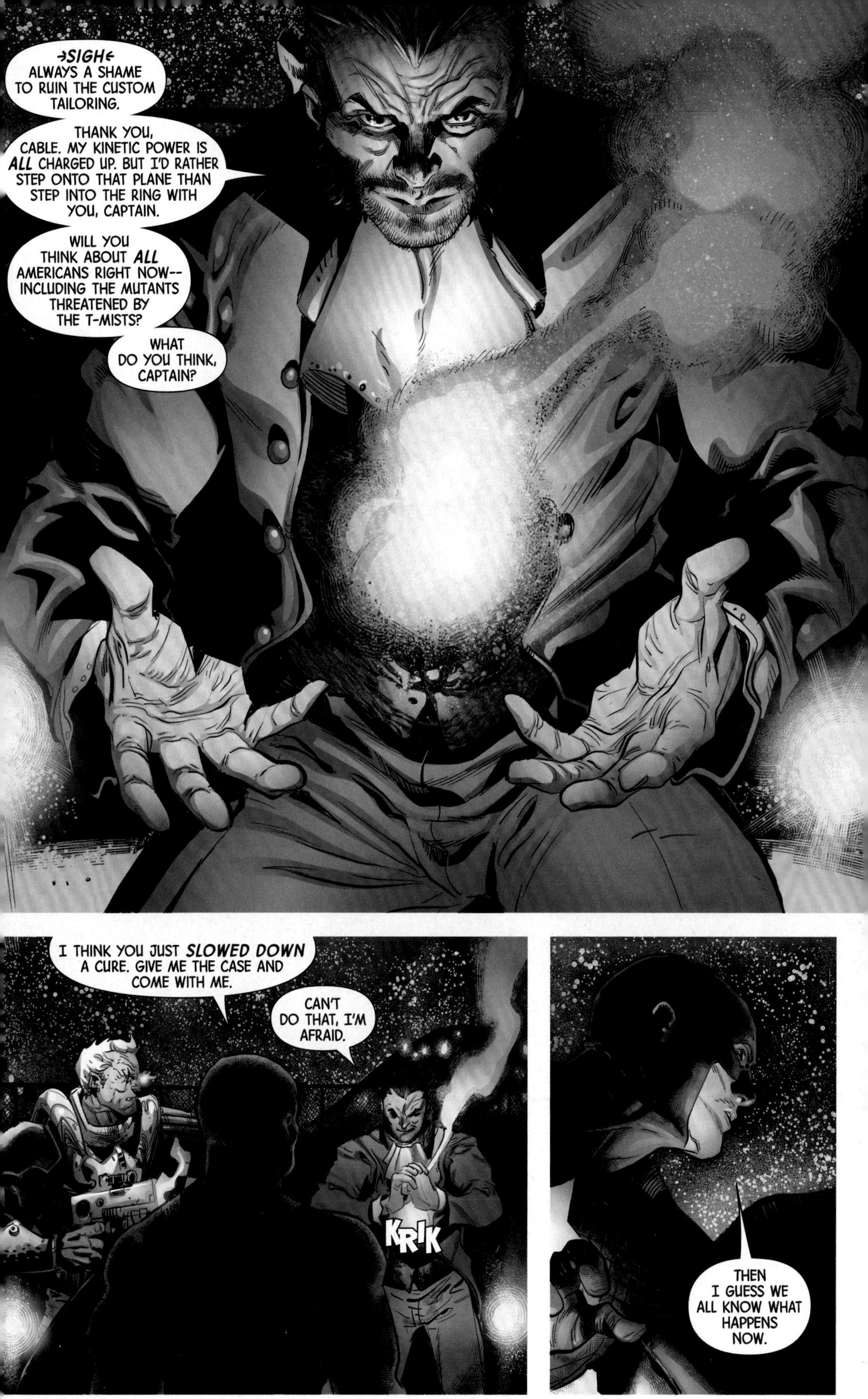
→SIGH← ALWAYS A SHAME TO RUIN THE CUSTOM TAILORING.
THANK YOU, CABLE. MY KINETIC POWER IS ALL CHARGED UP. BUT I'D RATHER STEP ONTO THAT PLANE THAN STEP INTO THE RING WITH YOU, CAPTAIN.
WILL YOU THINK ABOUT ALL AMERICANS RIGHT NOW-- INCLUDING THE MUTANTS THREATENED BY THE T-MISTS?
WHAT DO YOU THINK, CAPTAIN?
I THINK YOU JUST SLOWED DOWN A CURE. GIVE ME THE CASE AND COME WITH ME.
CAN'T DO THAT, I'M AFRAID.
KRIK
THEN I GUESS WE ALL KNOW WHAT HAPPENS NOW.

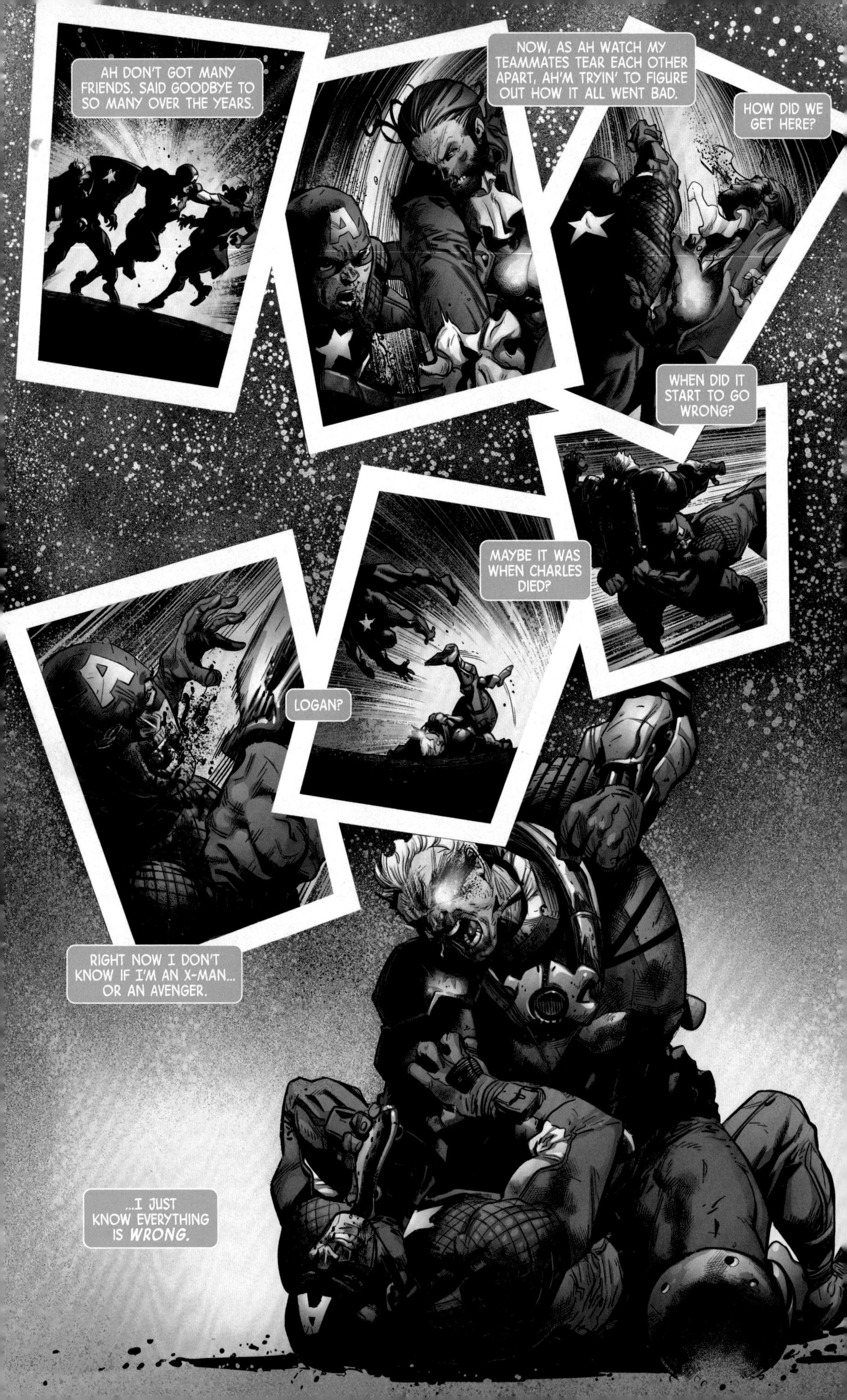
AH DON'T GOT MANY FRIENDS. SAID GOODBYE TO SO MANY OVER THE YEARS.
NOW, AS AH WATCH MY TEAMMATES TEAR EACH OTHER APART, AH'M TRYIN' TO FIGURE OUT HOW IT ALL WENT BAD.
HOW DID WE GET HERE?
WHEN DID IT START TO GO WRONG?
MAYBE IT WAS WHEN CHARLES DIED?
LOGAN?
RIGHT NOW I DON'T KNOW IF I'M AN X-MAN... OR AN AVENGER.
...I JUST KNOW EVERYTHING IS *WRONG.*

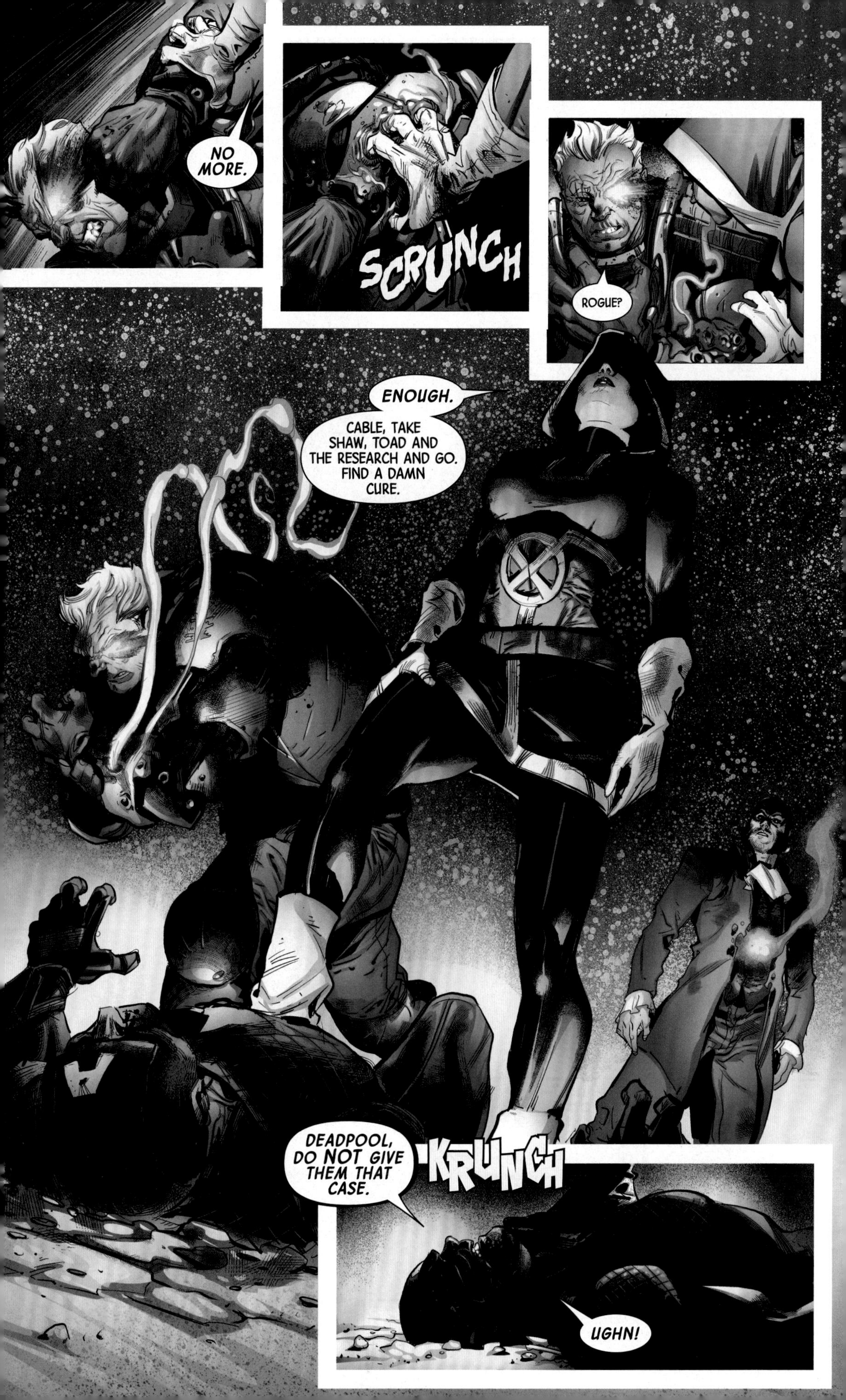
NO MORE.
SCRUNCH
ROGUE?
ENOUGH.
CABLE, TAKE SHAW, TOAD AND THE RESEARCH AND GO. FIND A DAMN CURE.
DEADPOOL, DO NOT GIVE THEM THAT CASE.
KRUNCH
UGHN!

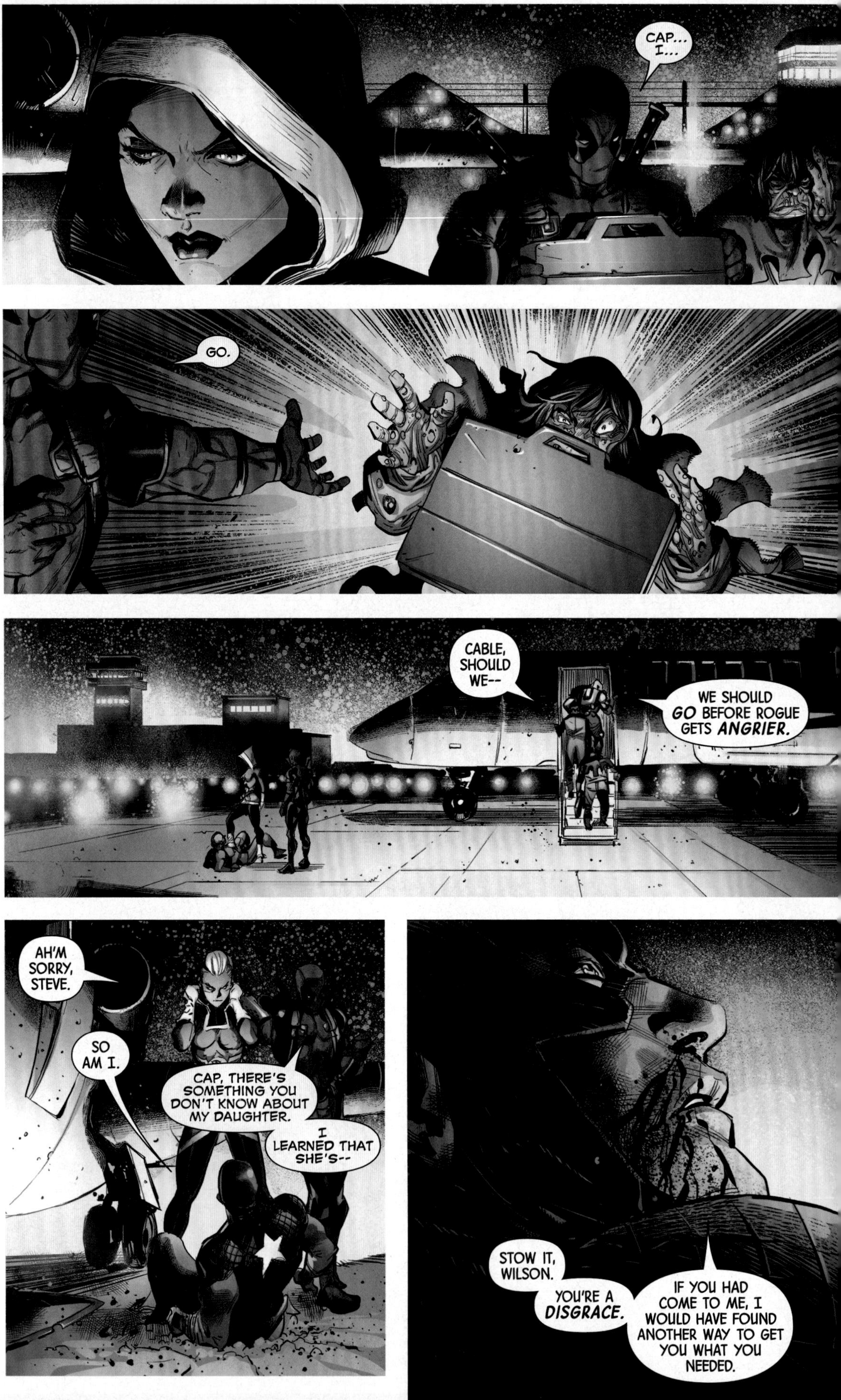

CAP... I...
GO.
CABLE, SHOULD WE--
WE SHOULD GO BEFORE ROGUE GETS ANGRIER.
AH'M SORRY, STEVE.
SO AM I.
CAP, THERE'S SOMETHING YOU DON'T KNOW ABOUT MY DAUGHTER.
I LEARNED THAT SHE'S--
STOW IT, WILSON.
YOU'RE A DISGRACE.
IF YOU HAD COME TO ME, I WOULD HAVE FOUND ANOTHER WAY TO GET YOU WHAT YOU NEEDED.

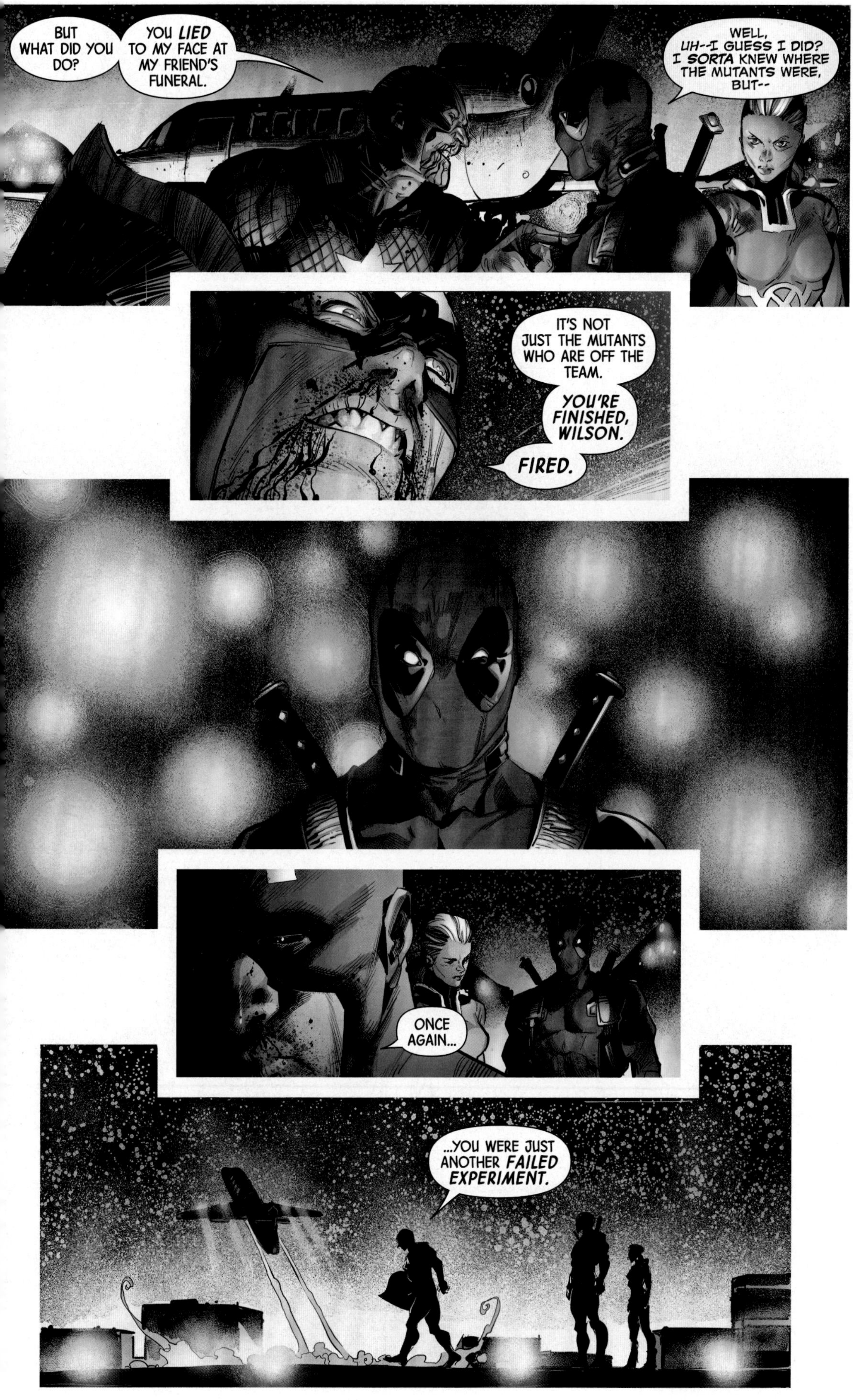
BUT WHAT DID YOU DO?
YOU LIED TO MY FACE AT MY FRIEND'S FUNERAL.
WELL, UH--I GUESS I DID? I SORTA KNEW WHERE THE MUTANTS WERE, BUT--
IT'S NOT JUST THE MUTANTS WHO ARE OFF THE TEAM.
YOU'RE FINISHED, WILSON.
FIRED.
ONCE AGAIN...
...YOU WERE JUST ANOTHER FAILED EXPERIMENT.

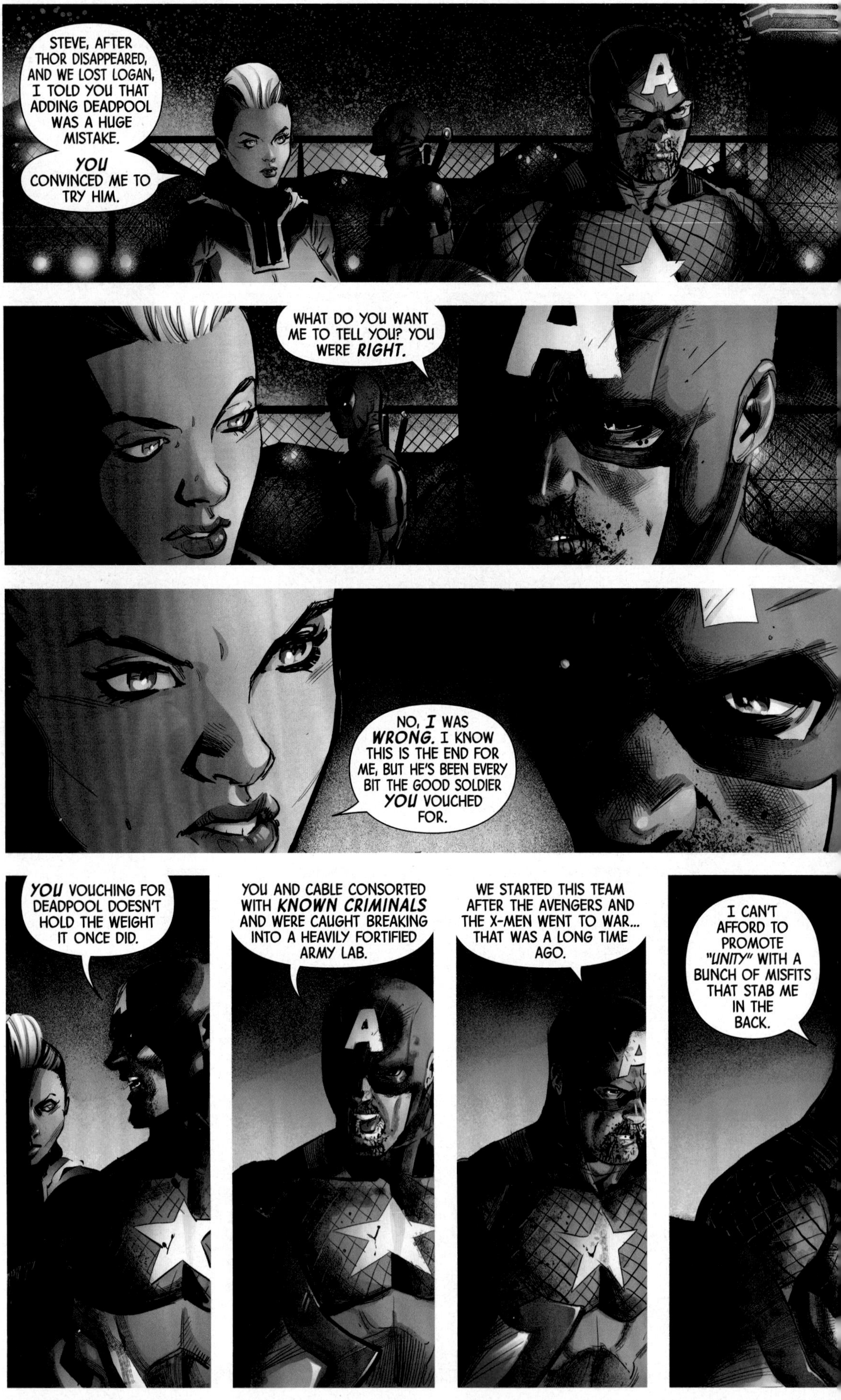
STEVE, AFTER THOR DISAPPEARED, AND WE LOST LOGAN, I TOLD YOU THAT ADDING DEADPOOL WAS A HUGE MISTAKE.
YOU CONVINCED ME TO TRY HIM.
WHAT DO YOU WANT ME TO TELL YOU? YOU WERE RIGHT.
NO, I WAS WRONG. I KNOW THIS IS THE END FOR ME, BUT HE'S BEEN EVERY BIT THE GOOD SOLDIER YOU VOUCHED FOR.
YOU VOUCHING FOR DEADPOOL DOESN'T HOLD THE WEIGHT IT ONCE DID.
YOU AND CABLE CONSORTED WITH KNOWN CRIMINALS AND WERE CAUGHT BREAKING INTO A HEAVILY FORTIFIED ARMY LAB.
WE STARTED THIS TEAM AFTER THE AVENGERS AND THE X-MEN WENT TO WAR... THAT WAS A LONG TIME AGO.
I CAN'T AFFORD TO PROMOTE "UNITY" WITH A BUNCH OF MISFITS THAT STAB ME IN THE BACK.

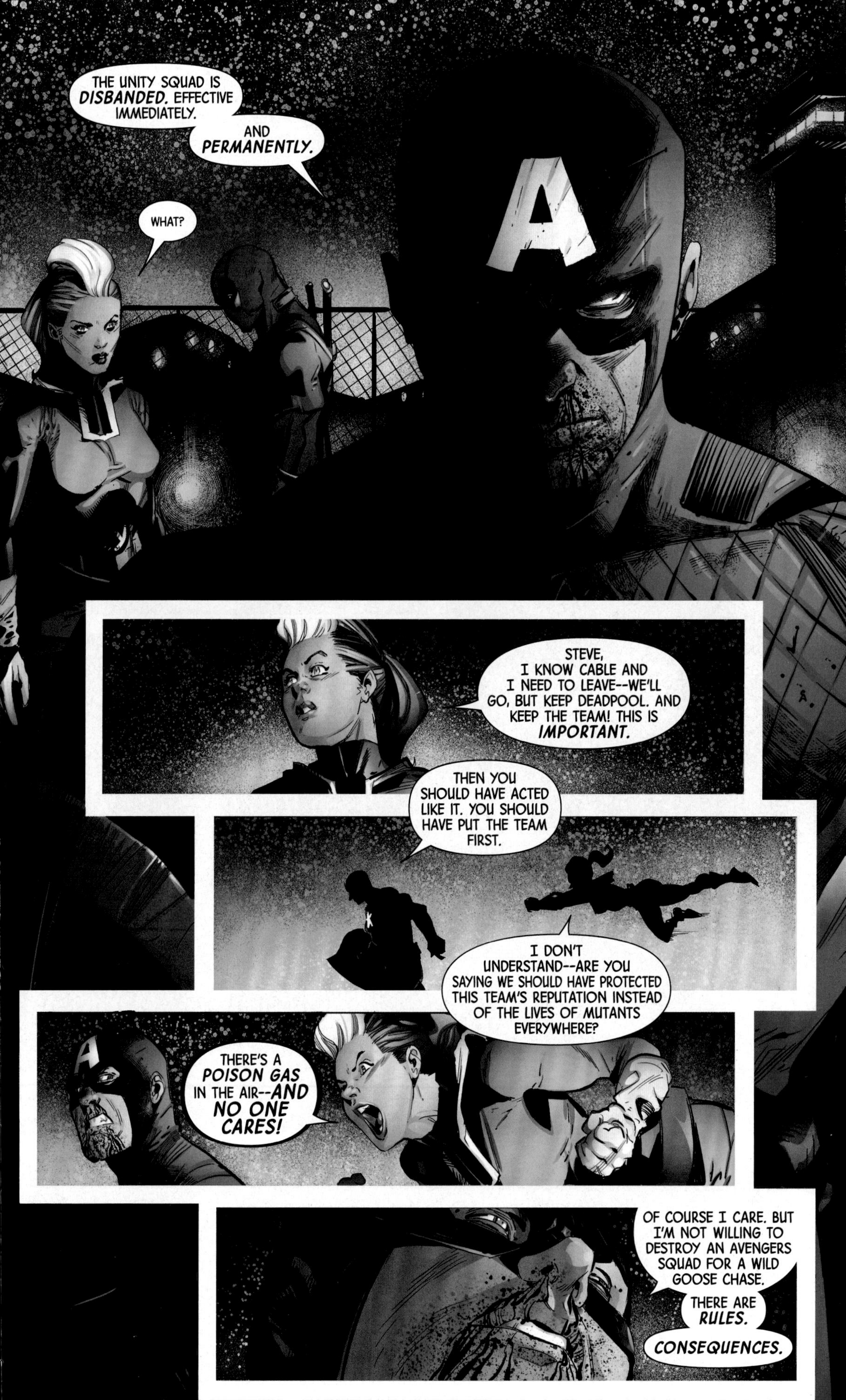
THE UNITY SQUAD IS DISBANDED. EFFECTIVE IMMEDIATELY.
AND PERMANENTLY.
WHAT?
STEVE, I KNOW CABLE AND I NEED TO LEAVE--WE'LL GO, BUT KEEP DEADPOOL. AND KEEP THE TEAM! THIS IS IMPORTANT.
THEN YOU SHOULD HAVE ACTED LIKE IT. YOU SHOULD HAVE PUT THE TEAM FIRST.
I DON'T UNDERSTAND--ARE YOU SAYING WE SHOULD HAVE PROTECTED THIS TEAM'S REPUTATION INSTEAD OF THE LIVES OF MUTANTS EVERYWHERE?
THERE'S A POISON GAS IN THE AIR--AND NO ONE CARES!
OF COURSE I CARE. BUT I'M NOT WILLING TO DESTROY AN AVENGERS SQUAD FOR A WILD GOOSE CHASE.
THERE ARE RULES.
CONSEQUENCES.

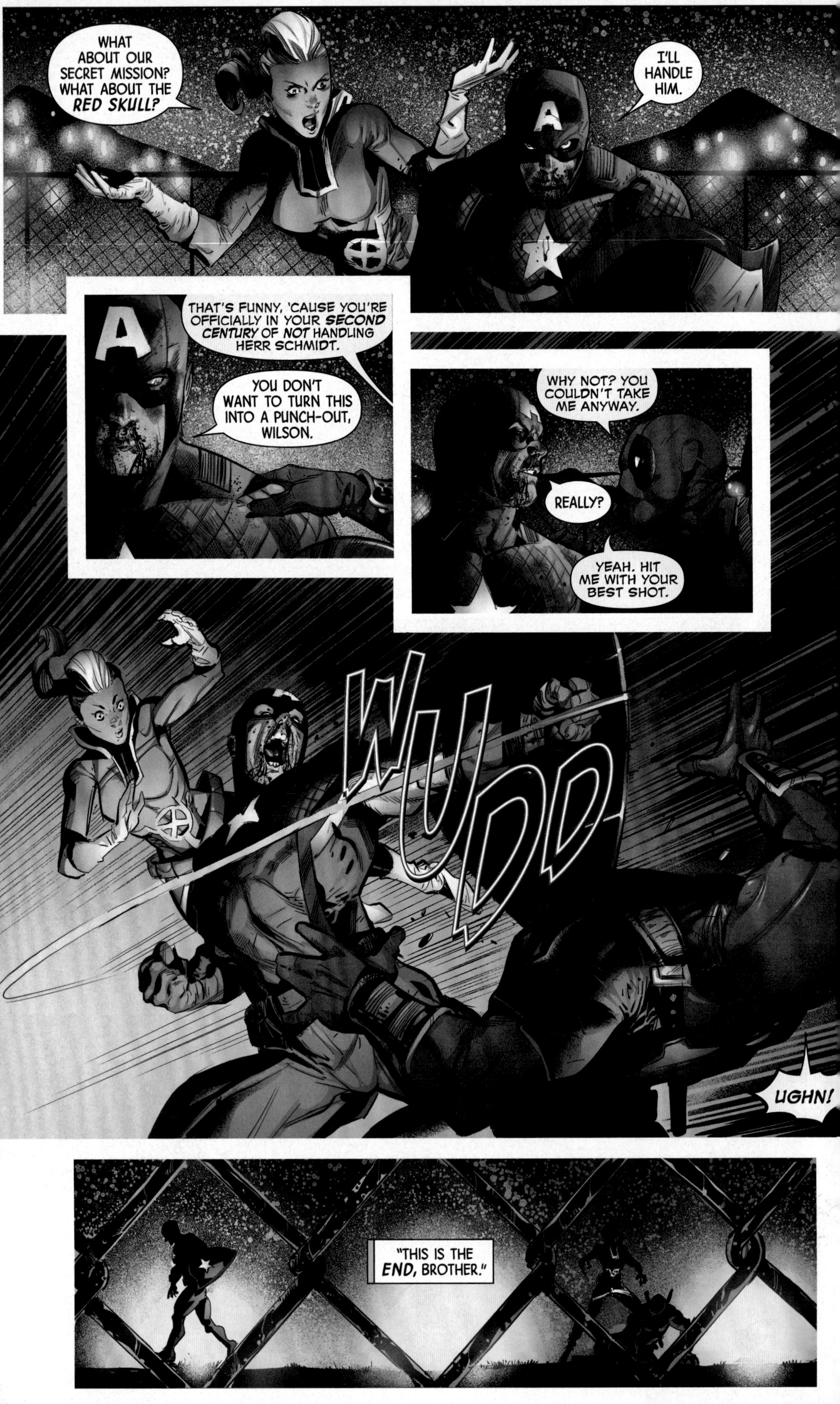
WHAT ABOUT OUR SECRET MISSION? WHAT ABOUT THE RED SKULL?
I'LL HANDLE HIM.
THAT'S FUNNY, 'CAUSE YOU'RE OFFICIALLY IN YOUR SECOND CENTURY OF NOT HANDLING HERR SCHMIDT.
YOU DON'T WANT TO TURN THIS INTO A PUNCH-OUT, WILSON.
WHY NOT? YOU COULDN'T TAKE ME ANYWAY.
REALLY?
YEAH. HIT ME WITH YOUR BEST SHOT.
WUDD
UGHN!
"THIS IS THE END, BROTHER."

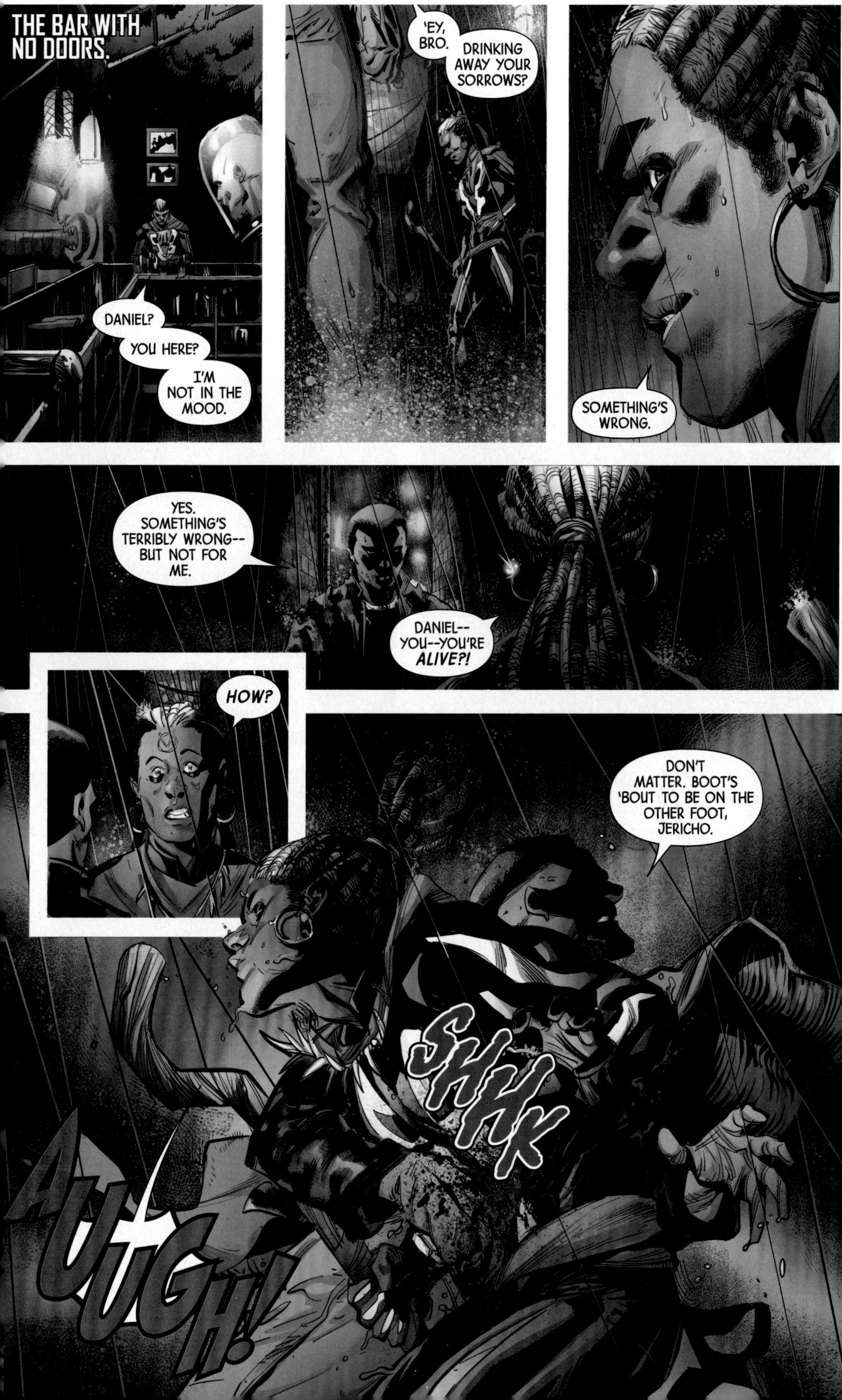
THE BAR WITH NO DOORS.
DANIEL?
YOU HERE?
I'M NOT IN THE MOOD.
'EY, BRO.
DRINKING AWAY YOUR SORROWS?
SOMETHING'S WRONG.
YES. SOMETHING'S TERRIBLY WRONG-- BUT NOT FOR ME.
DANIEL-- YOU--YOU'RE ALIVE?!
HOW?
DON'T MATTER. BOOT'S 'BOUT TO BE ON THE OTHER FOOT, JERICHO.
SHHK
AUUGH!

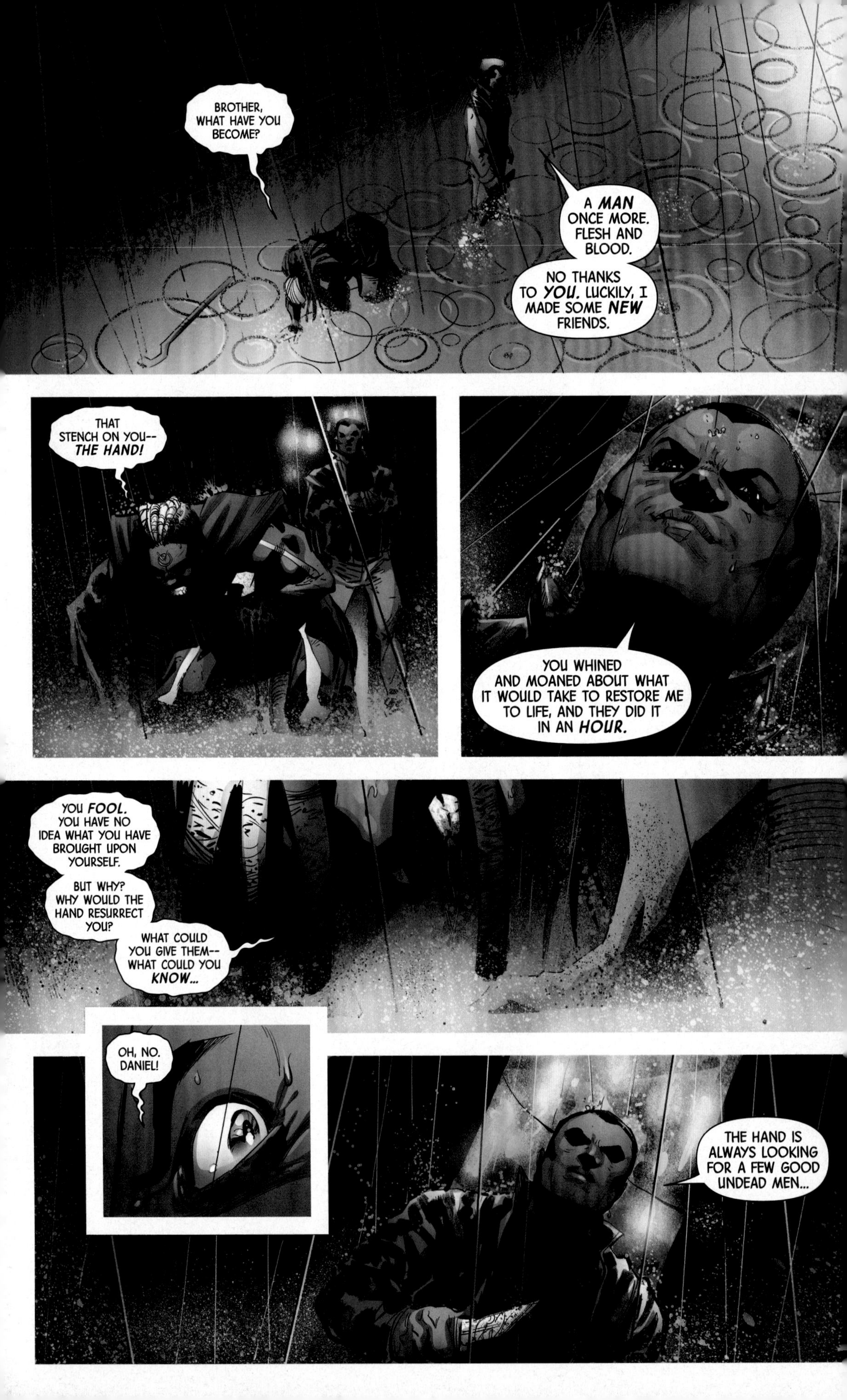
BROTHER, WHAT HAVE YOU BECOME?
A MAN ONCE MORE. FLESH AND BLOOD.
NO THANKS TO YOU. LUCKILY, I MADE SOME NEW FRIENDS.
THAT STENCH ON YOU-- THE HAND!
YOU WHINED AND MOANED ABOUT WHAT IT WOULD TAKE TO RESTORE ME TO LIFE, AND THEY DID IT IN AN HOUR.
YOU FOOL. YOU HAVE NO IDEA WHAT YOU HAVE BROUGHT UPON YOURSELF.
BUT WHY? WHY WOULD THE HAND RESURRECT YOU?
WHAT COULD YOU GIVE THEM-- WHAT COULD YOU KNOW...
OH, NO. DANIEL!
THE HAND IS ALWAYS LOOKING FOR A FEW GOOD UNDEAD MEN...

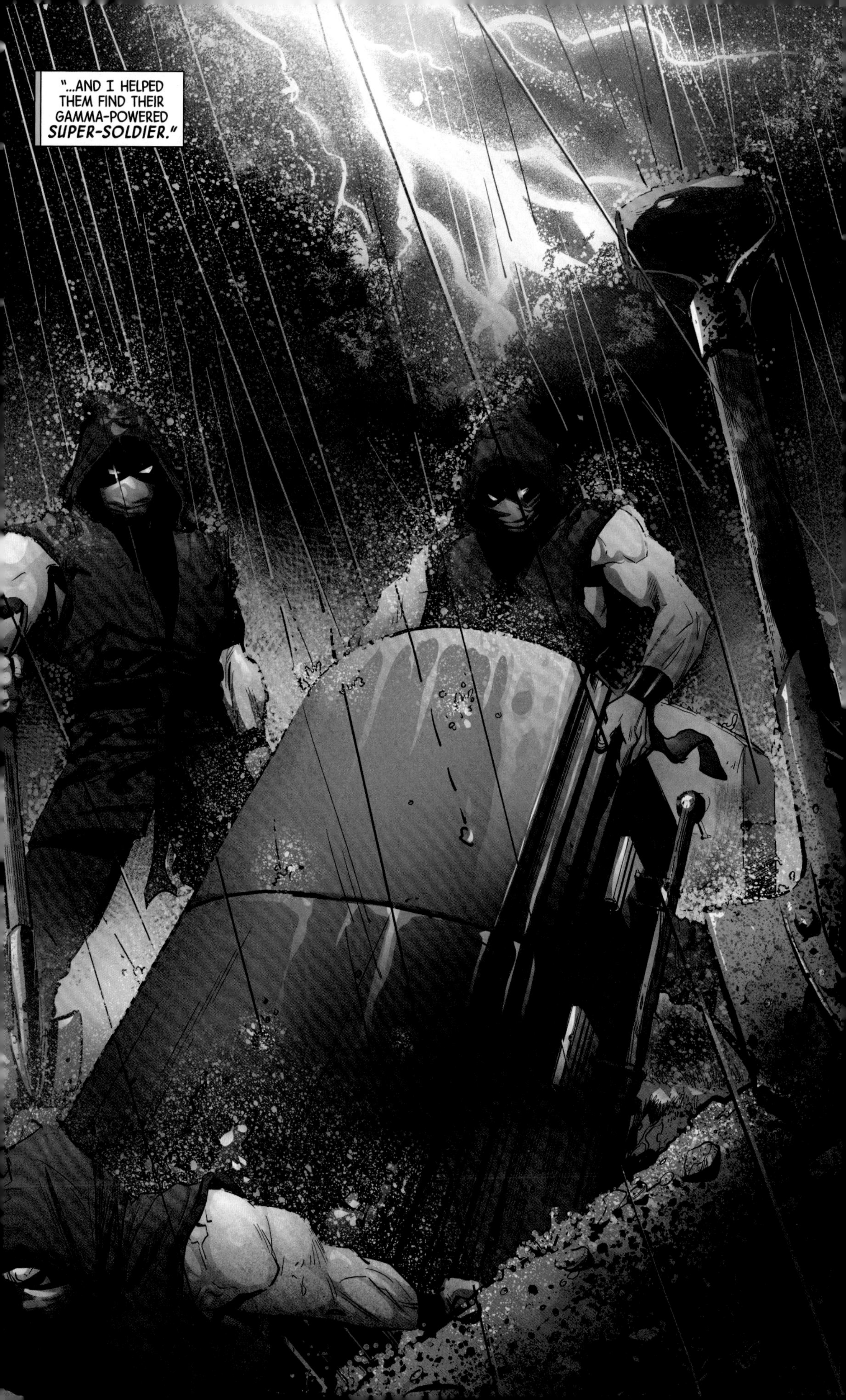
"...AND I HELPED THEM FIND THEIR GAMMA-POWERED SUPER-SOLDIER."

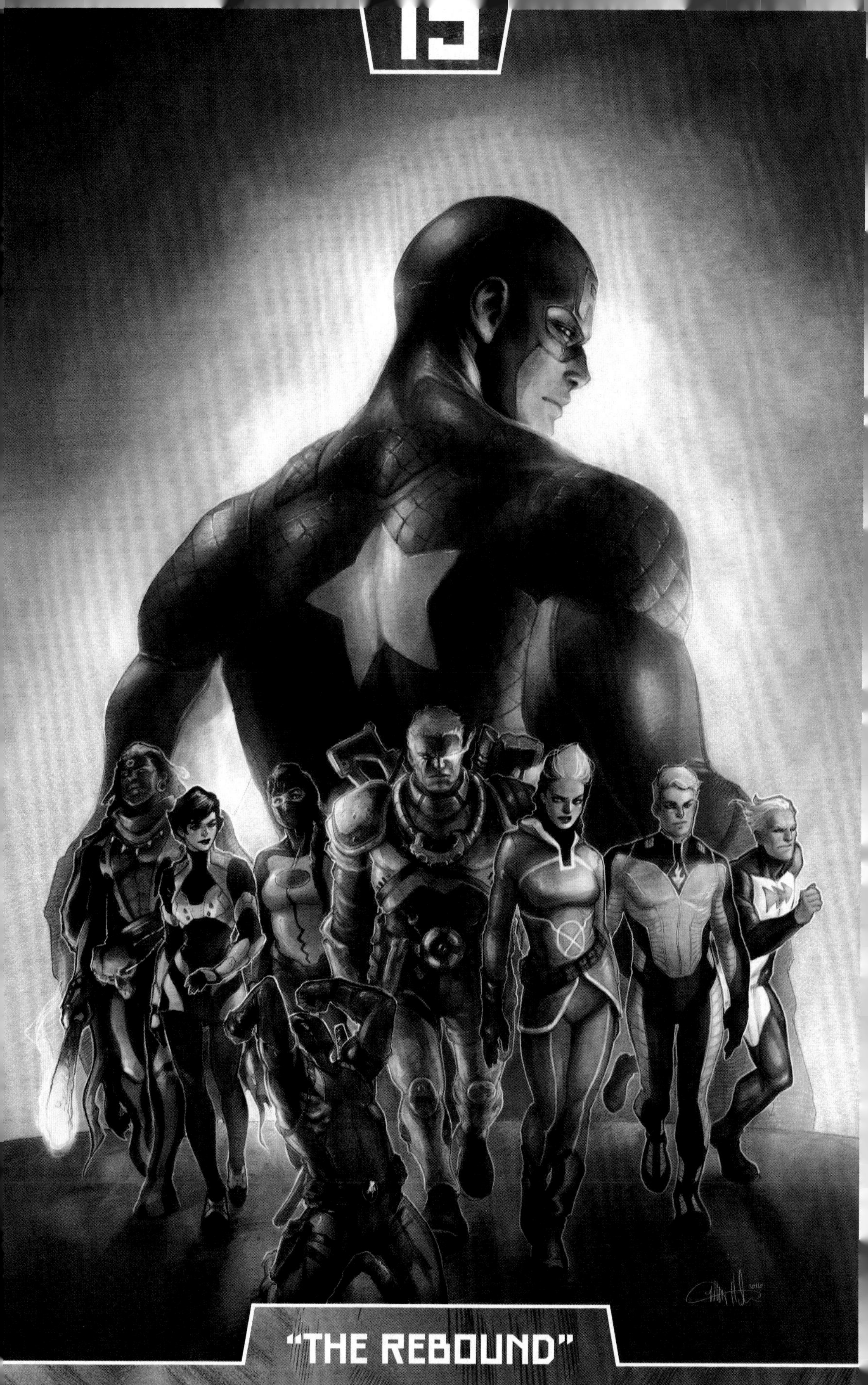
"THE REBOUND"

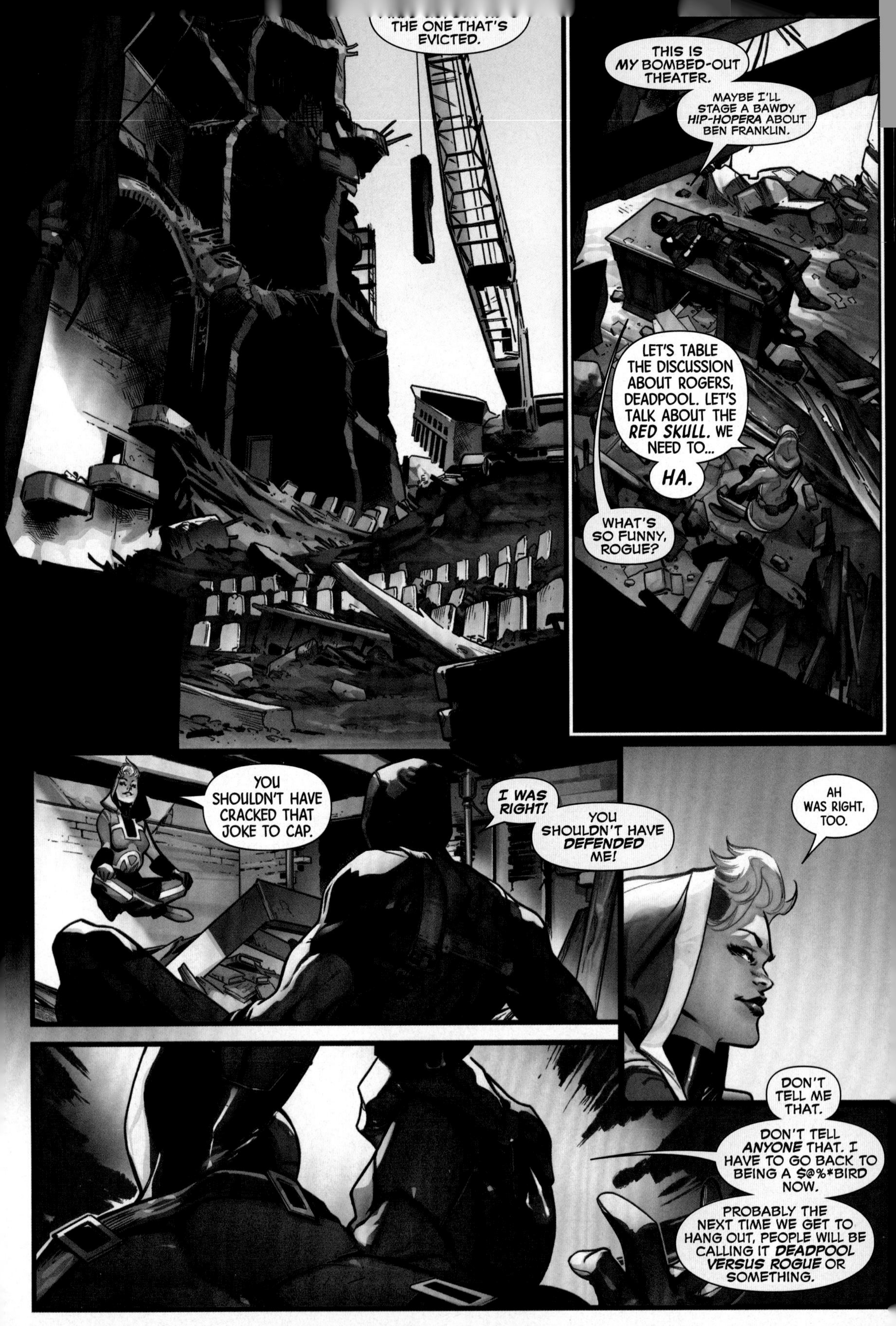
THE ONE THAT'S EVICTED.
THIS IS MY BOMBED-OUT THEATER.
MAYBE I'LL STAGE A BAWDY HIP-HOPERA ABOUT BEN FRANKLIN.
LET'S TABLE THE DISCUSSION ABOUT ROGERS, DEADPOOL. LET'S TALK ABOUT THE RED SKULL. WE NEED TO...
HA.
WHAT'S SO FUNNY, ROGUE?
YOU SHOULDN'T HAVE CRACKED THAT JOKE TO CAP.
I WAS RIGHT!
YOU SHOULDN'T HAVE DEFENDED ME!
AH WAS RIGHT, TOO.
DON'T TELL ME THAT.
DON'T TELL ANYONE THAT. I HAVE TO GO BACK TO BEING A $@%*BIRD NOW.
PROBABLY THE NEXT TIME WE GET TO HANG OUT, PEOPLE WILL BE CALLING IT DEADPOOL VERSUS ROGUE OR SOMETHING.

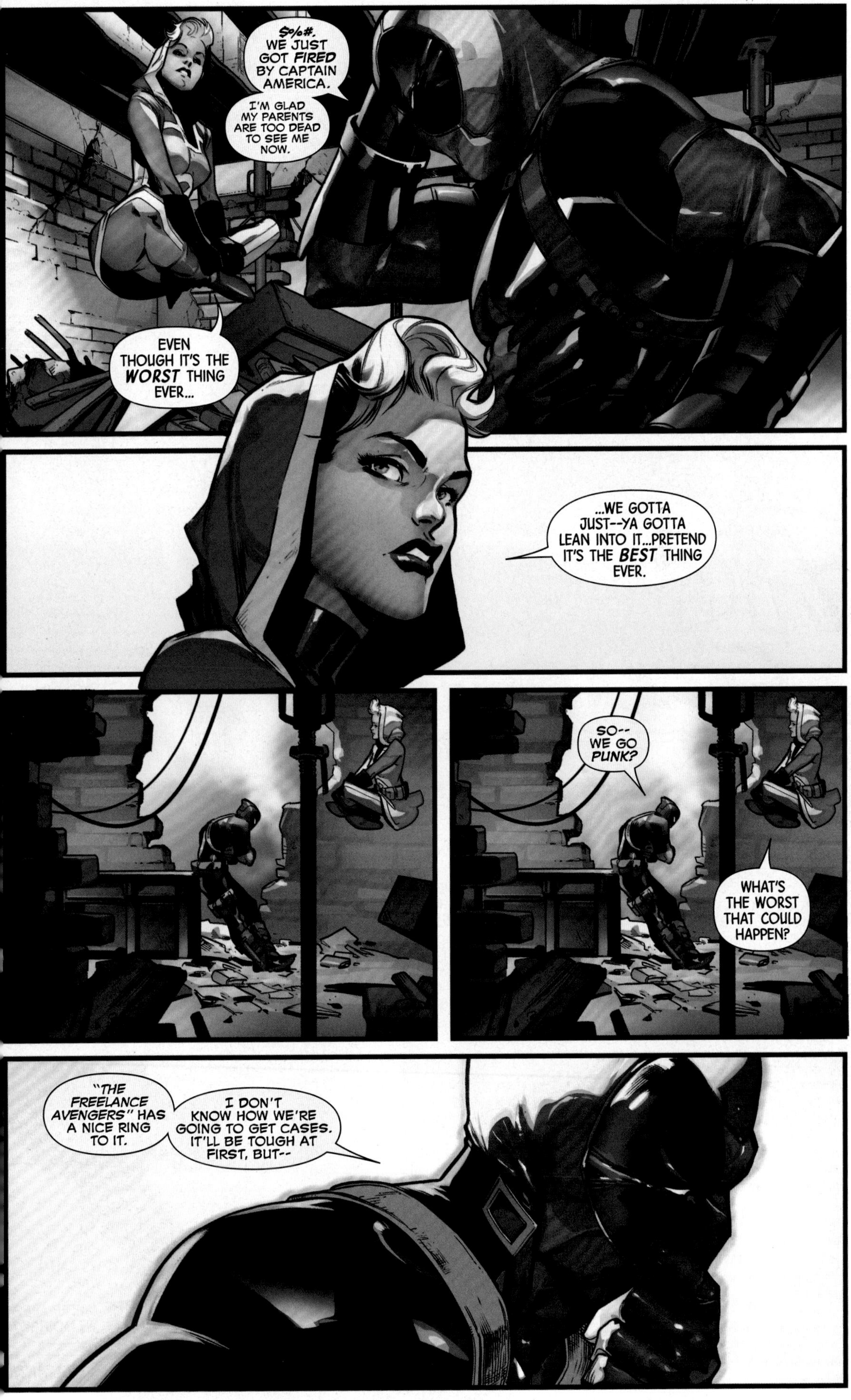
$%#. WE JUST GOT FIRED BY CAPTAIN AMERICA.
I'M GLAD MY PARENTS ARE TOO DEAD TO SEE ME NOW.
EVEN THOUGH IT'S THE WORST THING EVER...
...WE GOTTA JUST--YA GOTTA LEAN INTO IT...PRETEND IT'S THE BEST THING EVER.
SO-- WE GO PUNK?
WHAT'S THE WORST THAT COULD HAPPEN?
"THE FREELANCE AVENGERS" HAS A NICE RING TO IT.
I DON'T KNOW HOW WE'RE GOING TO GET CASES. IT'LL BE TOUGH AT FIRST, BUT--

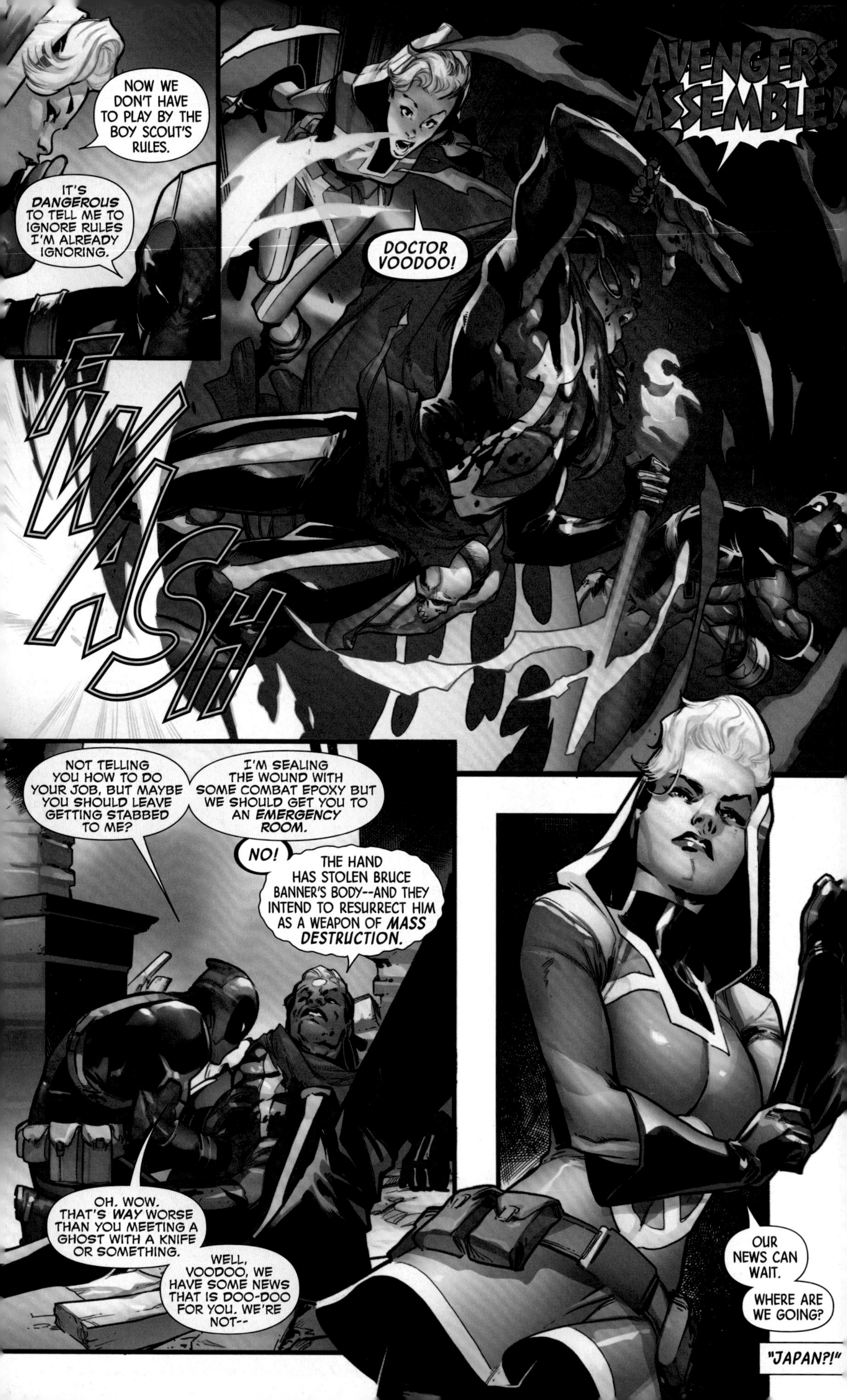
NOW WE DON'T HAVE TO PLAY BY THE BOY SCOUT'S RULES.
IT'S DANGEROUS TO TELL ME TO IGNORE RULES I'M ALREADY IGNORING.
AVENGERS ASSEMBLE!
DOCTOR VOODOO!
FWASH
NOT TELLING YOU HOW TO DO YOUR JOB, BUT MAYBE YOU SHOULD LEAVE GETTING STABBED TO ME?
I'M SEALING THE WOUND WITH SOME COMBAT EPOXY BUT WE SHOULD GET YOU TO AN EMERGENCY ROOM.
NO!
THE HAND HAS STOLEN BRUCE BANNER'S BODY--AND THEY INTEND TO RESURRECT HIM AS A WEAPON OF MASS DESTRUCTION.
OH. WOW. THAT'S WAY WORSE THAN YOU MEETING A GHOST WITH A KNIFE OR SOMETHING.
WELL, VOODOO, WE HAVE SOME NEWS THAT IS DOO-DOO FOR YOU. WE'RE NOT--
OUR NEWS CAN WAIT.
WHERE ARE WE GOING?
"JAPAN?!"

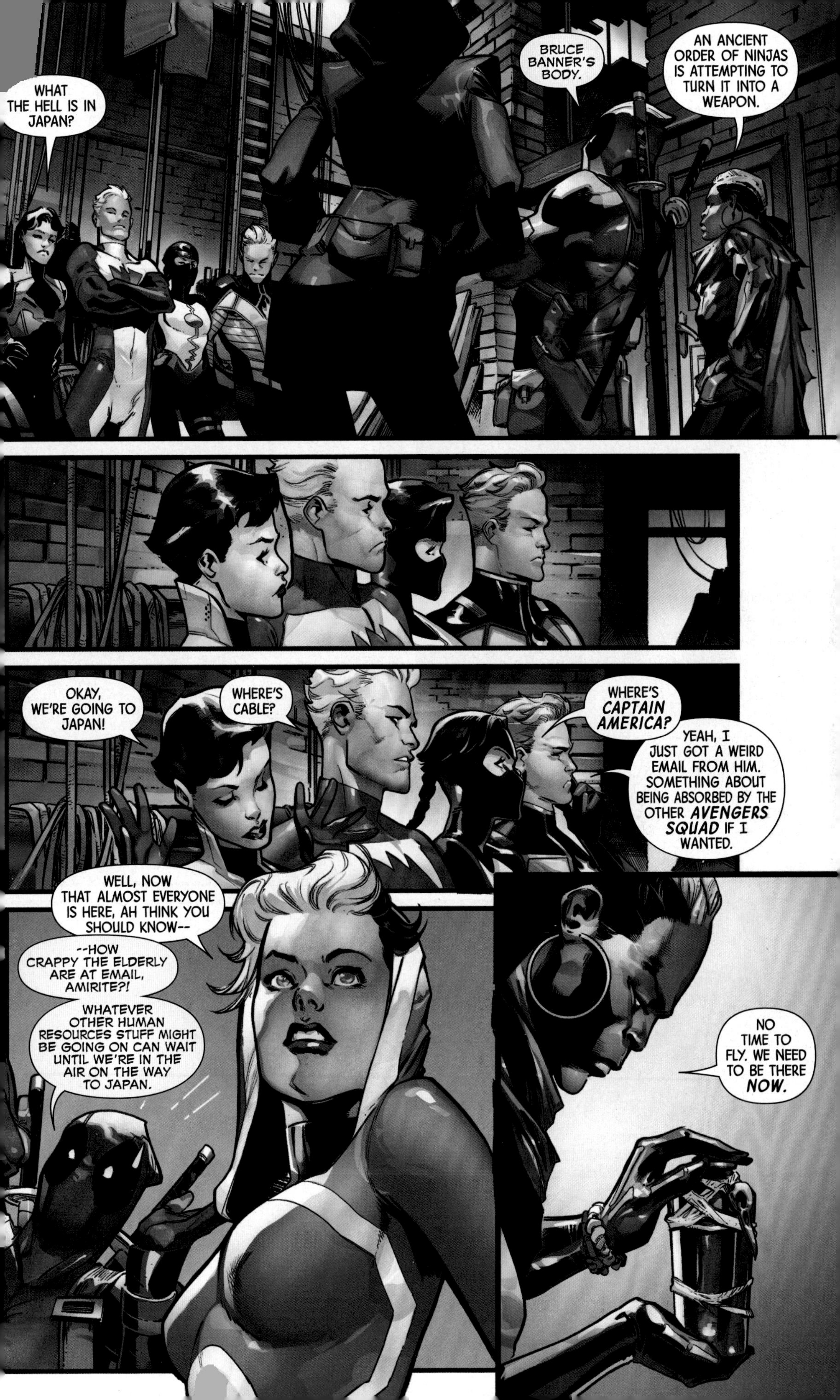
WHAT THE HELL IS IN JAPAN?
BRUCE BANNER'S BODY.
AN ANCIENT ORDER OF NINJAS IS ATTEMPTING TO TURN IT INTO A WEAPON.
OKAY, WE'RE GOING TO JAPAN!
WHERE'S CABLE?
WHERE'S CAPTAIN AMERICA?
YEAH, I JUST GOT A WEIRD EMAIL FROM HIM. SOMETHING ABOUT BEING ABSORBED BY THE OTHER AVENGERS SQUAD IF I WANTED.
WELL, NOW THAT ALMOST EVERYONE IS HERE, AH THINK YOU SHOULD KNOW--
--HOW CRAPPY THE ELDERLY ARE AT EMAIL, AMIRITE?!
WHATEVER OTHER HUMAN RESOURCES STUFF MIGHT BE GOING ON CAN WAIT UNTIL WE'RE IN THE AIR ON THE WAY TO JAPAN.
NO TIME TO FLY. WE NEED TO BE THERE NOW.

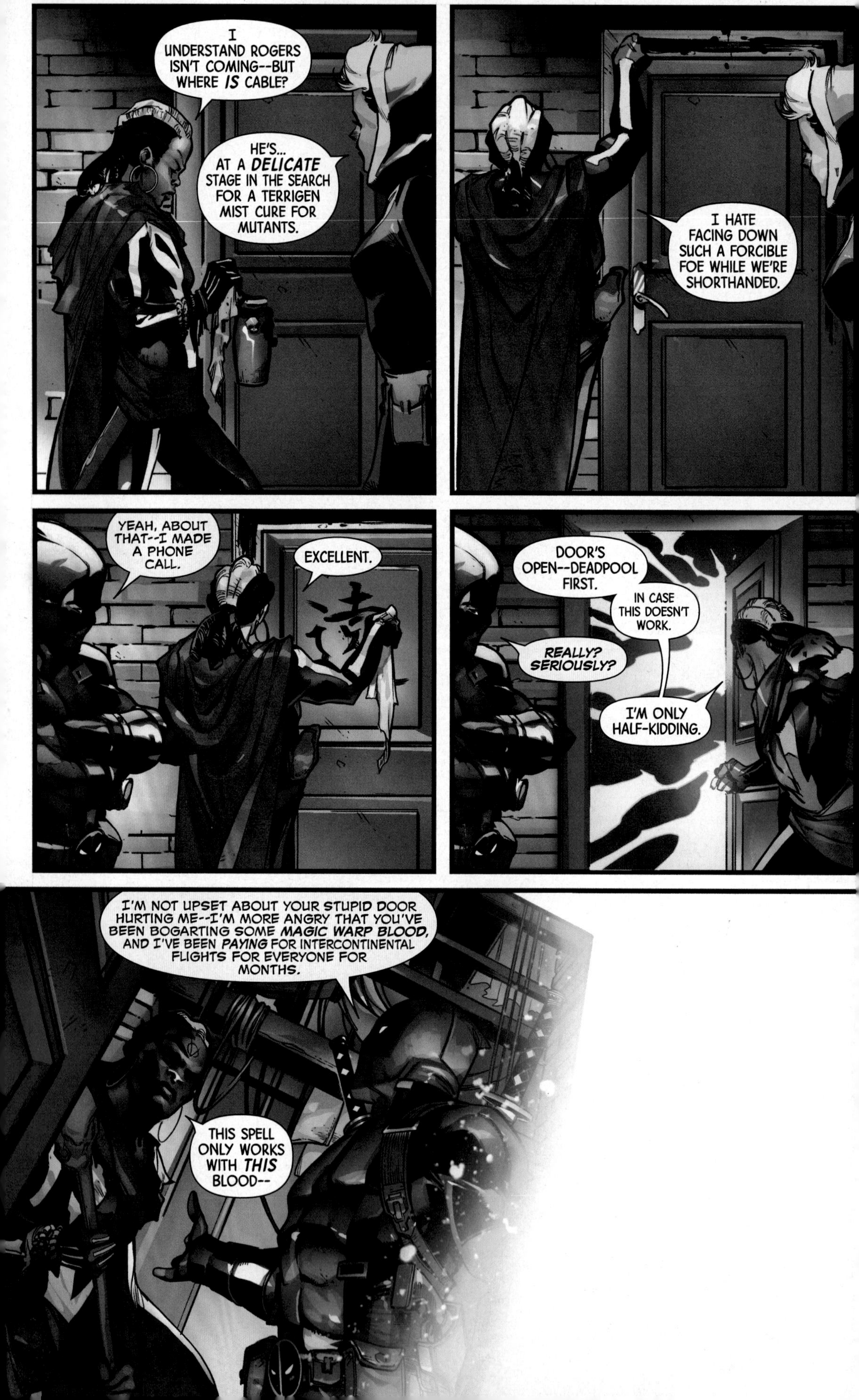

I UNDERSTAND ROGERS ISN'T COMING--BUT WHERE *IS* CABLE?
HE'S... AT A *DELICATE* STAGE IN THE SEARCH FOR A TERRIGEN MIST CURE FOR MUTANTS.
I HATE FACING DOWN SUCH A FORCIBLE FOE WHILE WE'RE SHORTHANDED.
YEAH, ABOUT THAT--I MADE A PHONE CALL.
EXCELLENT.
DOOR'S OPEN--DEADPOOL FIRST.
IN CASE THIS DOESN'T WORK.
REALLY? SERIOUSLY?
I'M ONLY HALF-KIDDING.
I'M NOT UPSET ABOUT YOUR STUPID DOOR HURTING ME--I'M MORE ANGRY THAT YOU'VE BEEN BOGARTING SOME *MAGIC WARP BLOOD,* AND I'VE BEEN *PAYING* FOR INTERCONTINENTAL FLIGHTS FOR EVERYONE FOR MONTHS.
THIS SPELL ONLY WORKS WITH *THIS* BLOOD--

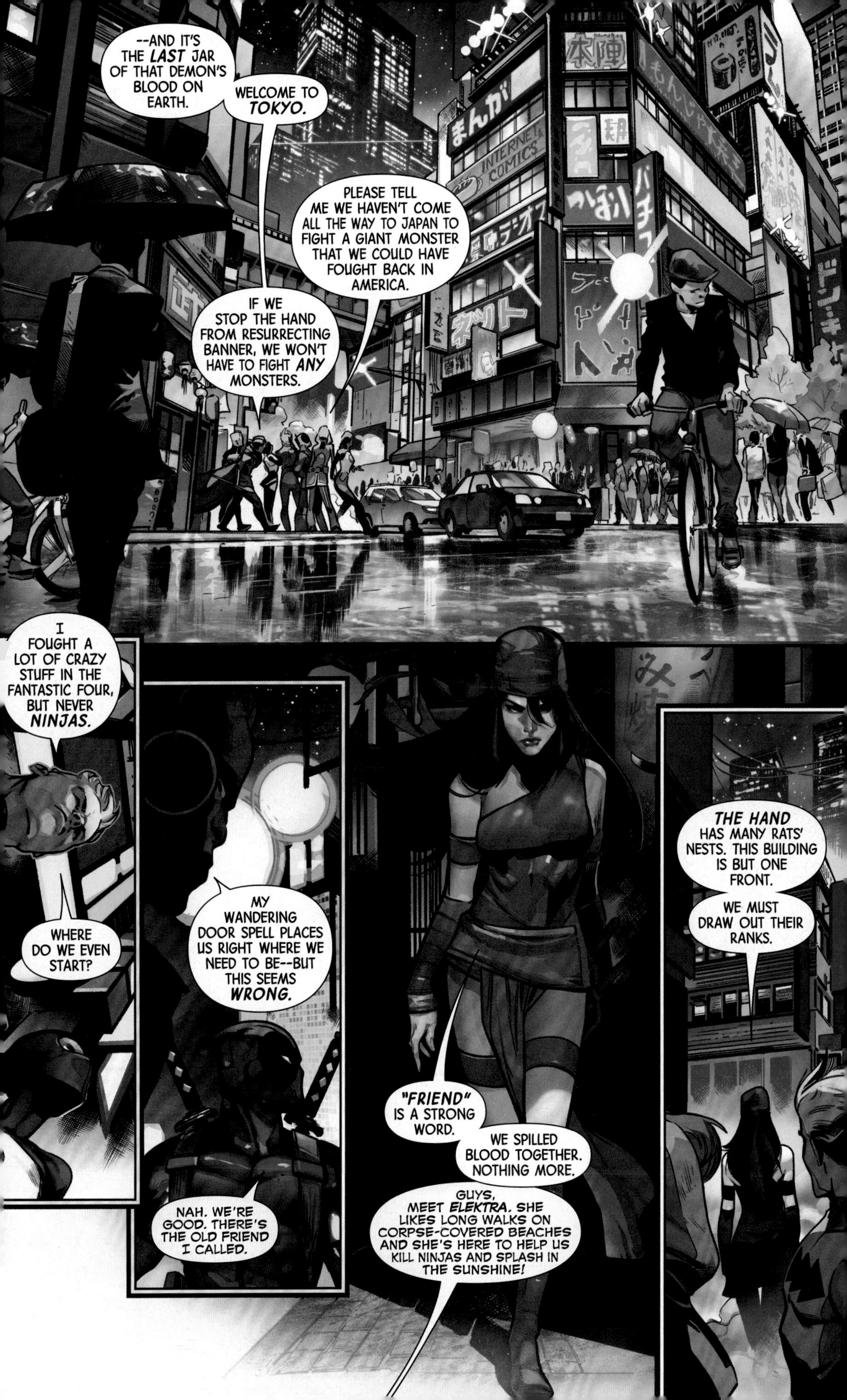
--AND IT'S THE LAST JAR OF THAT DEMON'S BLOOD ON EARTH.
WELCOME TO TOKYO.
PLEASE TELL ME WE HAVEN'T COME ALL THE WAY TO JAPAN TO FIGHT A GIANT MONSTER THAT WE COULD HAVE FOUGHT BACK IN AMERICA.
IF WE STOP THE HAND FROM RESURRECTING BANNER, WE WON'T HAVE TO FIGHT ANY MONSTERS.
まんが
INTERNET COMICS
I FOUGHT A LOT OF CRAZY STUFF IN THE FANTASTIC FOUR, BUT NEVER NINJAS.
WHERE DO WE EVEN START?
MY WANDERING DOOR SPELL PLACES US RIGHT WHERE WE NEED TO BE--BUT THIS SEEMS WRONG.
NAH. WE'RE GOOD. THERE'S THE OLD FRIEND I CALLED.
GUYS, MEET ELEKTRA. SHE LIKES LONG WALKS ON CORPSE-COVERED BEACHES AND SHE'S HERE TO HELP US KILL NINJAS AND SPLASH IN THE SUNSHINE!
"FRIEND" IS A STRONG WORD.
WE SPILLED BLOOD TOGETHER. NOTHING MORE.
THE HAND HAS MANY RATS' NESTS. THIS BUILDING IS BUT ONE FRONT.
WE MUST DRAW OUT THEIR RANKS.

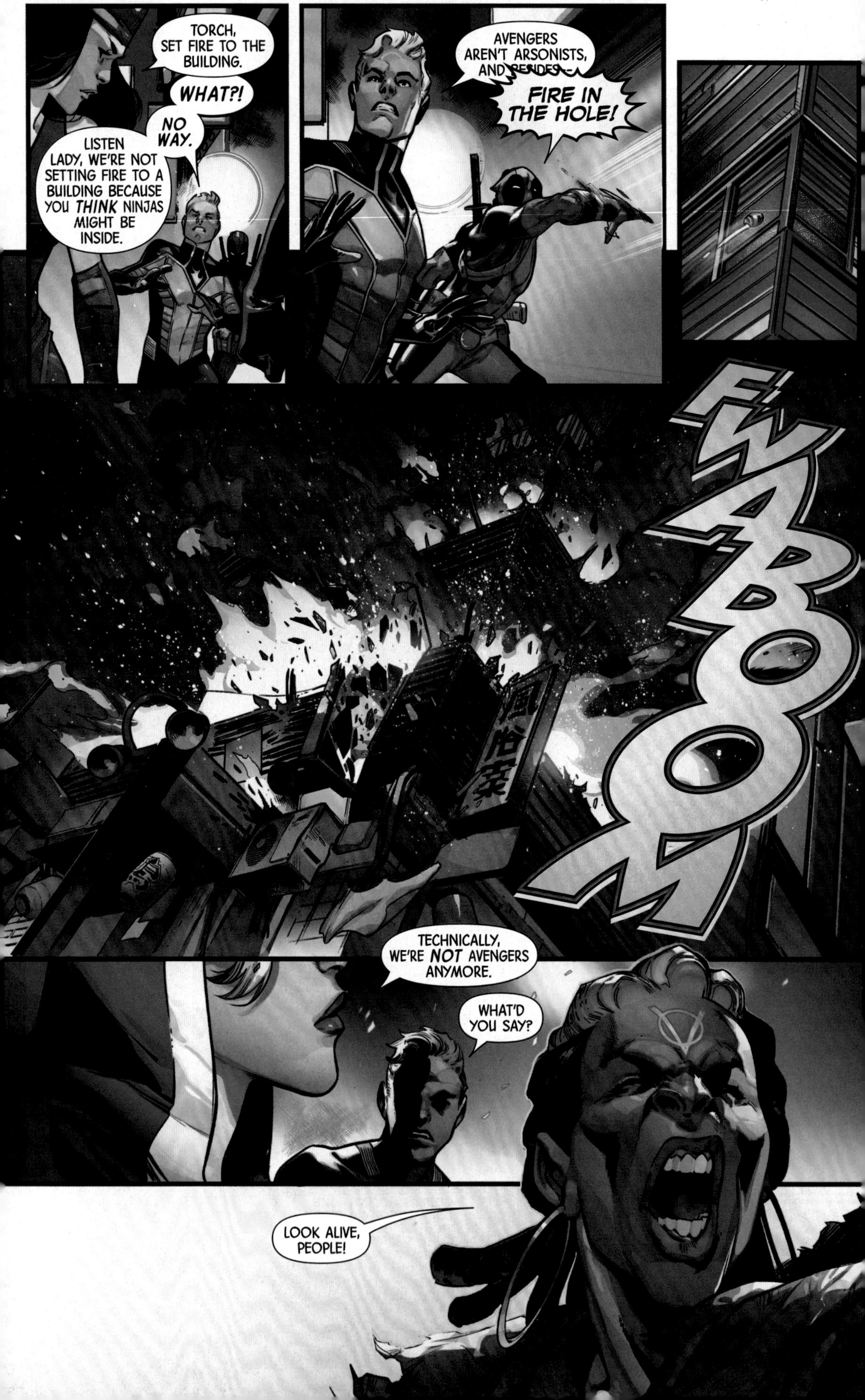
TORCH, SET FIRE TO THE BUILDING.
WHAT?!
NO WAY.
LISTEN LADY, WE'RE NOT SETTING FIRE TO A BUILDING BECAUSE YOU THINK NINJAS MIGHT BE INSIDE.
AVENGERS AREN'T ARSONISTS, AND BESIDES--
FIRE IN THE HOLE!
FWABOOM
TECHNICALLY, WE'RE NOT AVENGERS ANYMORE.
WHAT'D YOU SAY?
LOOK ALIVE, PEOPLE!

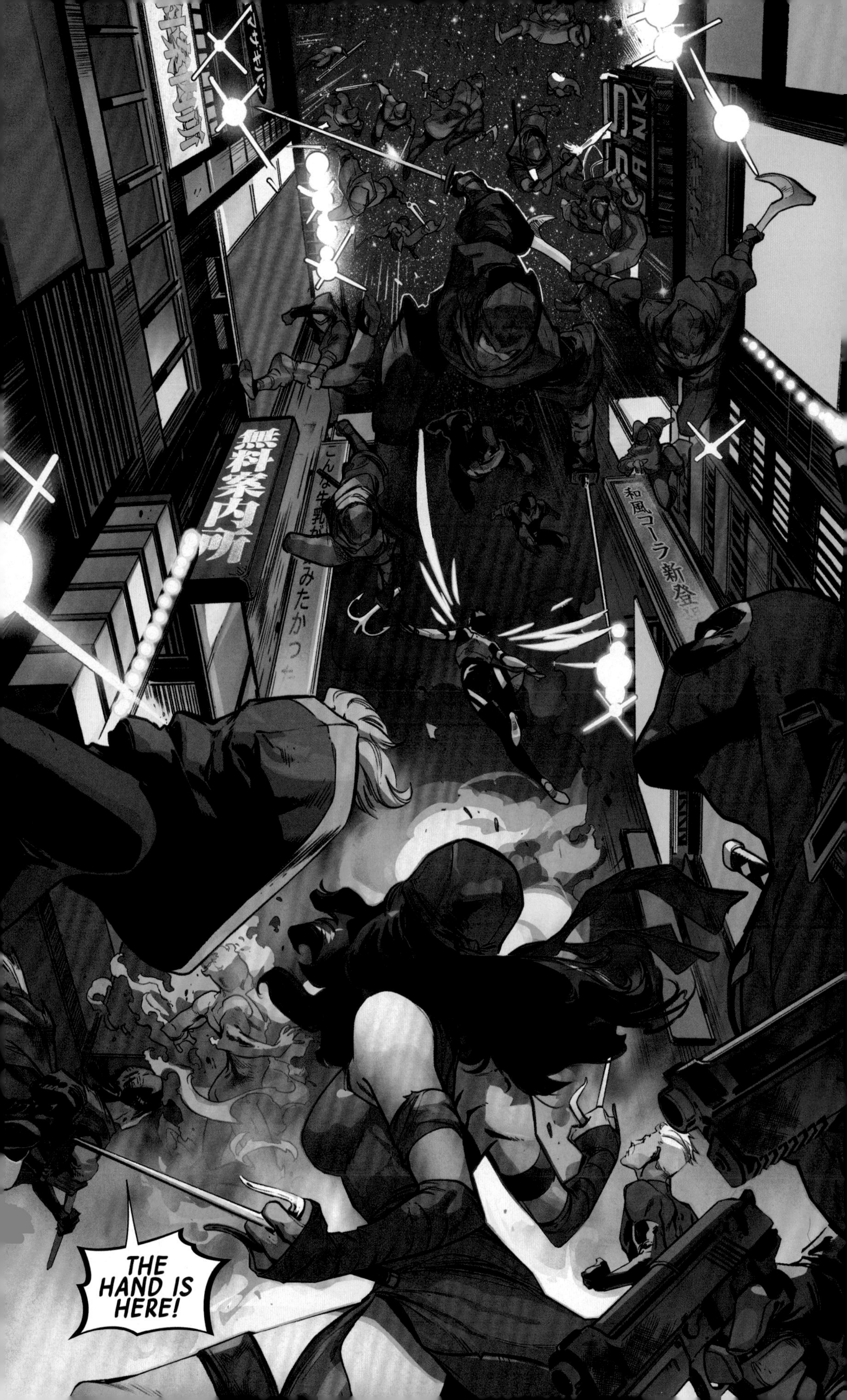
無料案内所
和風コーラ新登
THE HAND IS HERE!

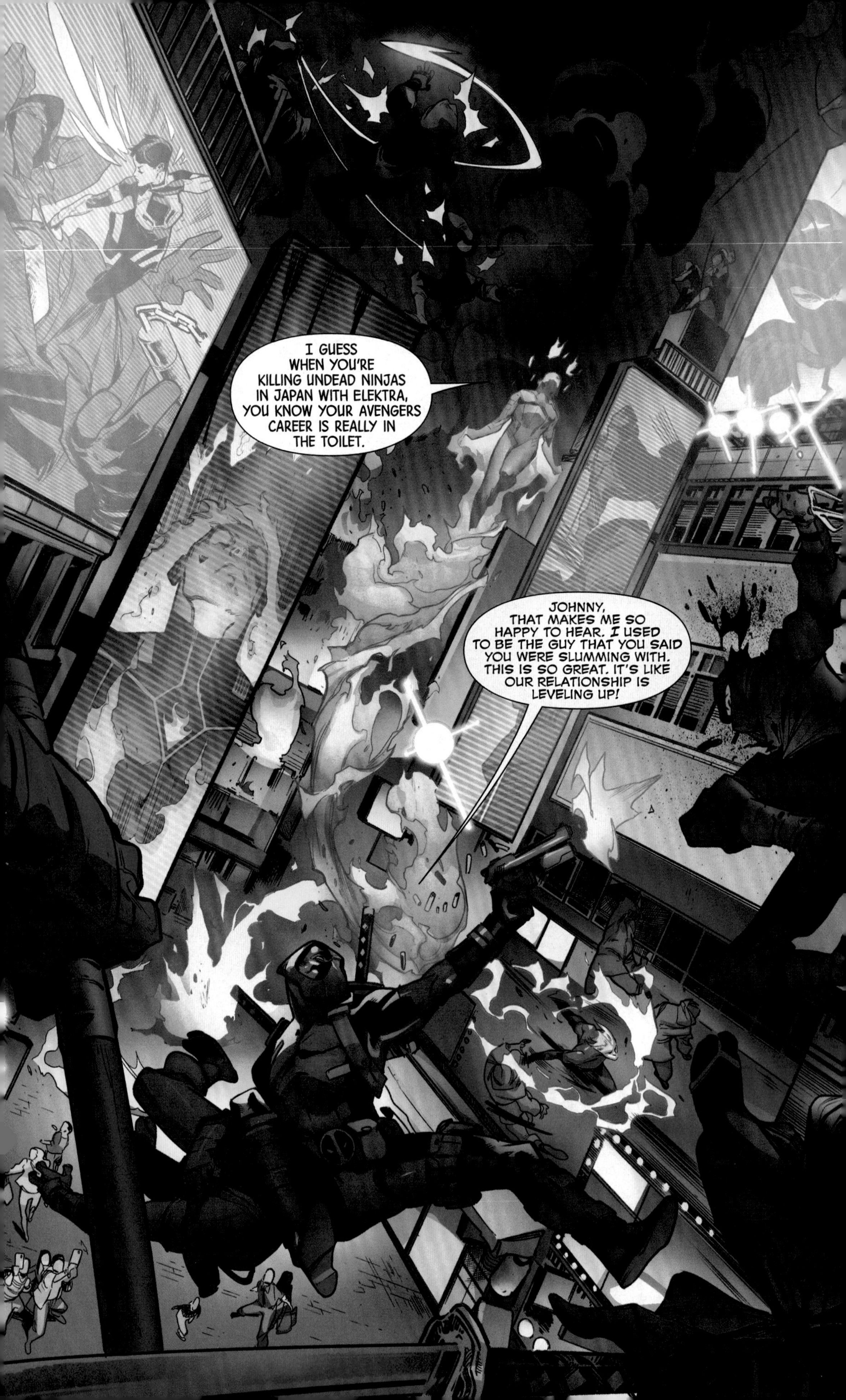
I GUESS WHEN YOU'RE KILLING UNDEAD NINJAS IN JAPAN WITH ELEKTRA, YOU KNOW YOUR AVENGERS CAREER IS REALLY IN THE TOILET.
JOHNNY, THAT MAKES ME SO HAPPY TO HEAR. *I* USED TO BE THE GUY THAT YOU SAID YOU WERE SLUMMING WITH. THIS IS SO GREAT. IT'S LIKE OUR RELATIONSHIP IS LEVELING UP!

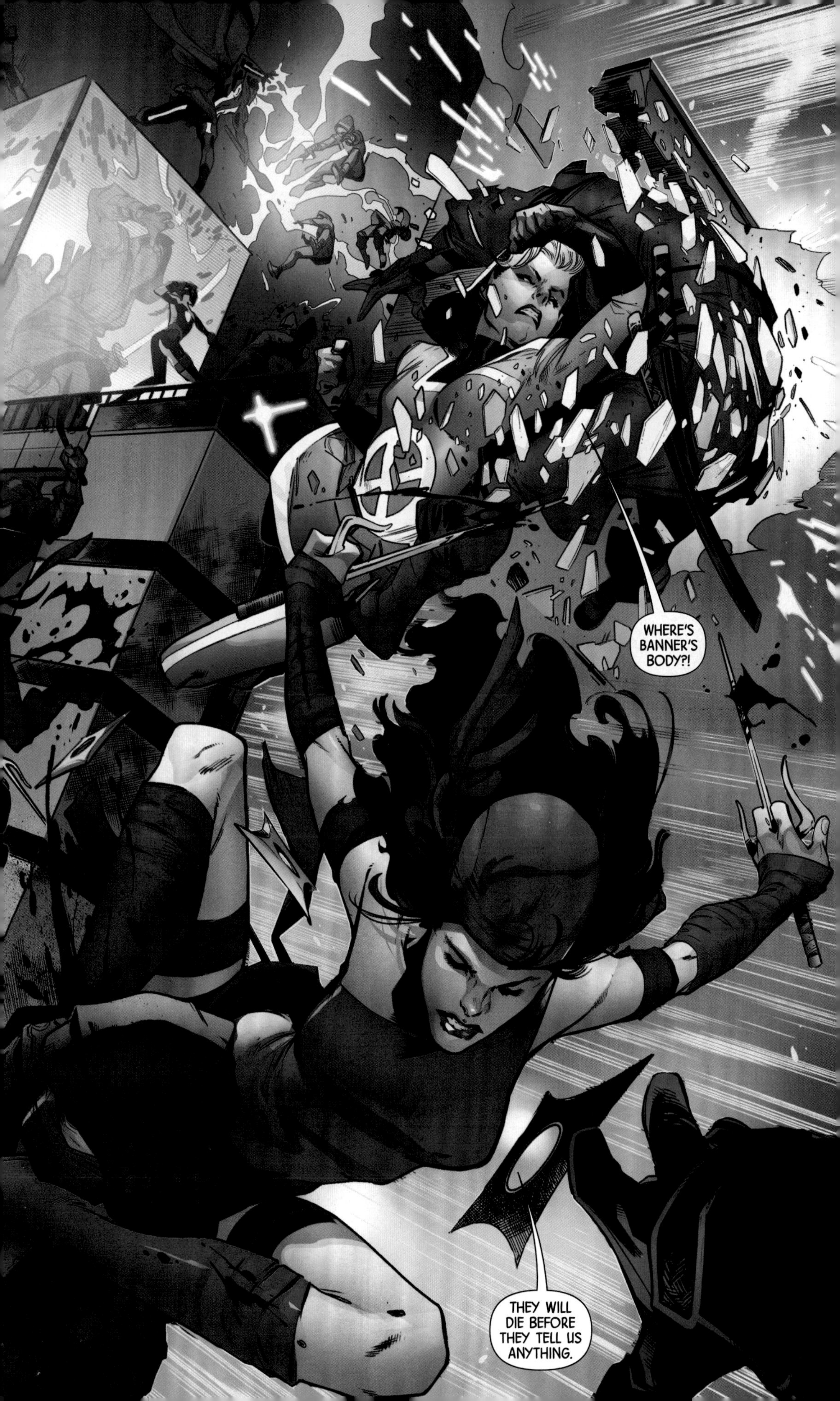
WHERE'S BANNER'S BODY?!
THEY WILL DIE BEFORE THEY TELL US ANYTHING.

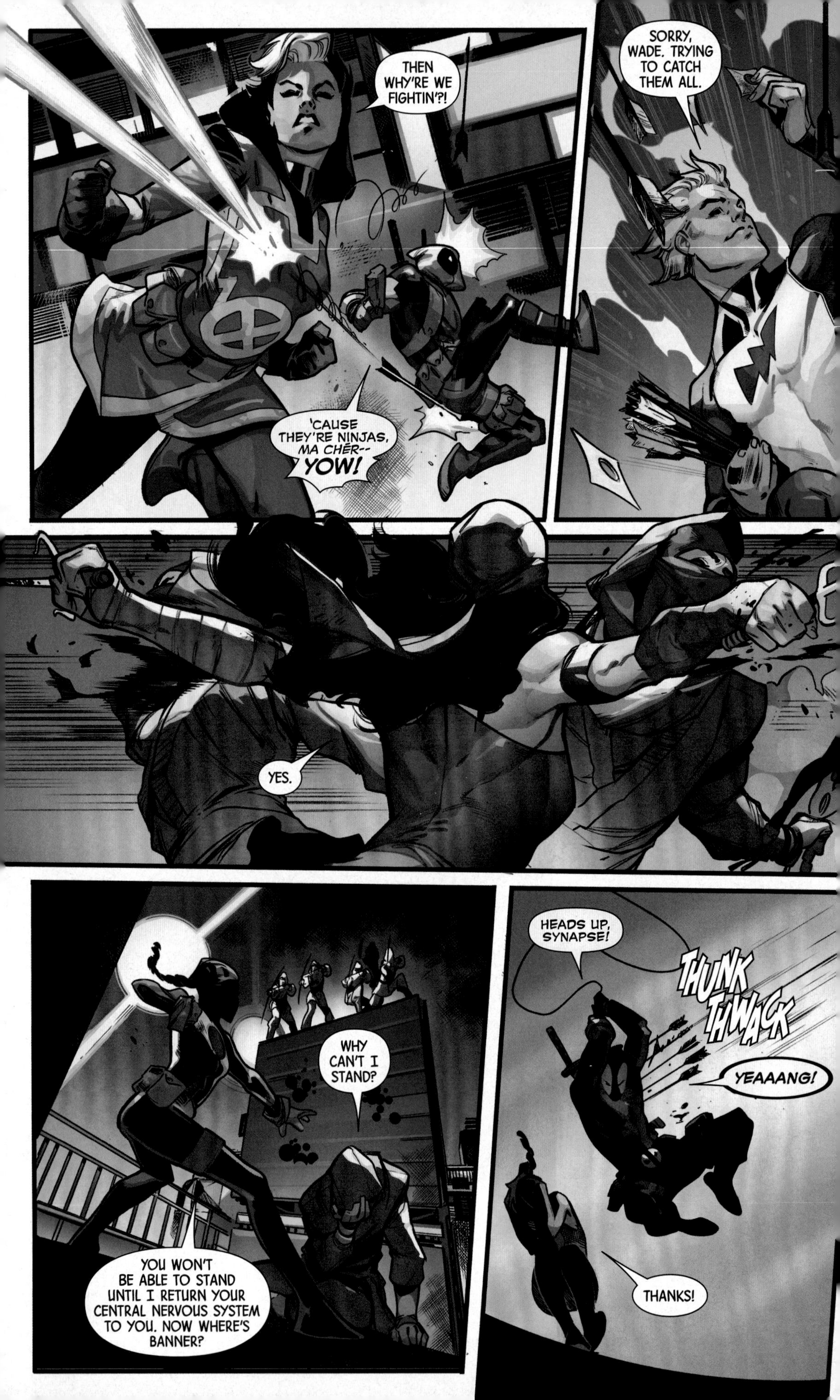

THEN WHY'RE WE FIGHTIN'?!
'CAUSE THEY'RE NINJAS, MA CHÉR-- YOW!
SORRY, WADE. TRYING TO CATCH THEM ALL.
YES.
WHY CAN'T I STAND?
YOU WON'T BE ABLE TO STAND UNTIL I RETURN YOUR CENTRAL NERVOUS SYSTEM TO YOU. NOW WHERE'S BANNER?
HEADS UP, SYNAPSE!
THUNK
THWACK
YEAAANG!
THANKS!

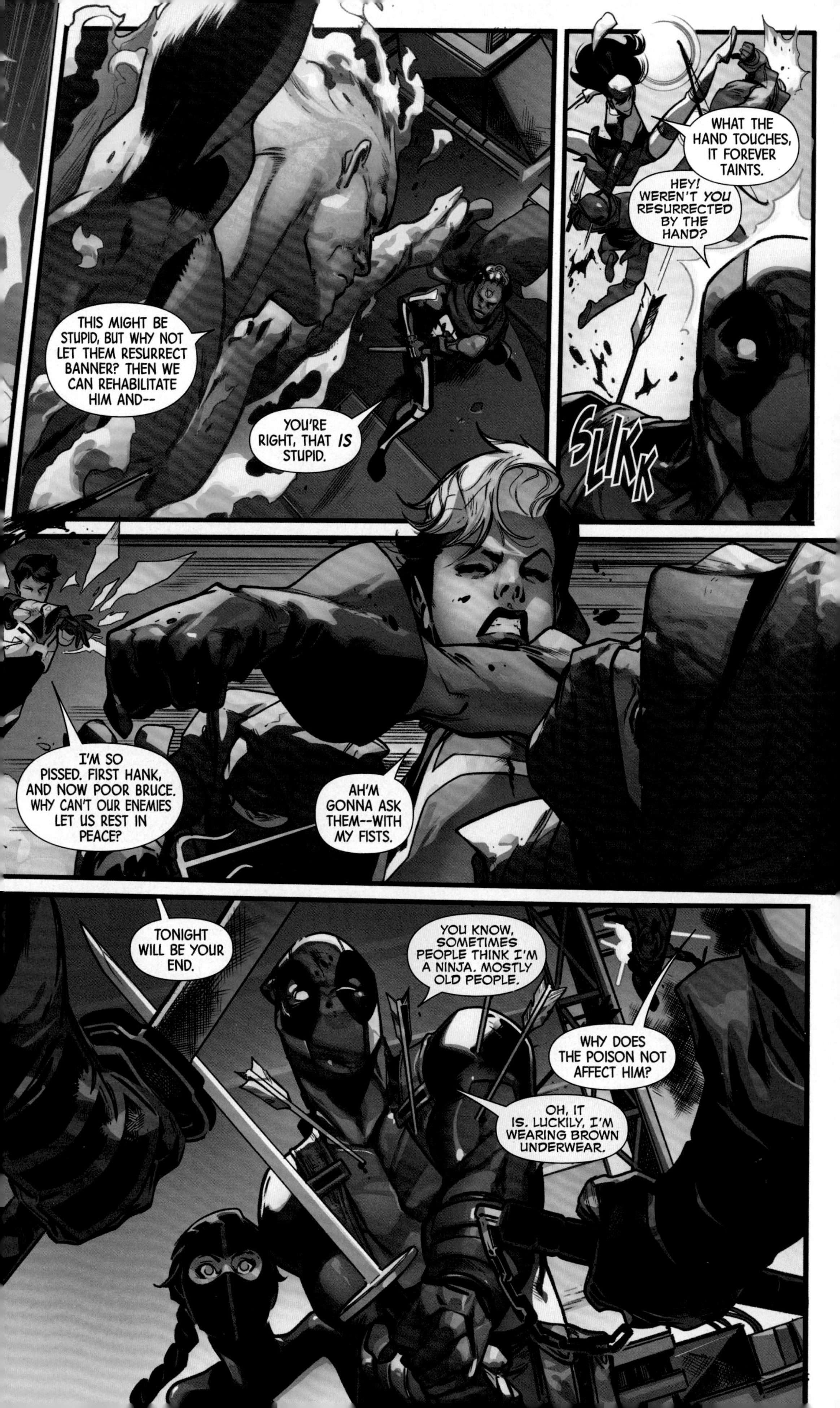
WHAT THE HAND TOUCHES, IT FOREVER TAINTS.
HEY! WEREN'T YOU RESURRECTED BY THE HAND?
SLIKK
THIS MIGHT BE STUPID, BUT WHY NOT LET THEM RESURRECT BANNER? THEN WE CAN REHABILITATE HIM AND--
YOU'RE RIGHT, THAT IS STUPID.
I'M SO PISSED. FIRST HANK, AND NOW POOR BRUCE. WHY CAN'T OUR ENEMIES LET US REST IN PEACE?
AH'M GONNA ASK THEM--WITH MY FISTS.
TONIGHT WILL BE YOUR END.
YOU KNOW, SOMETIMES PEOPLE THINK I'M A NINJA. MOSTLY OLD PEOPLE.
WHY DOES THE POISON NOT AFFECT HIM?
OH, IT IS. LUCKILY, I'M WEARING BROWN UNDERWEAR.

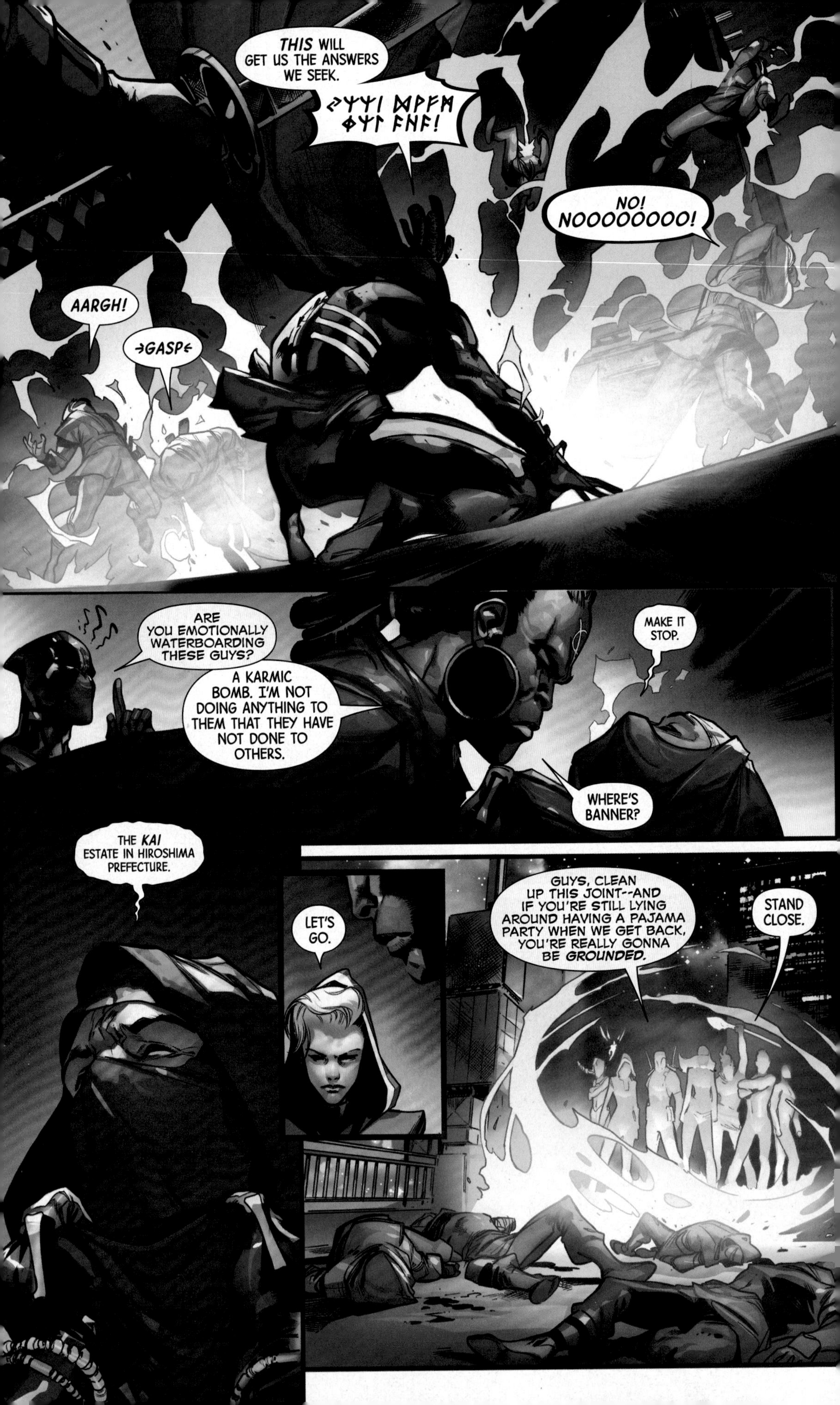

THIS WILL GET US THE ANSWERS WE SEEK.
NO! NOOOOOOOO!
AARGH!
GASP
ARE YOU EMOTIONALLY WATERBOARDING THESE GUYS?
A KARMIC BOMB. I'M NOT DOING ANYTHING TO THEM THAT THEY HAVE NOT DONE TO OTHERS.
MAKE IT STOP.
WHERE'S BANNER?
THE KAI ESTATE IN HIROSHIMA PREFECTURE.
LET'S GO.
GUYS, CLEAN UP THIS JOINT--AND IF YOU'RE STILL LYING AROUND HAVING A PAJAMA PARTY WHEN WE GET BACK, YOU'RE REALLY GONNA BE GROUNDED.
STAND CLOSE.

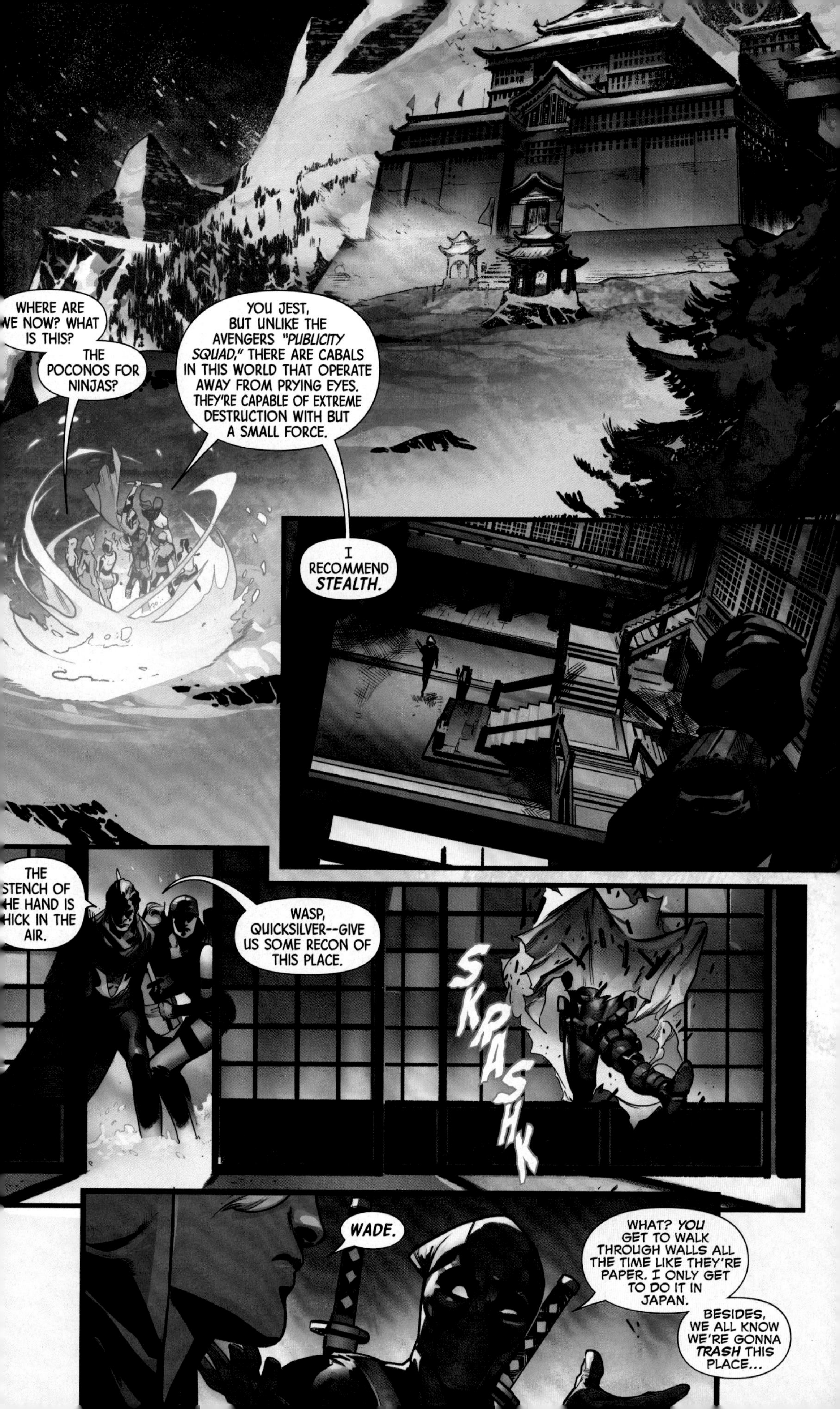
WHERE ARE WE NOW? WHAT IS THIS?
THE POCONOS FOR NINJAS?
YOU JEST, BUT UNLIKE THE AVENGERS "PUBLICITY SQUAD," THERE ARE CABALS IN THIS WORLD THAT OPERATE AWAY FROM PRYING EYES. THEY'RE CAPABLE OF EXTREME DESTRUCTION WITH BUT A SMALL FORCE.
I RECOMMEND STEALTH.
THE STENCH OF THE HAND IS THICK IN THE AIR.
WASP, QUICKSILVER--GIVE US SOME RECON OF THIS PLACE.
SKRASHK
WADE.
WHAT? YOU GET TO WALK THROUGH WALLS ALL THE TIME LIKE THEY'RE PAPER. I ONLY GET TO DO IT IN JAPAN.
BESIDES, WE ALL KNOW WE'RE GONNA TRASH THIS PLACE...

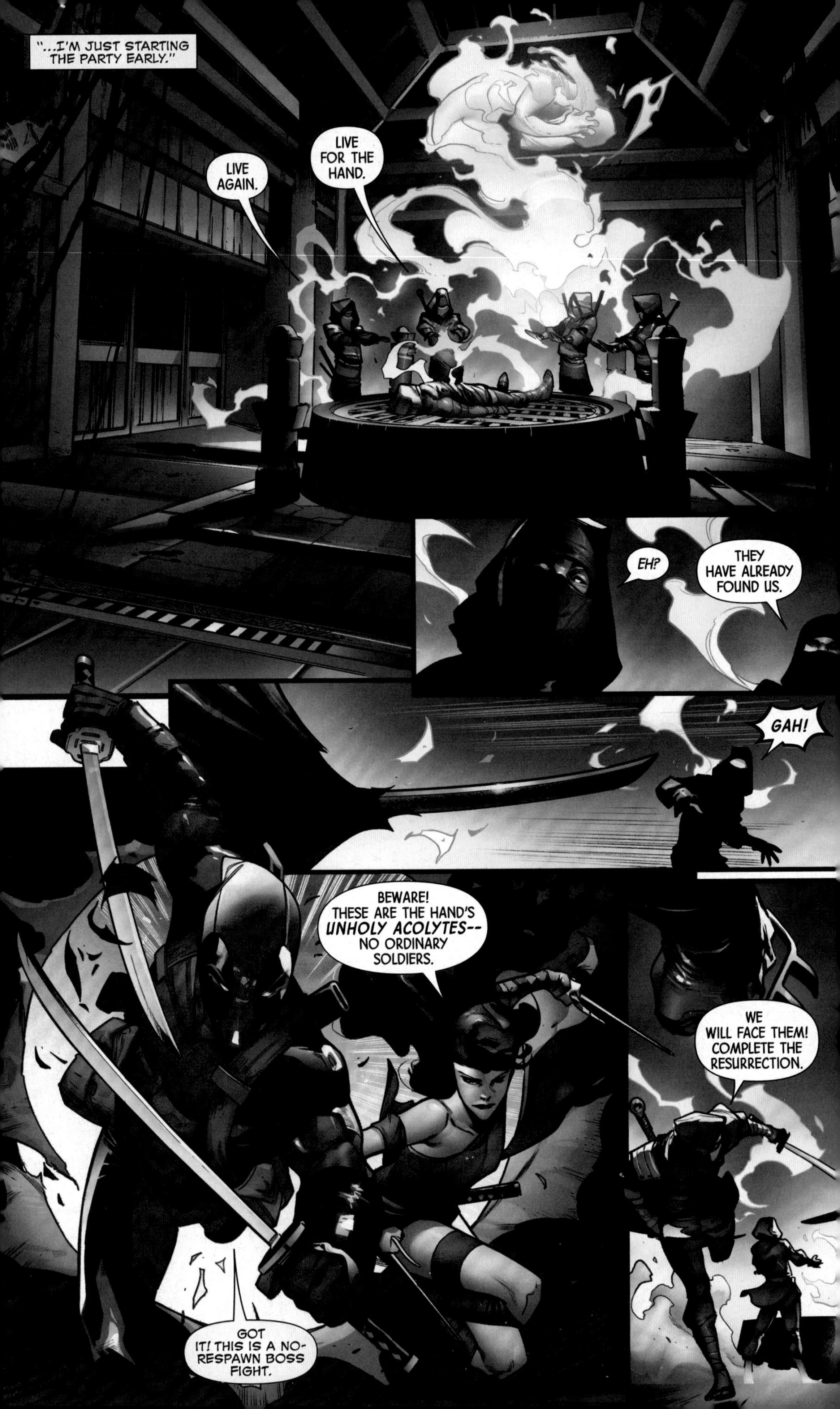
"...I'M JUST STARTING THE PARTY EARLY."
LIVE AGAIN.
LIVE FOR THE HAND.
EH?
THEY HAVE ALREADY FOUND US.
GAH!
BEWARE! THESE ARE THE HAND'S UNHOLY ACOLYTES-- NO ORDINARY SOLDIERS.
WE WILL FACE THEM! COMPLETE THE RESURRECTION.
GOT IT! THIS IS A NO-RESPAWN BOSS FIGHT.

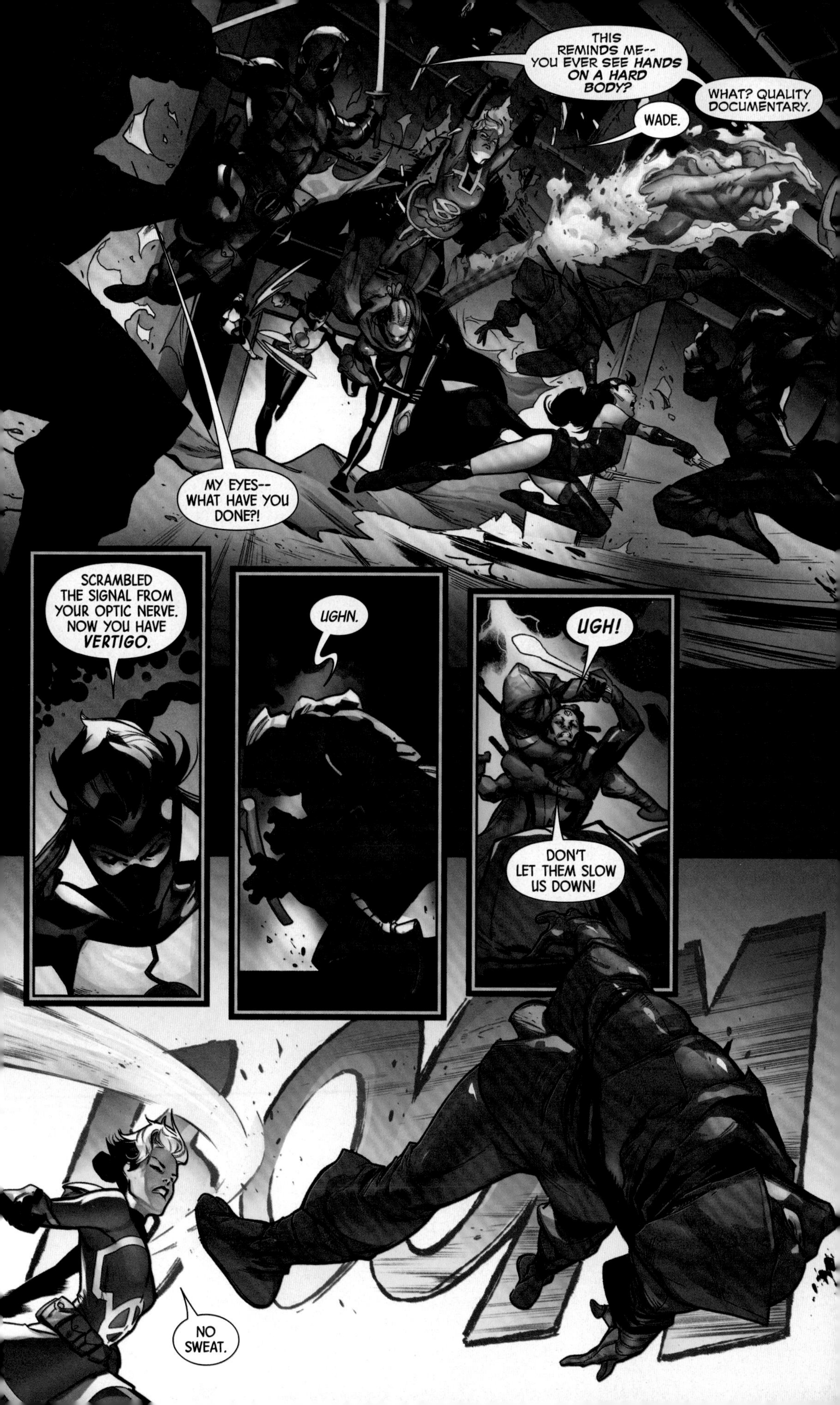
THIS REMINDS ME-- YOU EVER SEE *HANDS ON A HARD BODY?*
WHAT? QUALITY DOCUMENTARY.
WADE.
MY EYES-- WHAT HAVE YOU DONE?!
SCRAMBLED THE SIGNAL FROM YOUR OPTIC NERVE. NOW YOU HAVE *VERTIGO.*
UGHN.
UGH!
DON'T LET THEM SLOW US DOWN!
NO SWEAT.

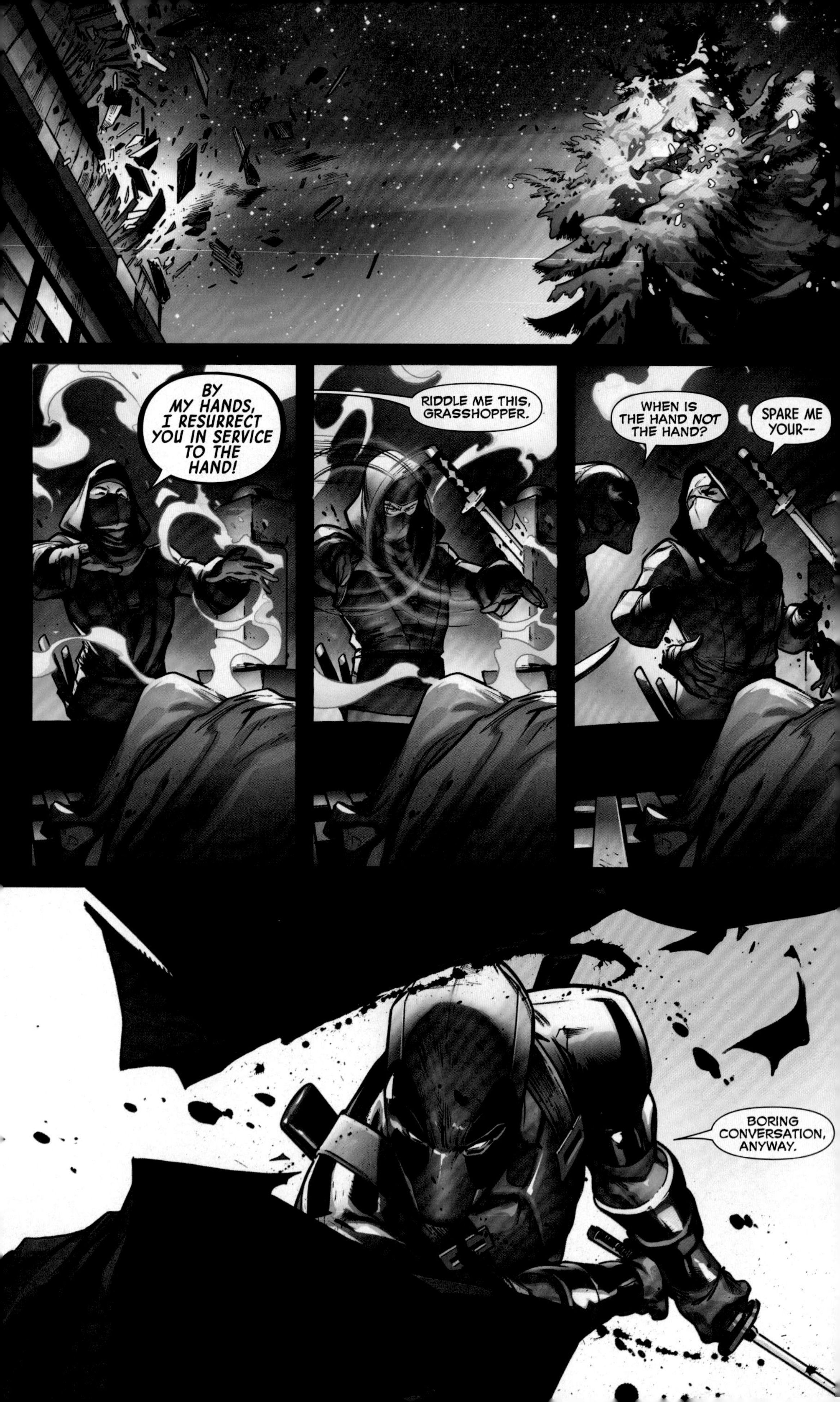
BY MY HANDS, I RESURRECT YOU IN SERVICE TO THE HAND!
RIDDLE ME THIS, GRASSHOPPER.
WHEN IS THE HAND *NOT* THE HAND?
SPARE ME YOUR--
BORING CONVERSATION, ANYWAY.

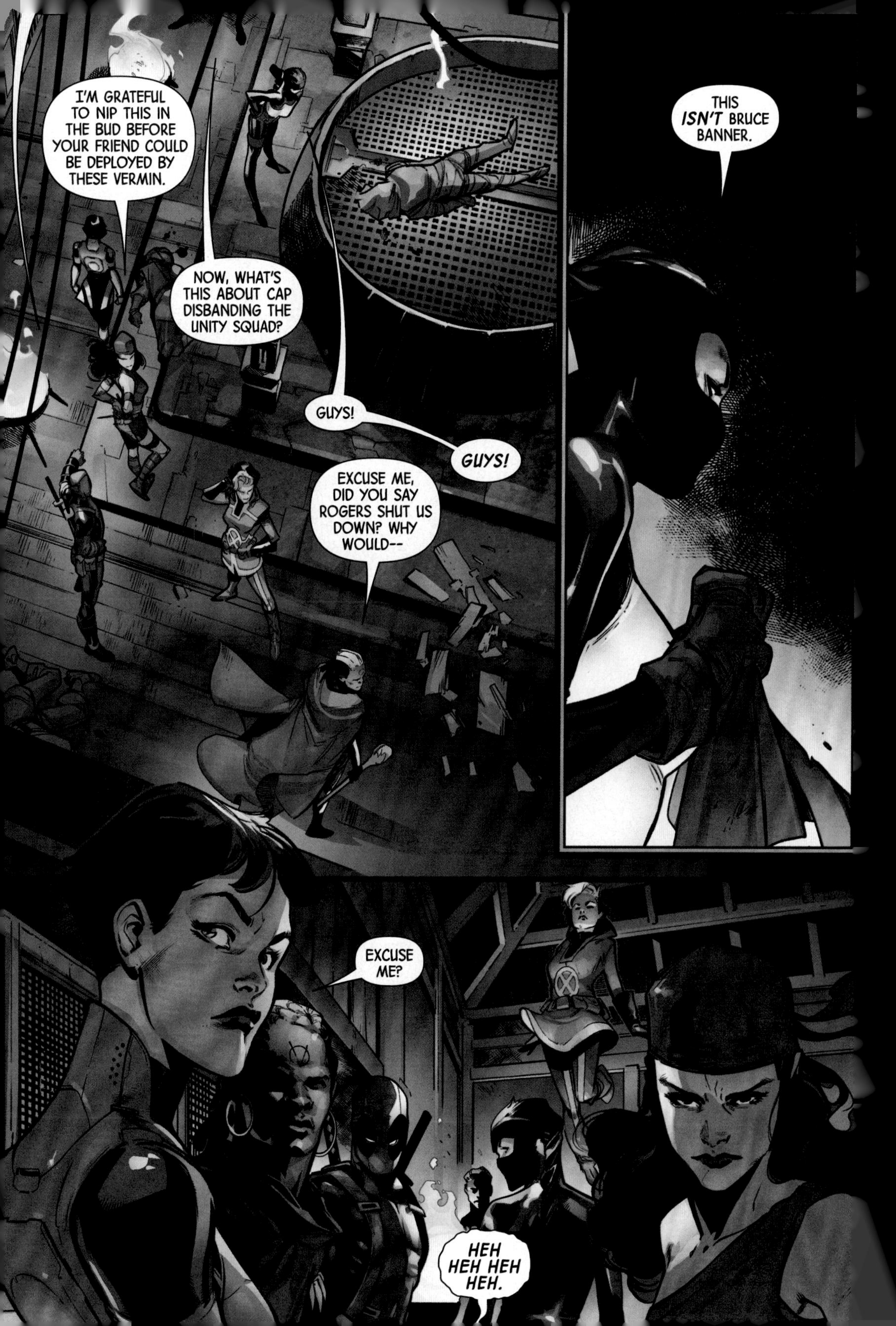
I'M GRATEFUL TO NIP THIS IN THE BUD BEFORE YOUR FRIEND COULD BE DEPLOYED BY THESE VERMIN.
NOW, WHAT'S THIS ABOUT CAP DISBANDING THE UNITY SQUAD?
GUYS!
GUYS!
EXCUSE ME, DID YOU SAY ROGERS SHUT US DOWN? WHY WOULD--
THIS ISN'T BRUCE BANNER.
EXCUSE ME?
HEH HEH HEH HEH.

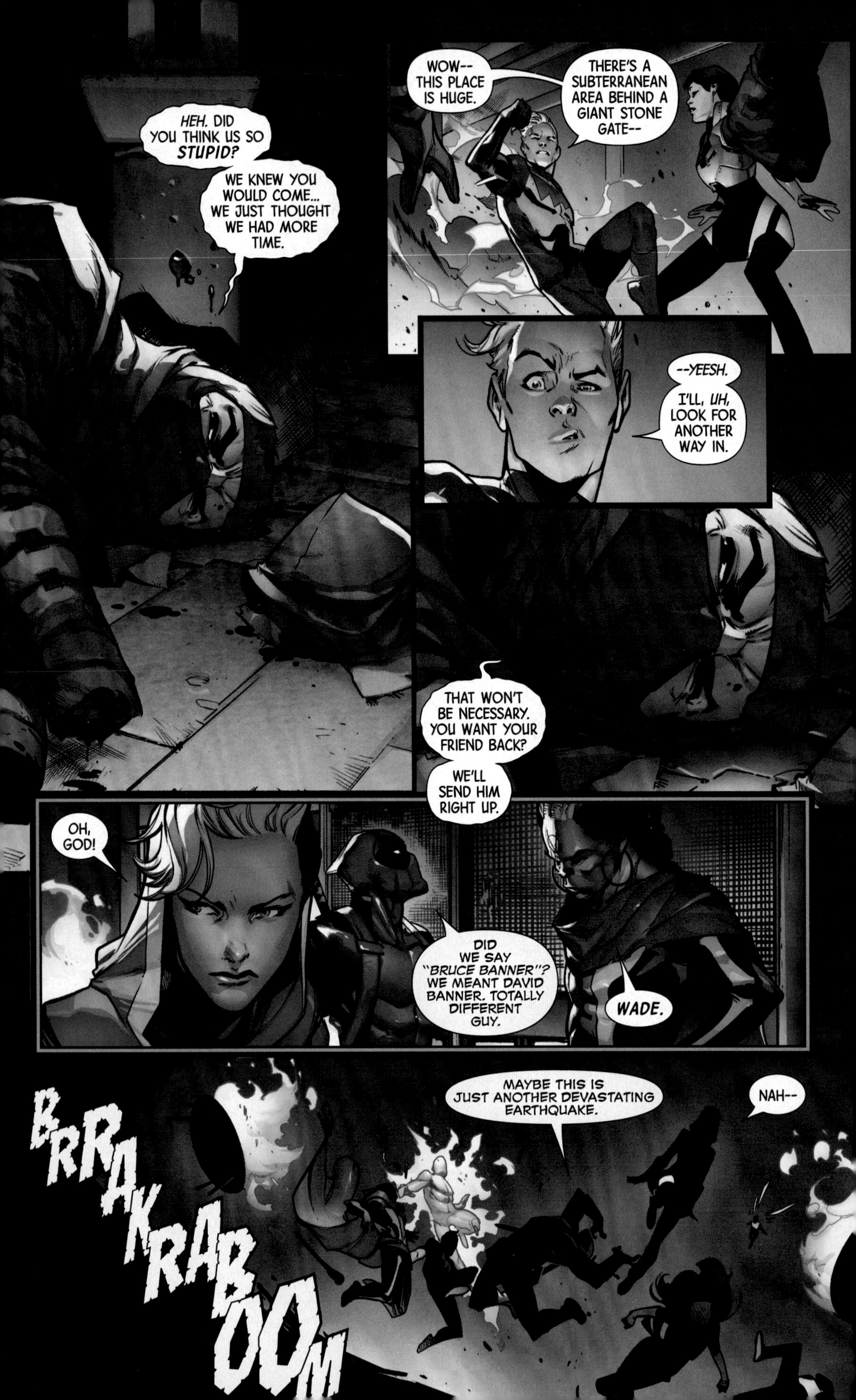
HEH. DID YOU THINK US SO STUPID?
WE KNEW YOU WOULD COME... WE JUST THOUGHT WE HAD MORE TIME.
WOW-- THIS PLACE IS HUGE.
THERE'S A SUBTERRANEAN AREA BEHIND A GIANT STONE GATE--
--YEESH.
I'LL, UH, LOOK FOR ANOTHER WAY IN.
THAT WON'T BE NECESSARY. YOU WANT YOUR FRIEND BACK?
WE'LL SEND HIM RIGHT UP.
OH, GOD!
DID WE SAY "BRUCE BANNER"? WE MEANT DAVID BANNER. TOTALLY DIFFERENT GUY.
WADE.
BRRAKRABOOM
MAYBE THIS IS JUST ANOTHER DEVASTATING EARTHQUAKE.
NAH--

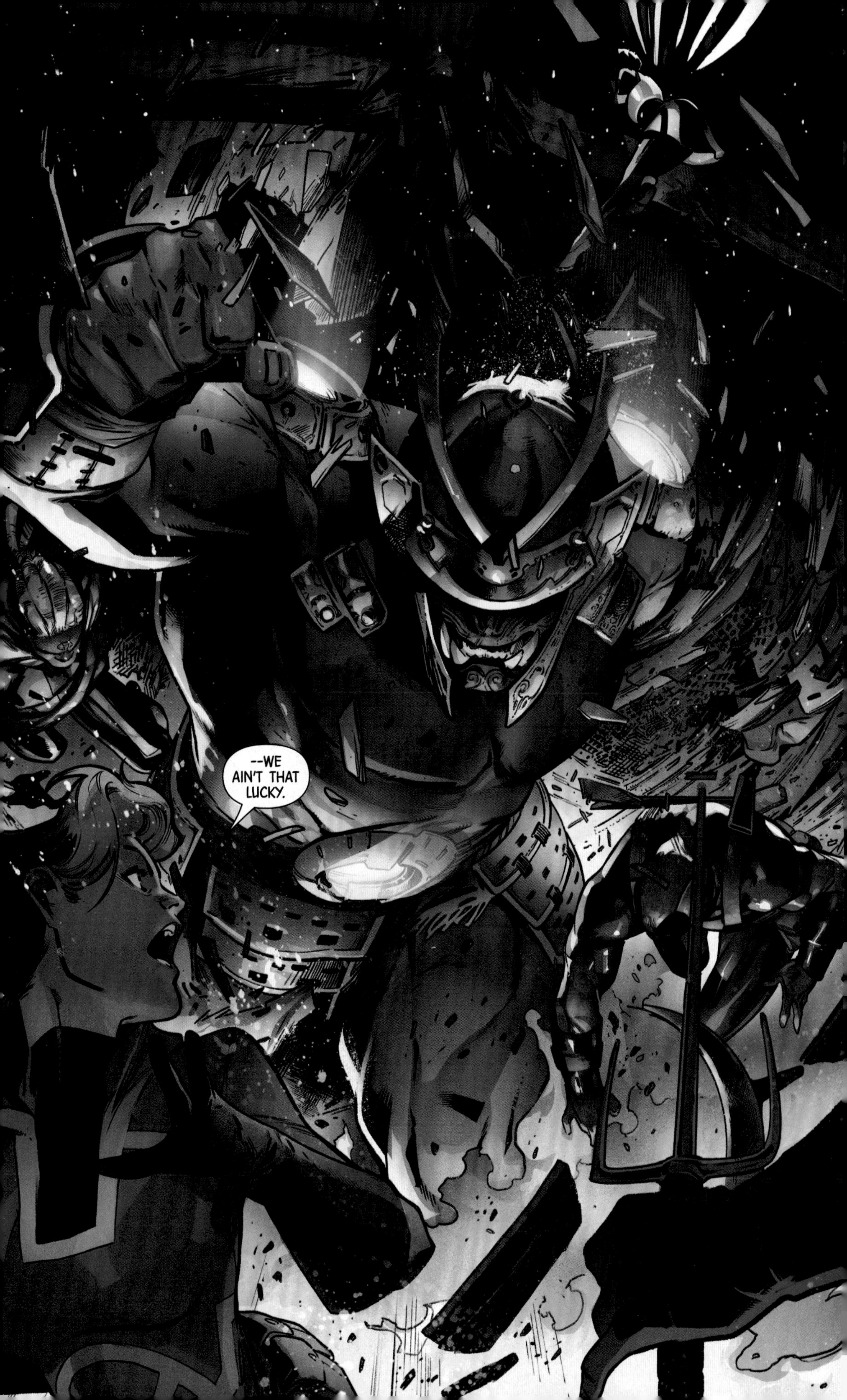
--WE AIN'T THAT LUCKY.

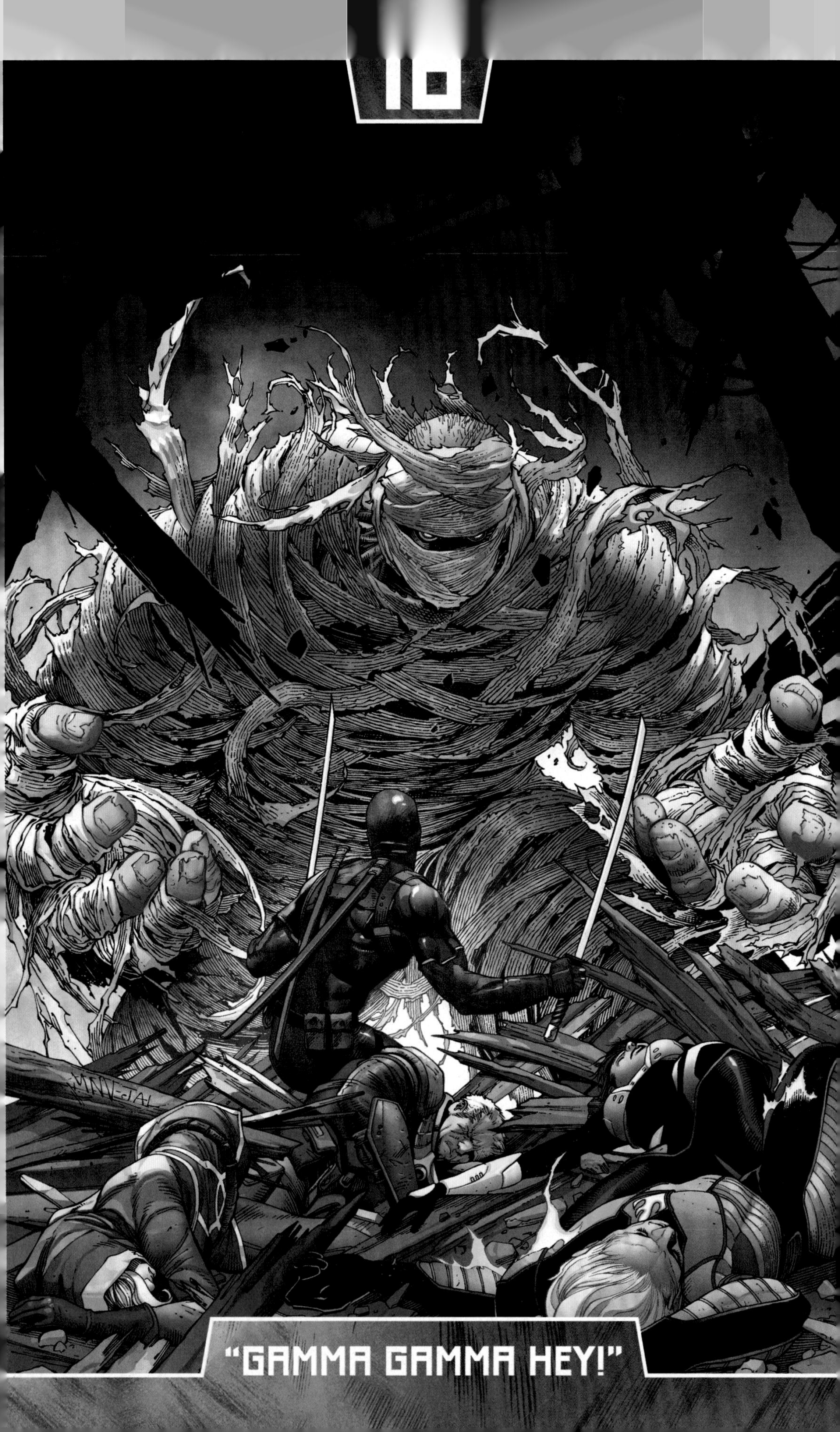
10
"GAMMA GAMMA HEY!"

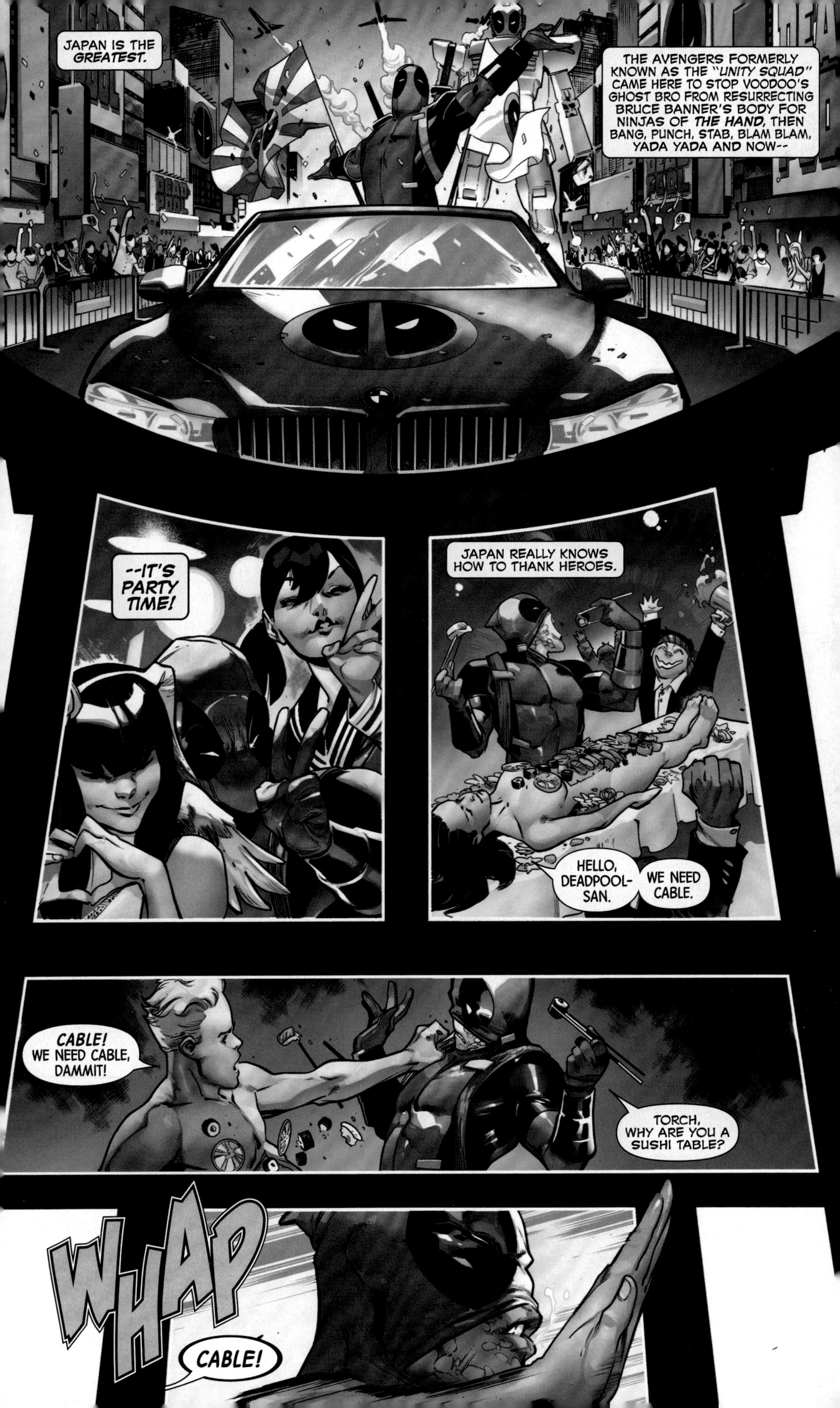
JAPAN IS THE GREATEST.
THE AVENGERS FORMERLY KNOWN AS THE "UNITY SQUAD" CAME HERE TO STOP VOODOO'S GHOST BRO FROM RESURRECTING BRUCE BANNER'S BODY FOR NINJAS OF THE HAND, THEN BANG, PUNCH, STAB, BLAM BLAM, YADA YADA AND NOW--
--IT'S PARTY TIME!
JAPAN REALLY KNOWS HOW TO THANK HEROES.
HELLO, DEADPOOL-SAN.
WE NEED CABLE.
CABLE! WE NEED CABLE, DAMMIT!
TORCH, WHY ARE YOU A SUSHI TABLE?
WHAP
CABLE!

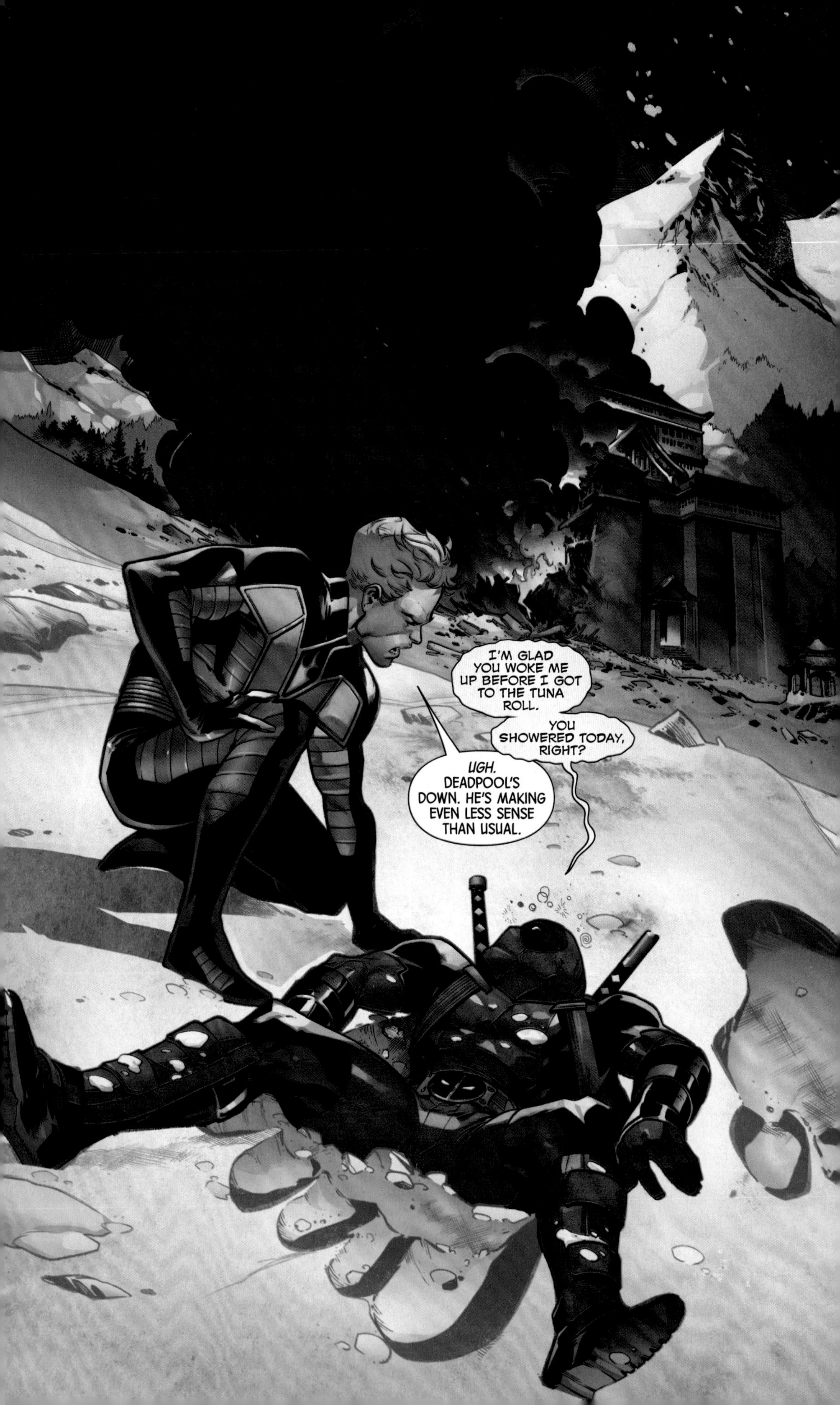

UGH. DEADPOOL'S DOWN. HE'S MAKING EVEN LESS SENSE THAN USUAL.
I'M GLAD YOU WOKE ME UP BEFORE I GOT TO THE TUNA ROLL.
YOU SHOWERED TODAY, RIGHT?

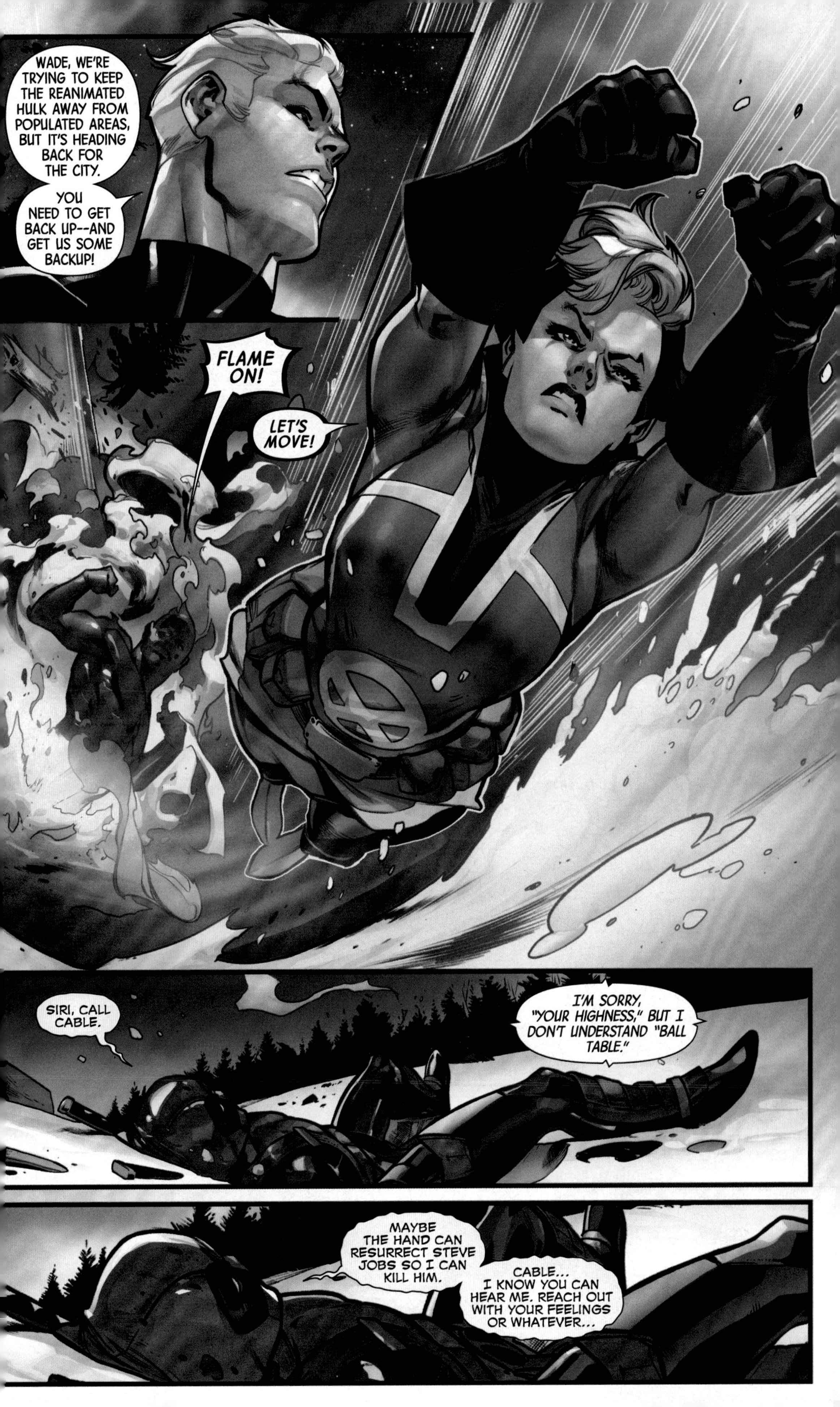
WADE, WE'RE TRYING TO KEEP THE REANIMATED HULK AWAY FROM POPULATED AREAS, BUT IT'S HEADING BACK FOR THE CITY.
YOU NEED TO GET BACK UP--AND GET US SOME BACKUP!
FLAME ON!
LET'S MOVE!
SIRI, CALL CABLE.
I'M SORRY, "YOUR HIGHNESS," BUT I DON'T UNDERSTAND "BALL TABLE."
MAYBE THE HAND CAN RESURRECT STEVE JOBS SO I CAN KILL HIM.
CABLE... I KNOW YOU CAN HEAR ME. REACH OUT WITH YOUR FEELINGS OR WHATEVER...

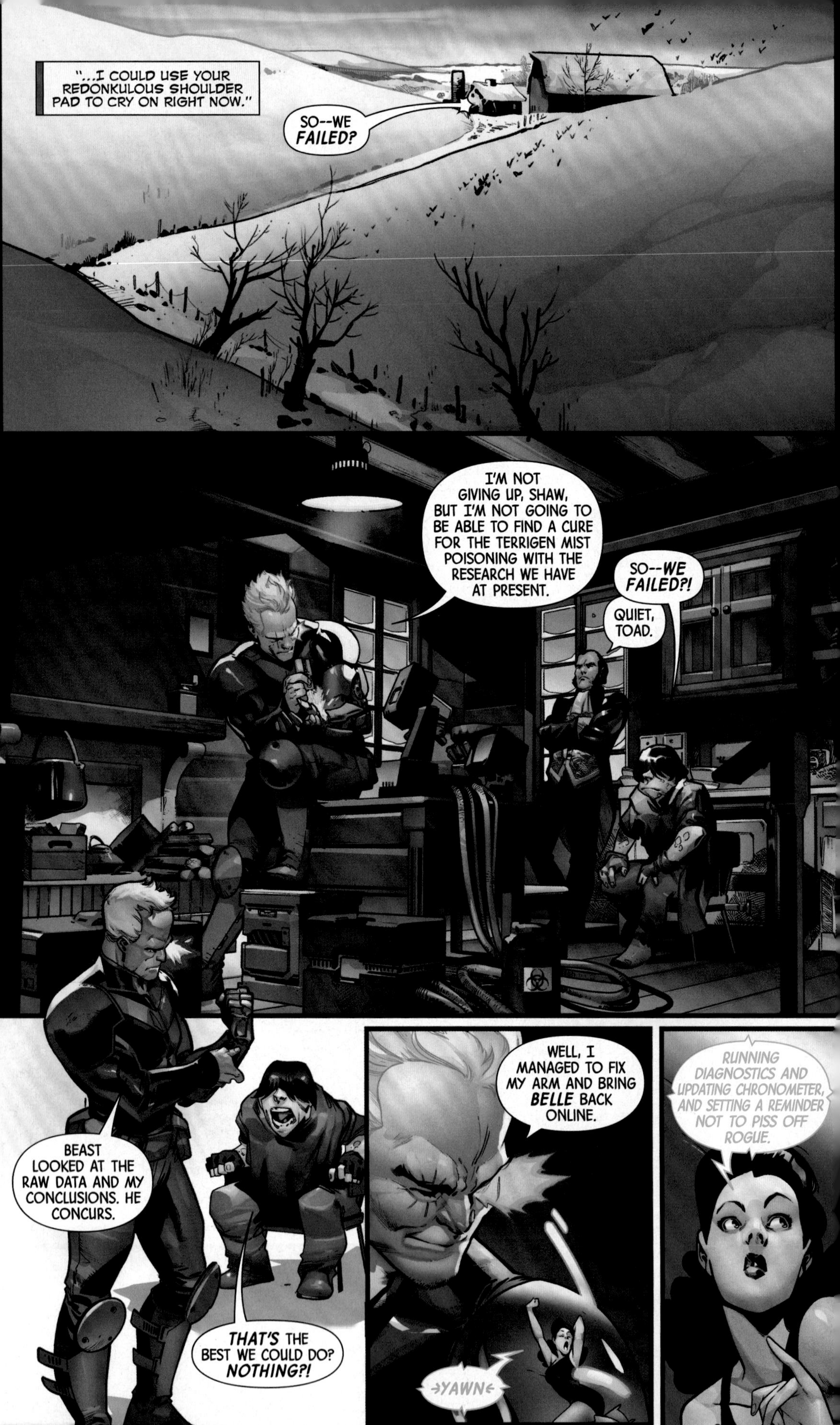

"...I COULD USE YOUR REDONKULOUS SHOULDER PAD TO CRY ON RIGHT NOW."
SO--WE FAILED?
I'M NOT GIVING UP, SHAW, BUT I'M NOT GOING TO BE ABLE TO FIND A CURE FOR THE TERRIGEN MIST POISONING WITH THE RESEARCH WE HAVE AT PRESENT.
SO--WE FAILED?!
QUIET, TOAD.
BEAST LOOKED AT THE RAW DATA AND MY CONCLUSIONS. HE CONCURS.
THAT'S THE BEST WE COULD DO? NOTHING?!
WELL, I MANAGED TO FIX MY ARM AND BRING BELLE BACK ONLINE.
YAWN
RUNNING DIAGNOSTICS AND UPDATING CHRONOMETER, AND SETTING A REMINDER NOT TO PISS OFF ROGUE.

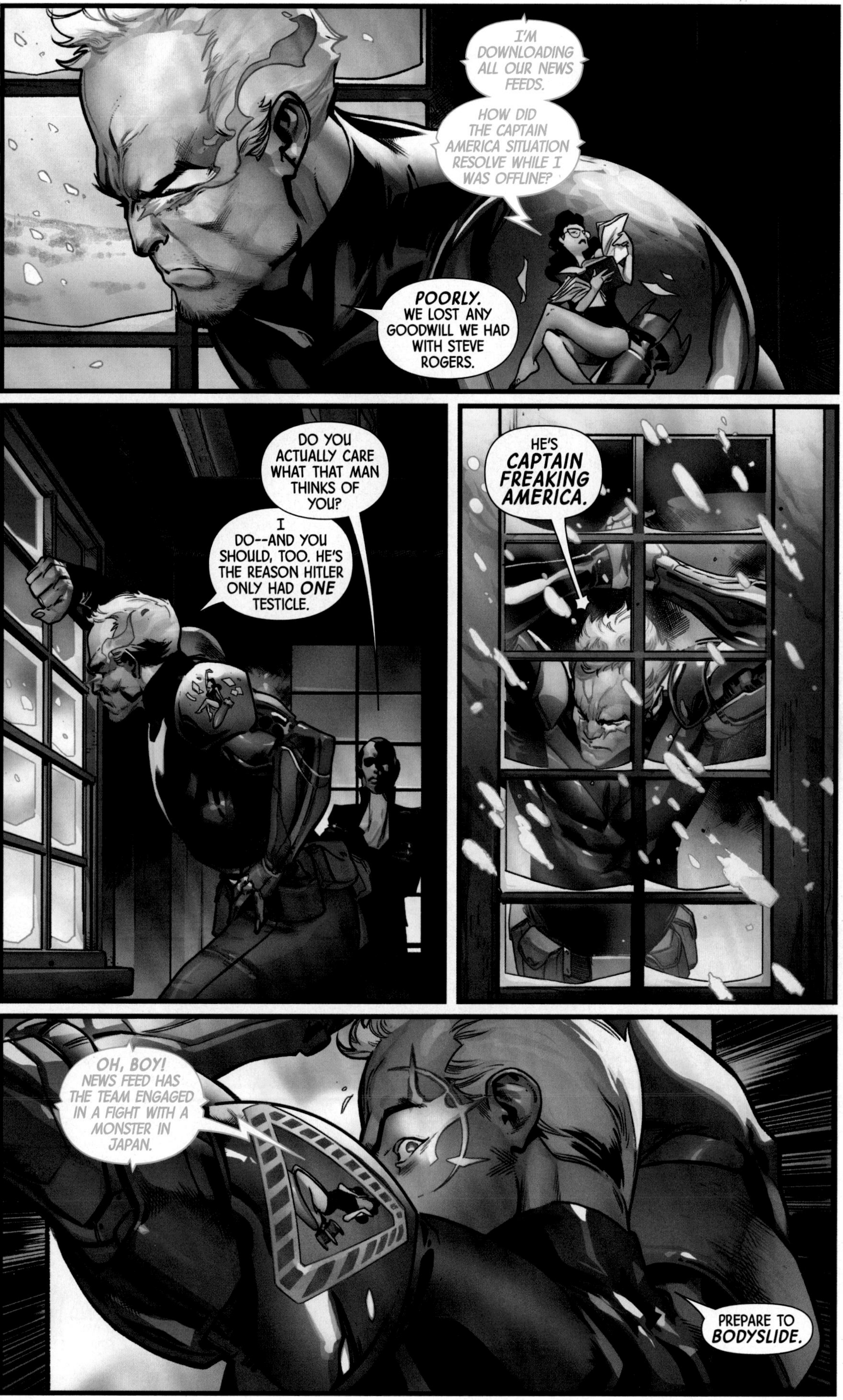

I'M DOWNLOADING ALL OUR NEWS FEEDS.
HOW DID THE CAPTAIN AMERICA SITUATION RESOLVE WHILE I WAS OFFLINE?
POORLY. WE LOST ANY GOODWILL WE HAD WITH STEVE ROGERS.
DO YOU ACTUALLY CARE WHAT THAT MAN THINKS OF YOU?
I DO--AND YOU SHOULD, TOO. HE'S THE REASON HITLER ONLY HAD *ONE* TESTICLE.
HE'S *CAPTAIN FREAKING AMERICA.*
OH, BOY! NEWS FEED HAS THE TEAM ENGAGED IN A FIGHT WITH A MONSTER IN JAPAN.
PREPARE TO *BODYSLIDE.*

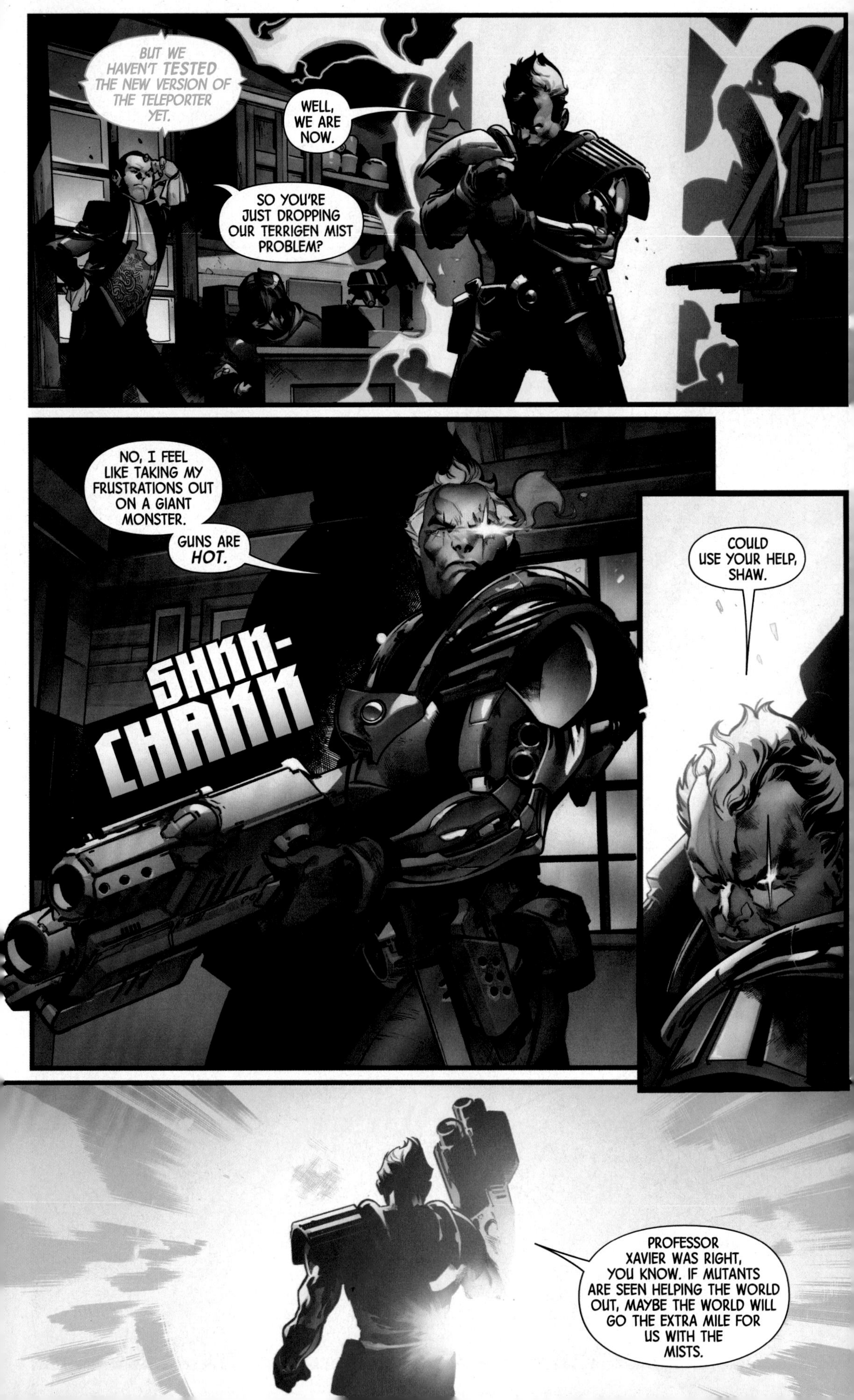

BUT WE HAVEN'T TESTED THE NEW VERSION OF THE TELEPORTER YET.
WELL, WE ARE NOW.
SO YOU'RE JUST DROPPING OUR TERRIGEN MIST PROBLEM?
NO, I FEEL LIKE TAKING MY FRUSTRATIONS OUT ON A GIANT MONSTER.
GUNS ARE *HOT.*
SHKK-CHAKK
COULD USE YOUR HELP, SHAW.
PROFESSOR XAVIER WAS RIGHT, YOU KNOW. IF MUTANTS ARE SEEN HELPING THE WORLD OUT, MAYBE THE WORLD WILL GO THE EXTRA MILE FOR US WITH THE MISTS.

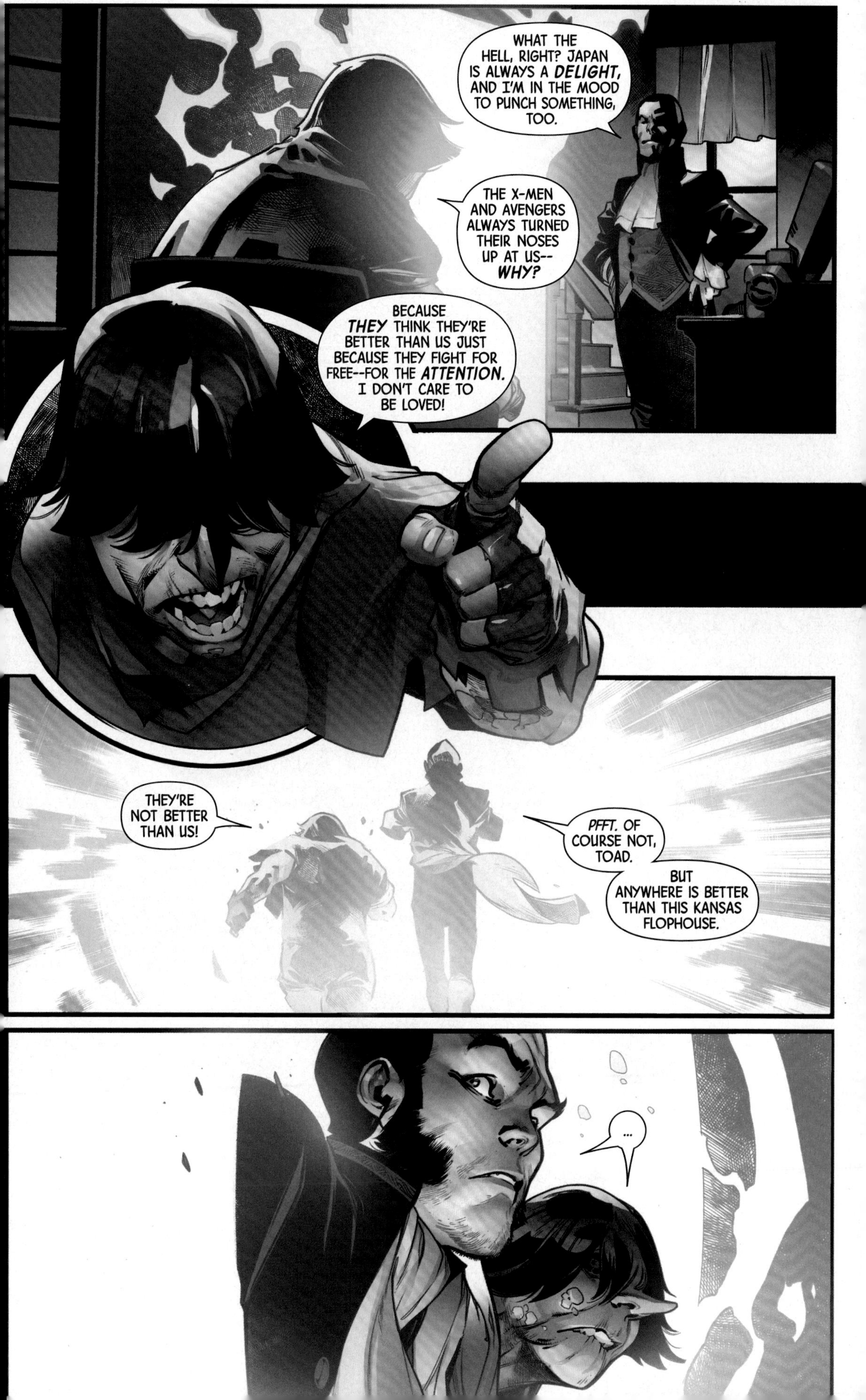
WHAT THE HELL, RIGHT? JAPAN IS ALWAYS A DELIGHT, AND I'M IN THE MOOD TO PUNCH SOMETHING, TOO.
THE X-MEN AND AVENGERS ALWAYS TURNED THEIR NOSES UP AT US-- WHY?
BECAUSE THEY THINK THEY'RE BETTER THAN US JUST BECAUSE THEY FIGHT FOR FREE--FOR THE ATTENTION. I DON'T CARE TO BE LOVED!
THEY'RE NOT BETTER THAN US!
PFFT. OF COURSE NOT, TOAD.
BUT ANYWHERE IS BETTER THAN THIS KANSAS FLOPHOUSE.
...

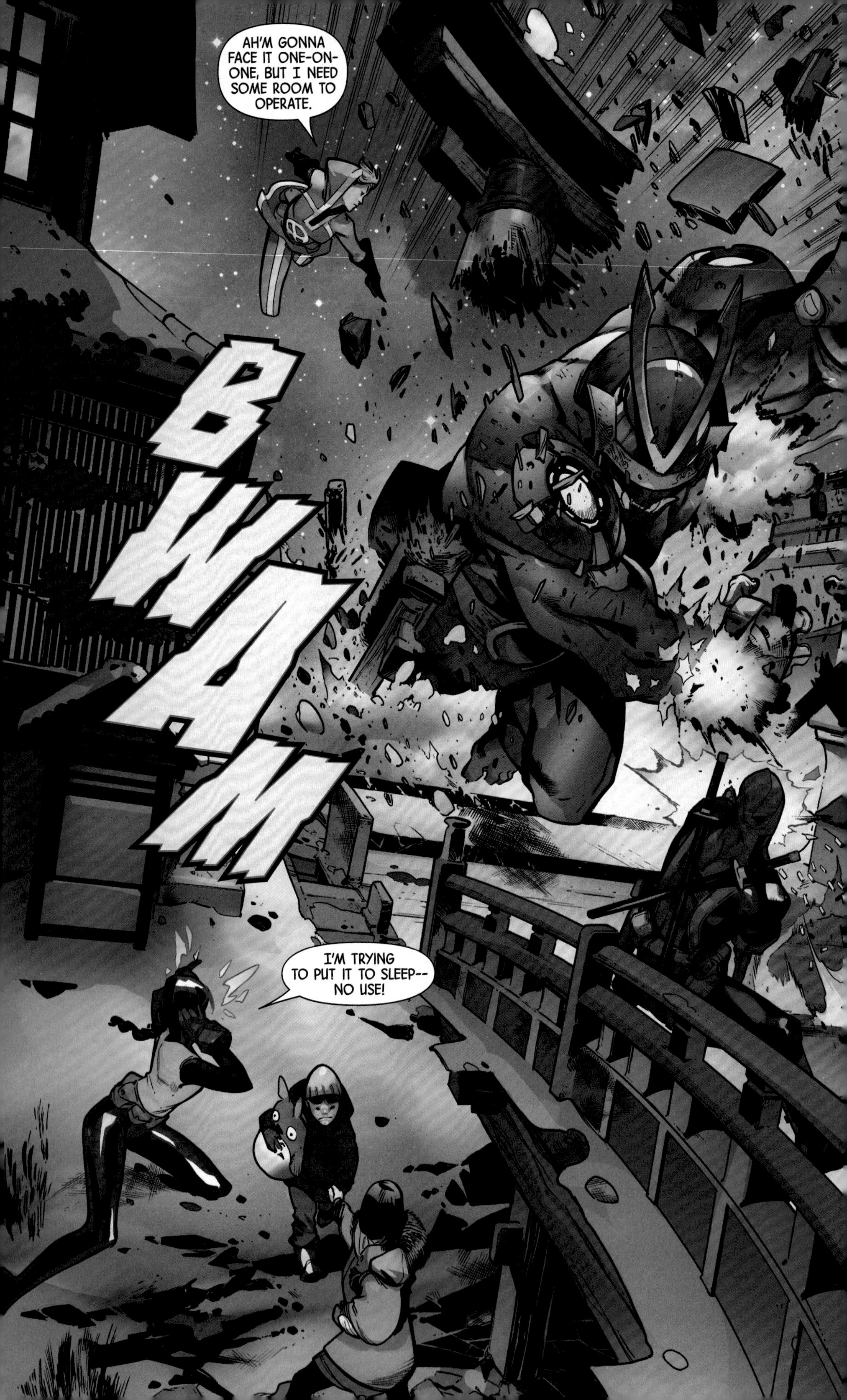
AH'M GONNA FACE IT ONE-ON-ONE, BUT I NEED SOME ROOM TO OPERATE.
BWAAM
I'M TRYING TO PUT IT TO SLEEP-- NO USE!

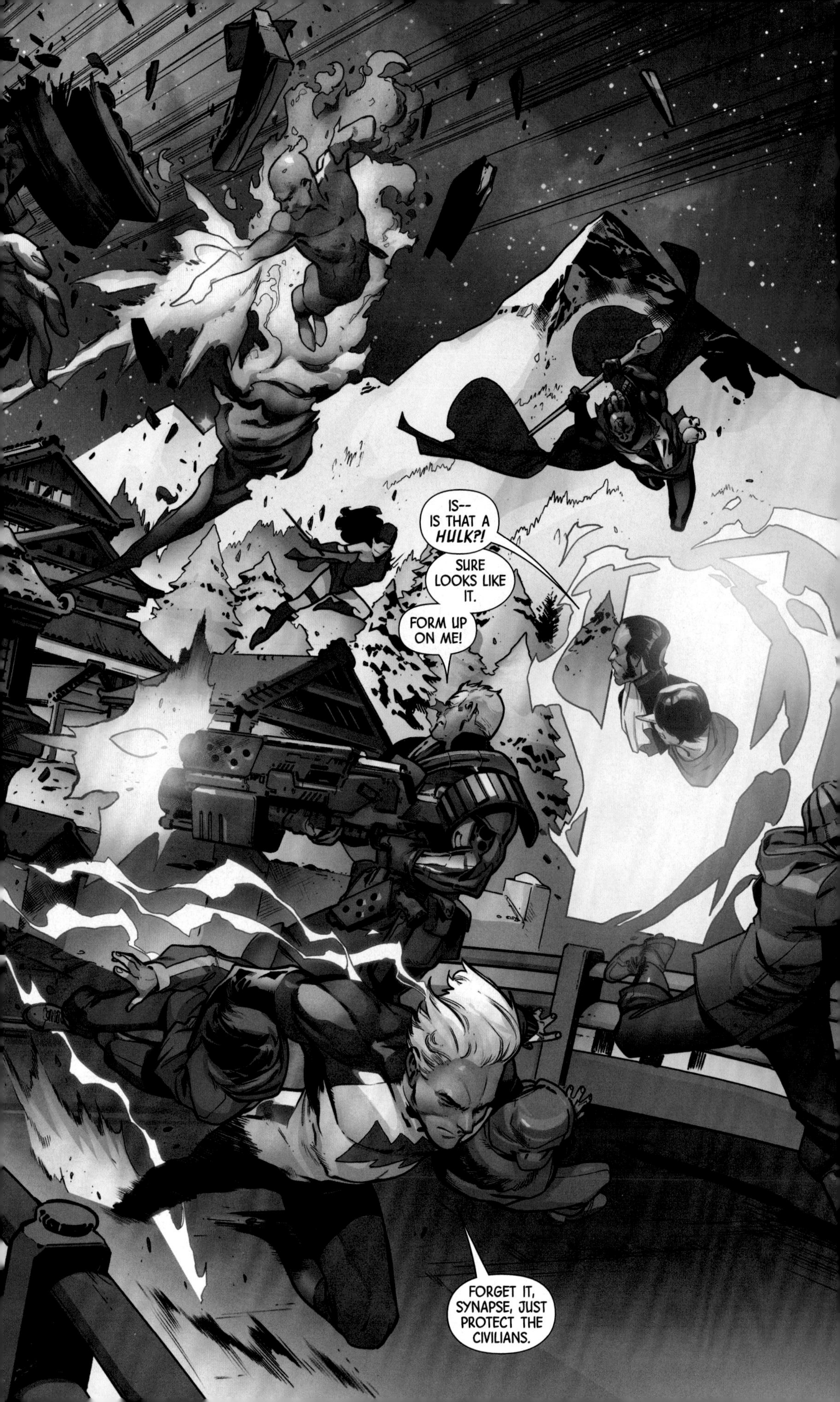
IS--
IS THAT A HULK?!
SURE LOOKS LIKE IT.
FORM UP ON ME!
FORGET IT, SYNAPSE, JUST PROTECT THE CIVILIANS.

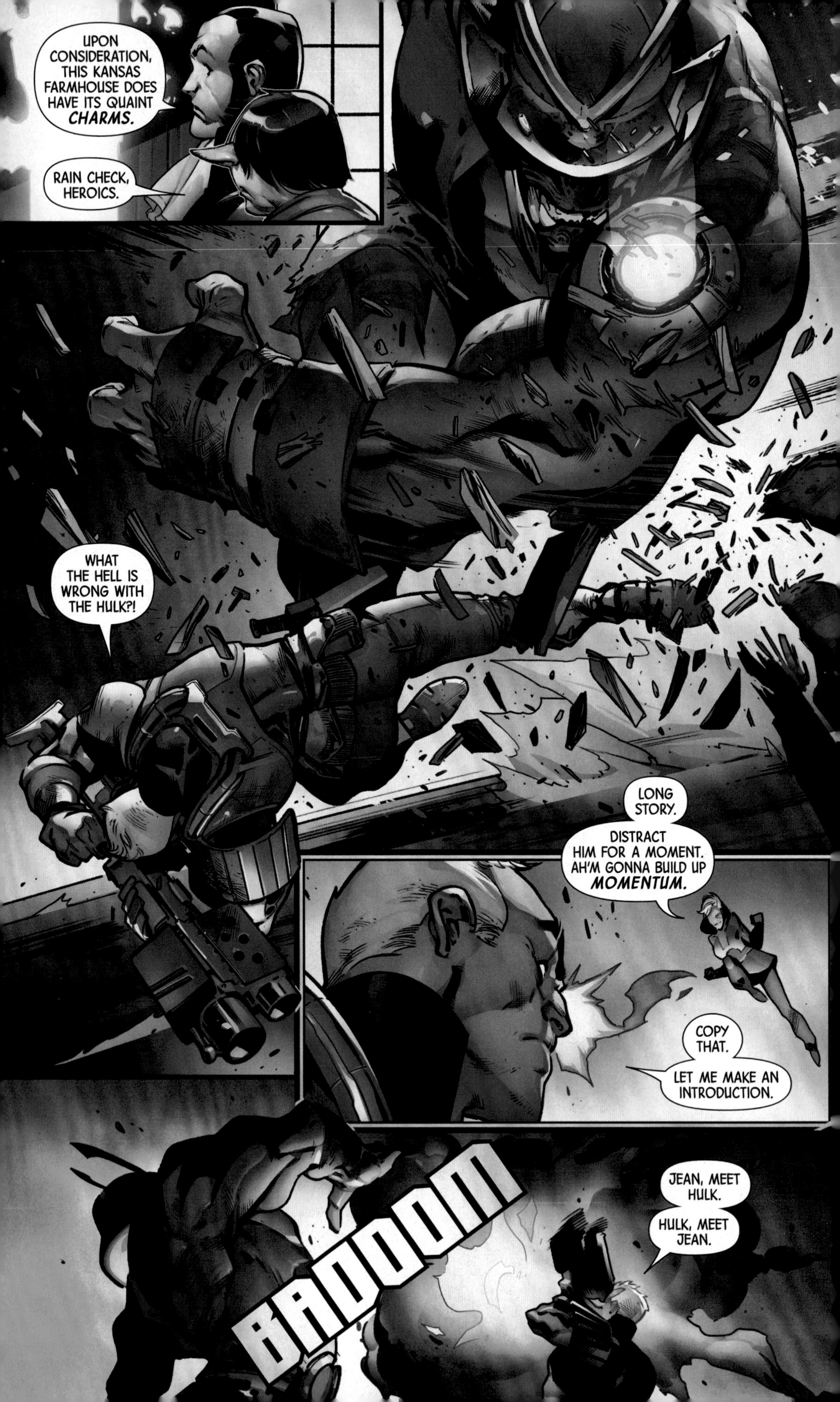
UPON CONSIDERATION, THIS KANSAS FARMHOUSE DOES HAVE ITS QUAINT CHARMS.
RAIN CHECK, HEROICS.
WHAT THE HELL IS WRONG WITH THE HULK?!
LONG STORY.
DISTRACT HIM FOR A MOMENT. AH'M GONNA BUILD UP MOMENTUM.
COPY THAT.
LET ME MAKE AN INTRODUCTION.
BADOOM
JEAN, MEET HULK.
HULK, MEET JEAN.

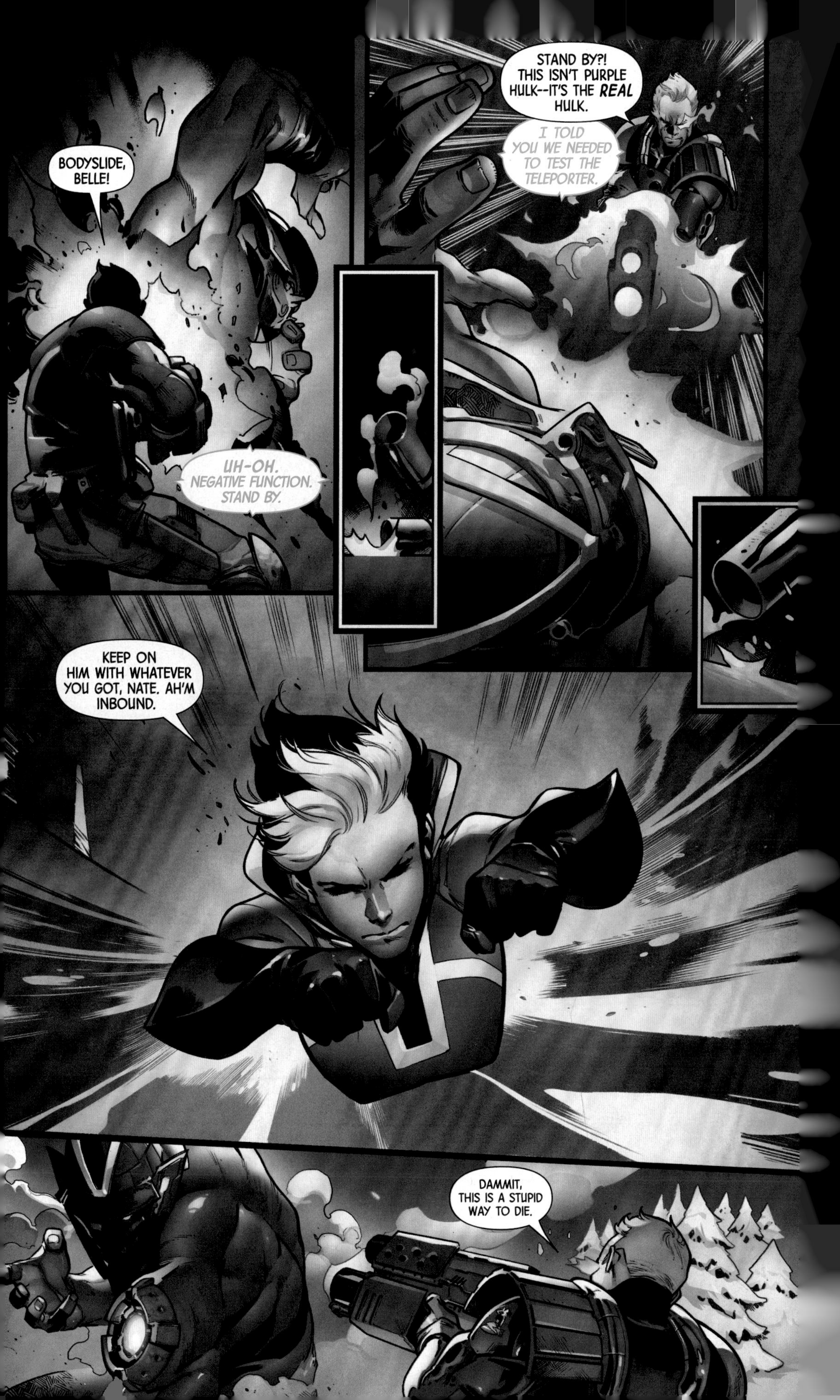
BODYSLIDE, BELLE!
UH-OH. NEGATIVE FUNCTION. STAND BY.
STAND BY?! THIS ISN'T PURPLE HULK--IT'S THE REAL HULK.
I TOLD YOU WE NEEDED TO TEST THE TELEPORTER.
KEEP ON HIM WITH WHATEVER YOU GOT, NATE. AH'M INBOUND.
DAMMIT, THIS IS A STUPID WAY TO DIE.

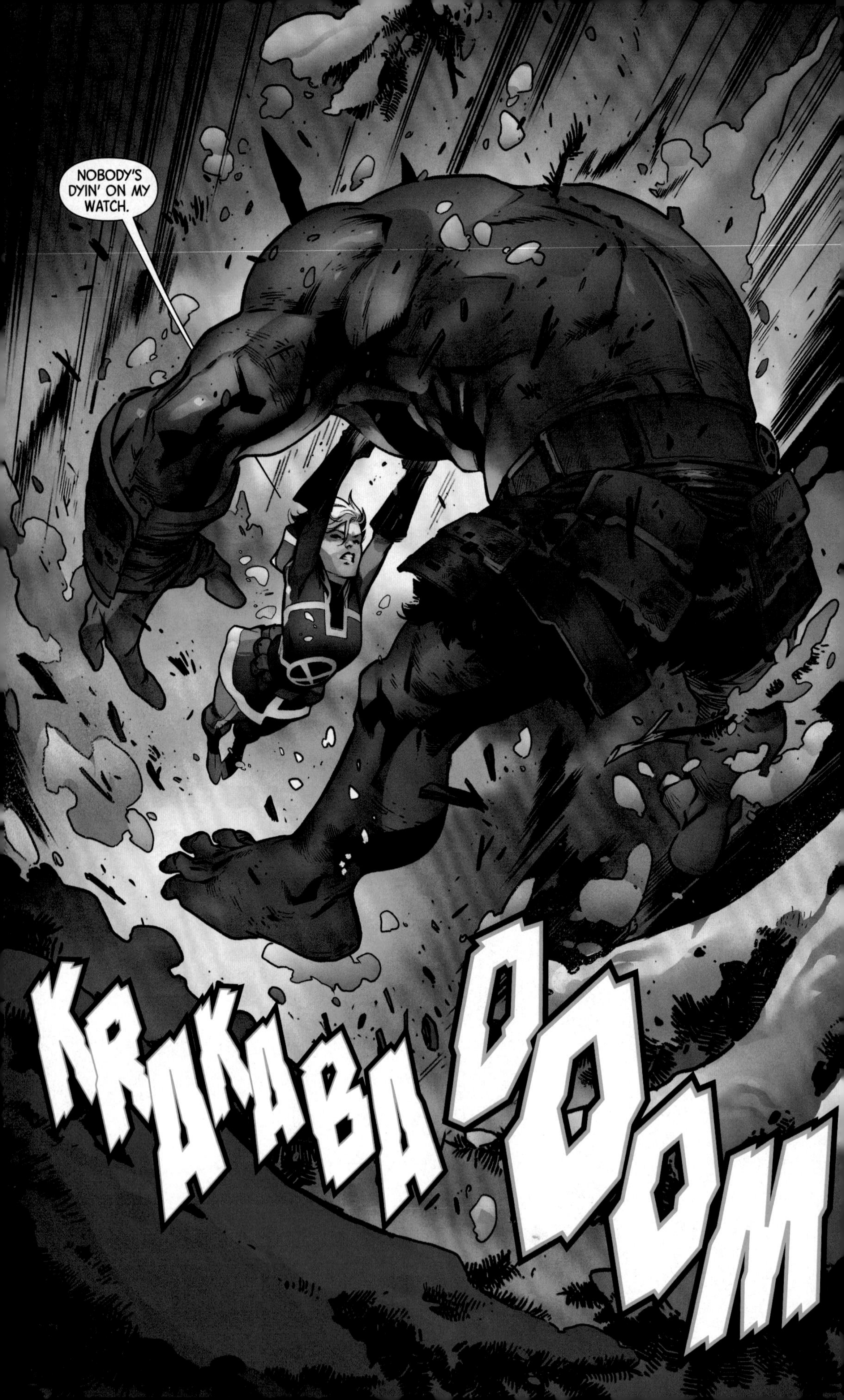
NOBODY'S DYIN' ON MY WATCH.
KRAKABADOOOM

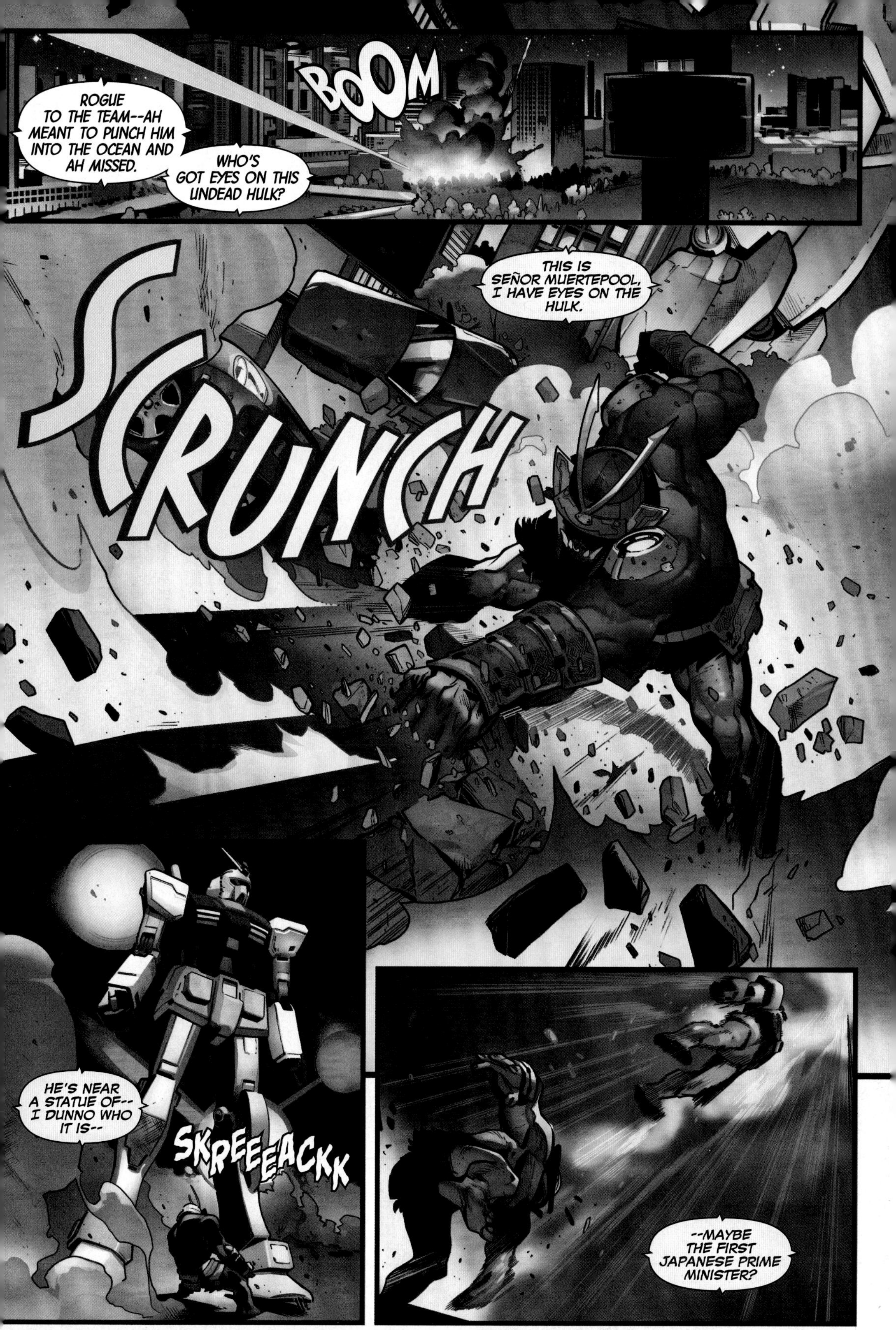

ROGUE TO THE TEAM--AH MEANT TO PUNCH HIM INTO THE OCEAN AND AH MISSED.
BOOM
WHO'S GOT EYES ON THIS UNDEAD HULK?
SCRUNCH
THIS IS SEÑOR MUERTEPOOL, I HAVE EYES ON THE HULK.
HE'S NEAR A STATUE OF-- I DUNNO WHO IT IS--
SKREEEEACKK
--MAYBE THE FIRST JAPANESE PRIME MINISTER?

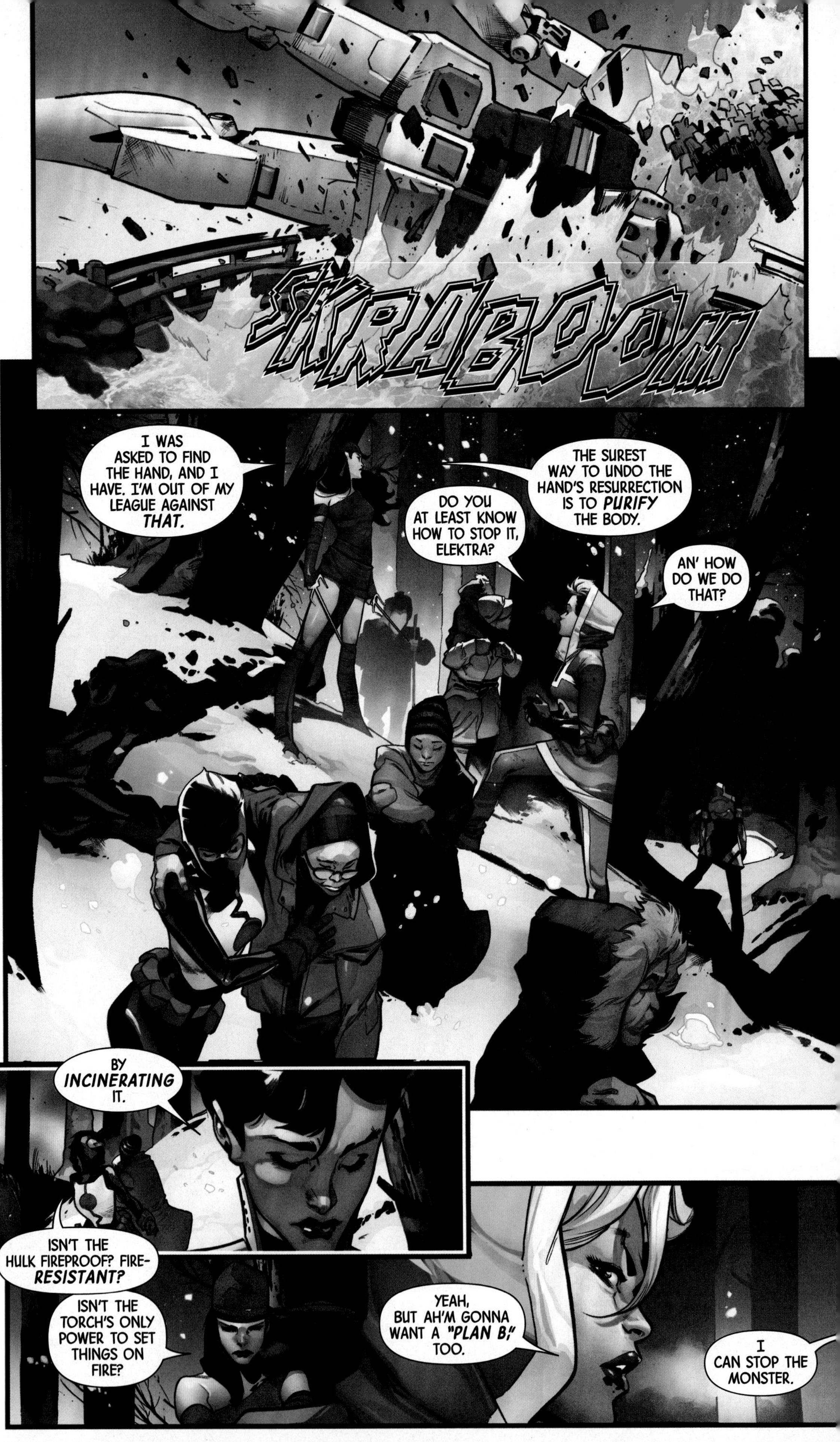

SKRABOOM
I WAS ASKED TO FIND THE HAND, AND I HAVE. I'M OUT OF MY LEAGUE AGAINST THAT.
DO YOU AT LEAST KNOW HOW TO STOP IT, ELEKTRA?
THE SUREST WAY TO UNDO THE HAND'S RESURRECTION IS TO PURIFY THE BODY.
AN' HOW DO WE DO THAT?
BY INCINERATING IT.
ISN'T THE HULK FIREPROOF? FIRE-RESISTANT?
ISN'T THE TORCH'S ONLY POWER TO SET THINGS ON FIRE?
YEAH, BUT AH'M GONNA WANT A "PLAN B," TOO.
I CAN STOP THE MONSTER.

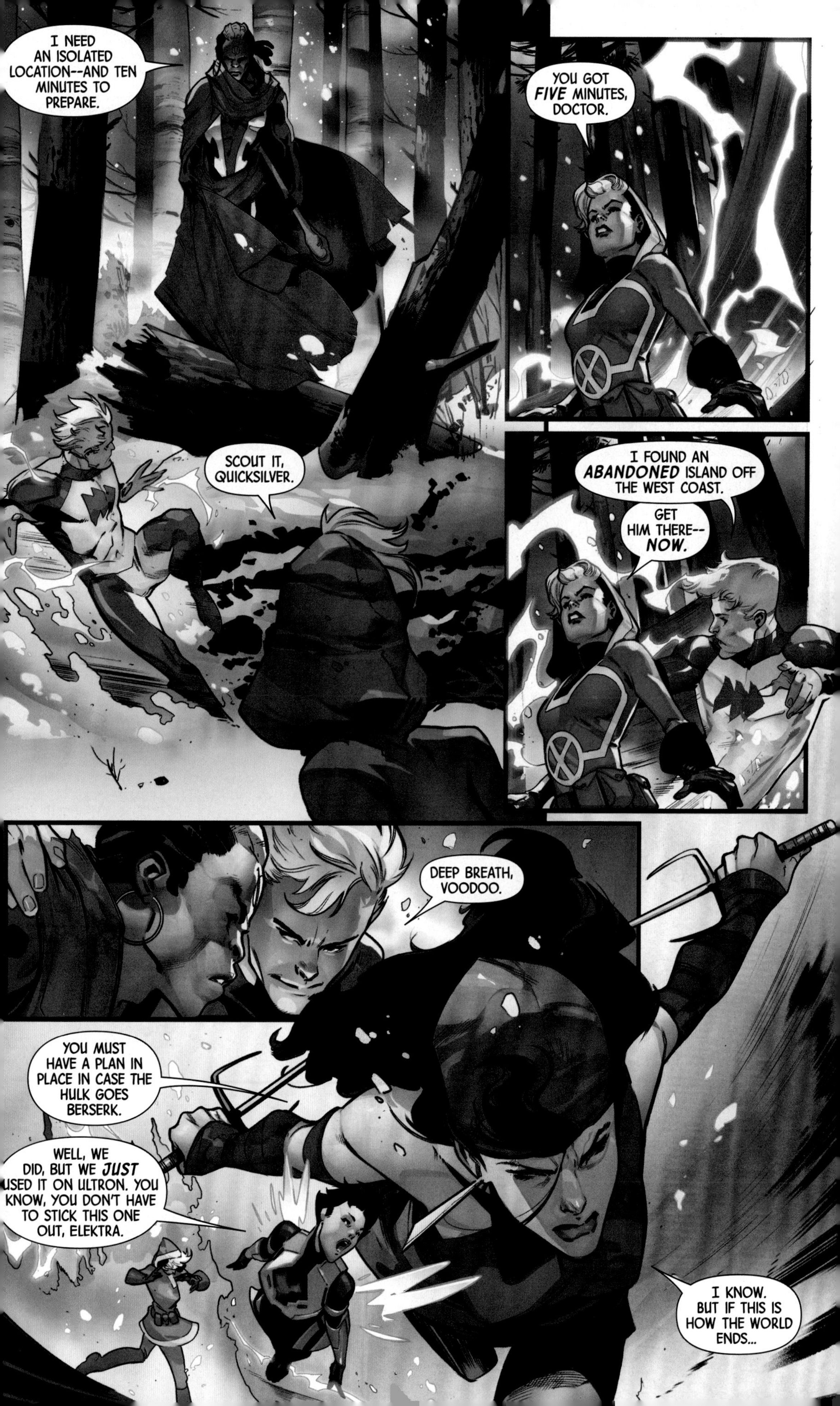
I NEED AN ISOLATED LOCATION--AND TEN MINUTES TO PREPARE.
YOU GOT FIVE MINUTES, DOCTOR.
SCOUT IT, QUICKSILVER.
I FOUND AN ABANDONED ISLAND OFF THE WEST COAST.
GET HIM THERE-- NOW.
DEEP BREATH, VOODOO.
YOU MUST HAVE A PLAN IN PLACE IN CASE THE HULK GOES BERSERK.
WELL, WE DID, BUT WE JUST USED IT ON ULTRON. YOU KNOW, YOU DON'T HAVE TO STICK THIS ONE OUT, ELEKTRA.
I KNOW. BUT IF THIS IS HOW THE WORLD ENDS...

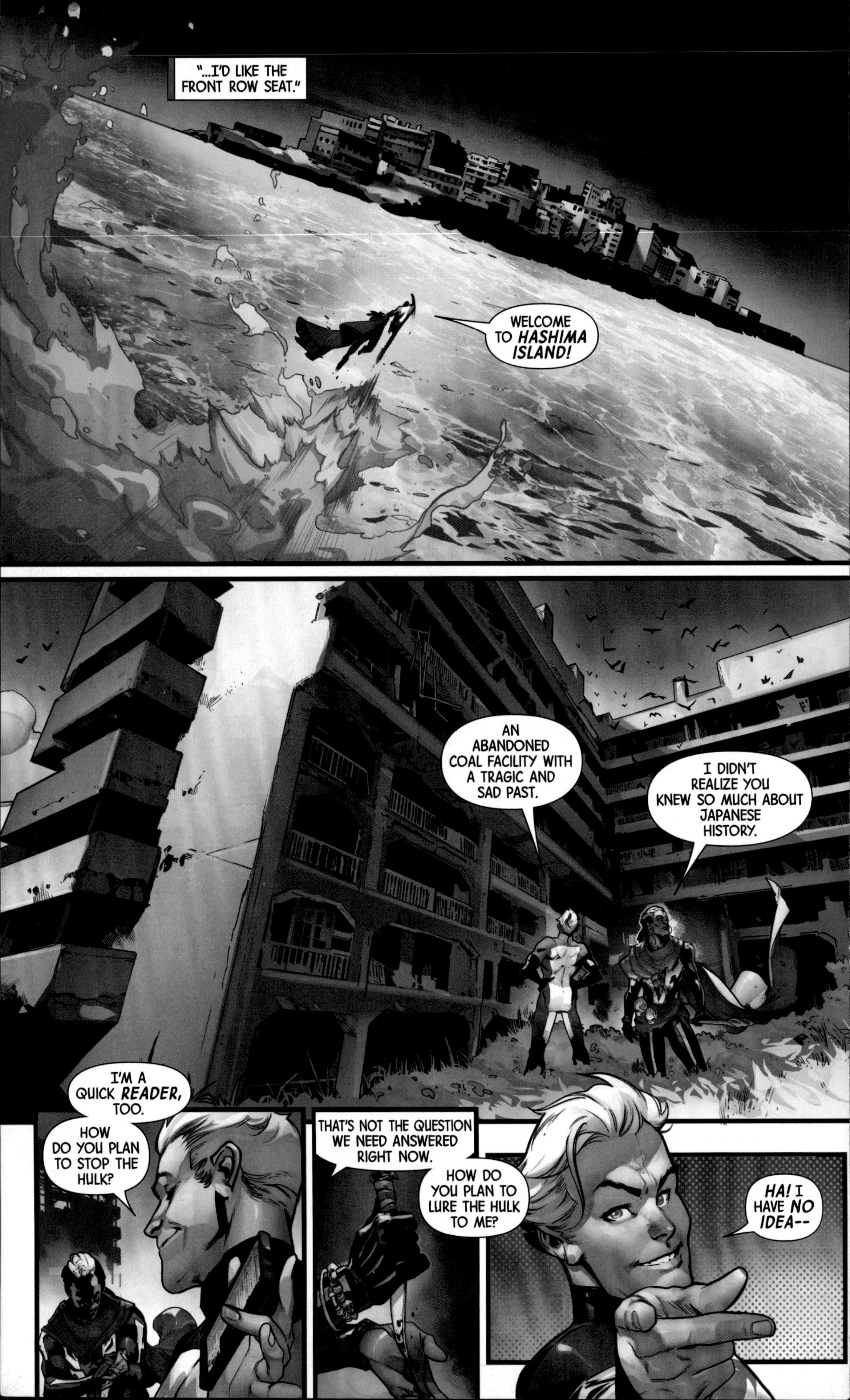
"...I'D LIKE THE FRONT ROW SEAT."
WELCOME TO HASHIMA ISLAND!
AN ABANDONED COAL FACILITY WITH A TRAGIC AND SAD PAST.
I DIDN'T REALIZE YOU KNEW SO MUCH ABOUT JAPANESE HISTORY.
I'M A QUICK READER, TOO.
HOW DO YOU PLAN TO STOP THE HULK?
THAT'S NOT THE QUESTION WE NEED ANSWERED RIGHT NOW.
HOW DO YOU PLAN TO LURE THE HULK TO ME?
HA! I HAVE NO IDEA--

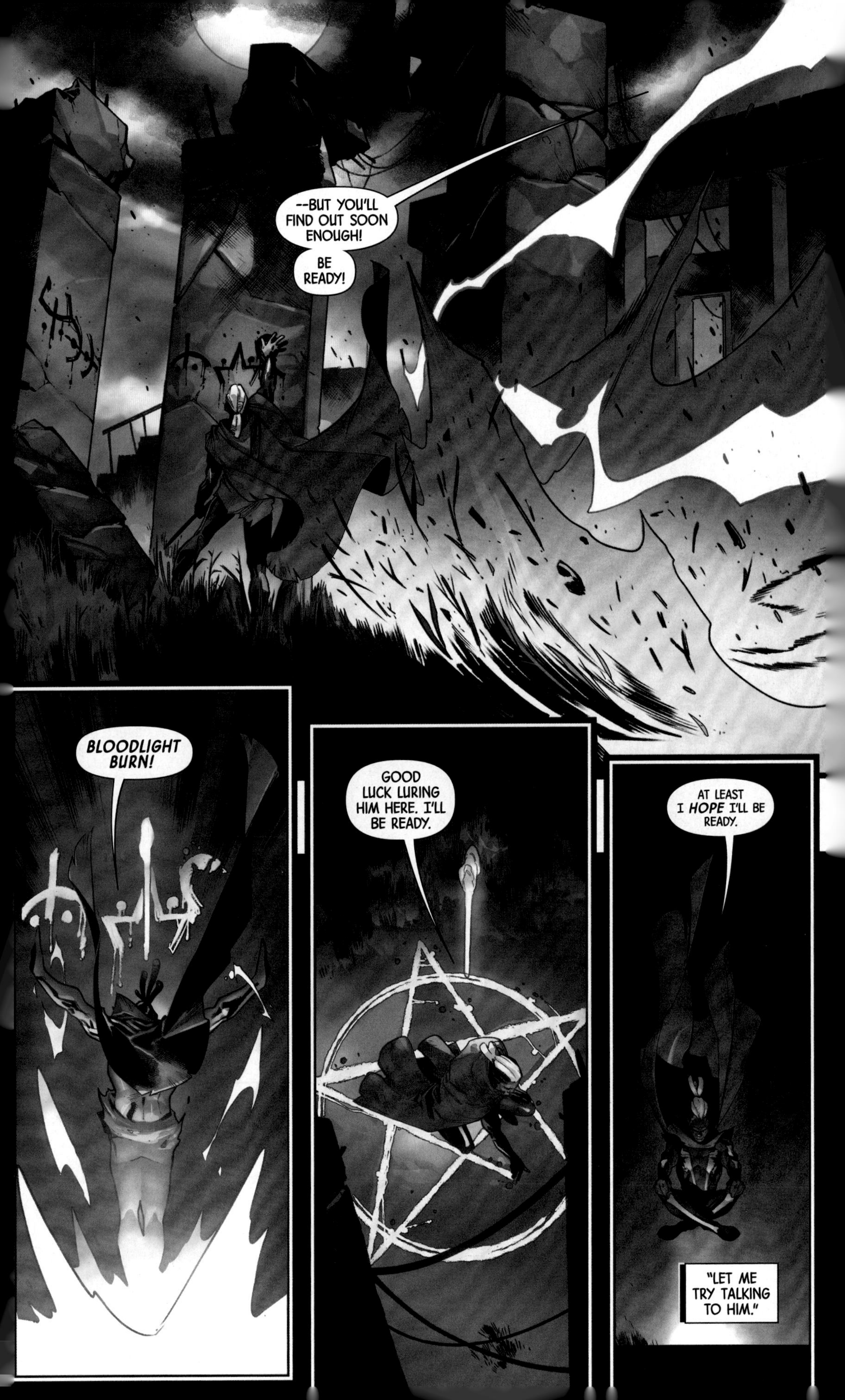
--BUT YOU'LL FIND OUT SOON ENOUGH!
BE READY!
BLOODLIGHT BURN!
GOOD LUCK LURING HIM HERE. I'LL BE READY.
AT LEAST I HOPE I'LL BE READY.
"LET ME TRY TALKING TO HIM."

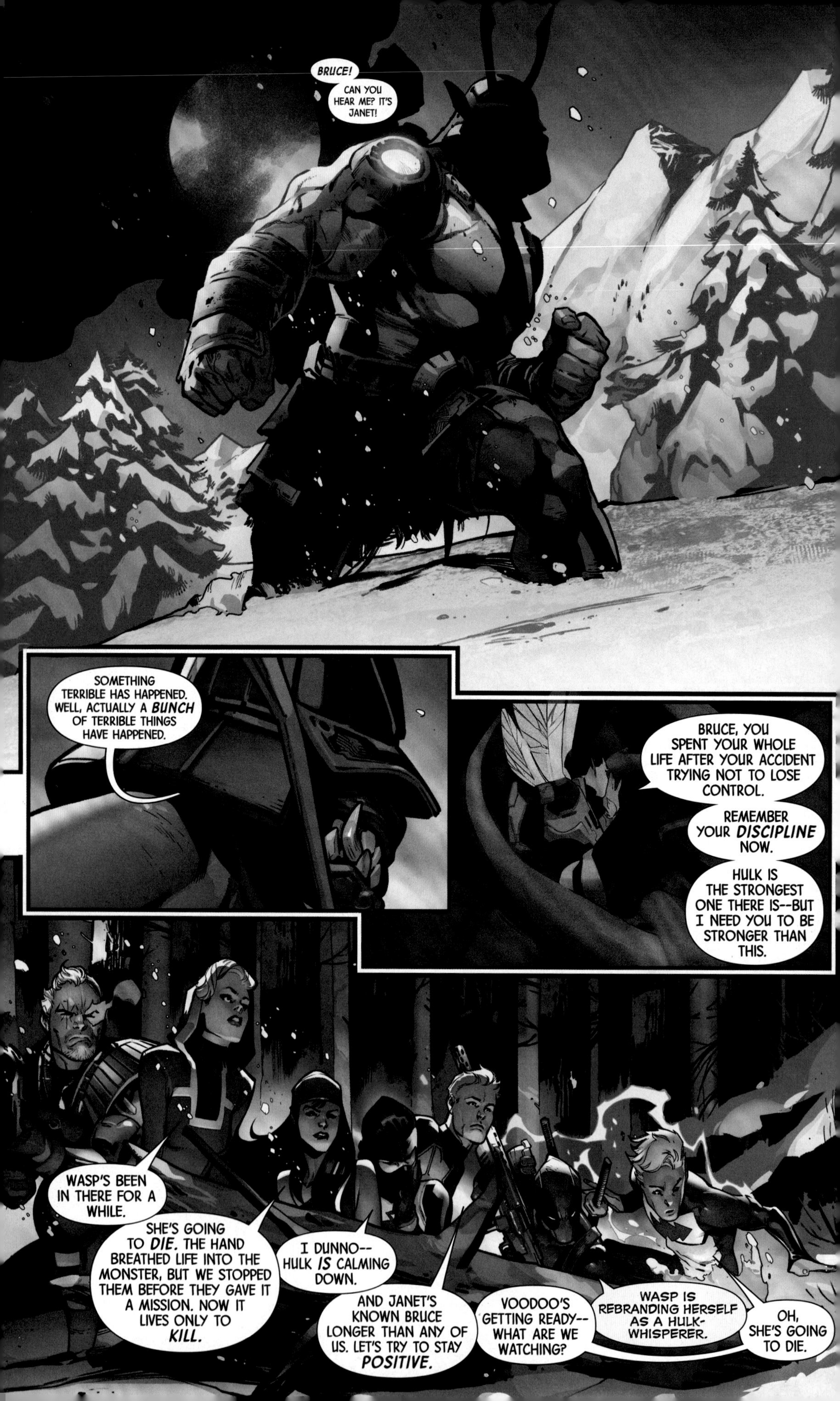
BRUCE!
CAN YOU HEAR ME? IT'S JANET!
SOMETHING TERRIBLE HAS HAPPENED. WELL, ACTUALLY A BUNCH OF TERRIBLE THINGS HAVE HAPPENED.
BRUCE, YOU SPENT YOUR WHOLE LIFE AFTER YOUR ACCIDENT TRYING NOT TO LOSE CONTROL.
REMEMBER YOUR DISCIPLINE NOW.
HULK IS THE STRONGEST ONE THERE IS--BUT I NEED YOU TO BE STRONGER THAN THIS.
WASP'S BEEN IN THERE FOR A WHILE.
SHE'S GOING TO DIE. THE HAND BREATHED LIFE INTO THE MONSTER, BUT WE STOPPED THEM BEFORE THEY GAVE IT A MISSION. NOW IT LIVES ONLY TO KILL.
I DUNNO-- HULK IS CALMING DOWN.
AND JANET'S KNOWN BRUCE LONGER THAN ANY OF US. LET'S TRY TO STAY POSITIVE.
VOODOO'S GETTING READY-- WHAT ARE WE WATCHING?
WASP IS REBRANDING HERSELF AS A HULK-WHISPERER.
OH, SHE'S GOING TO DIE.

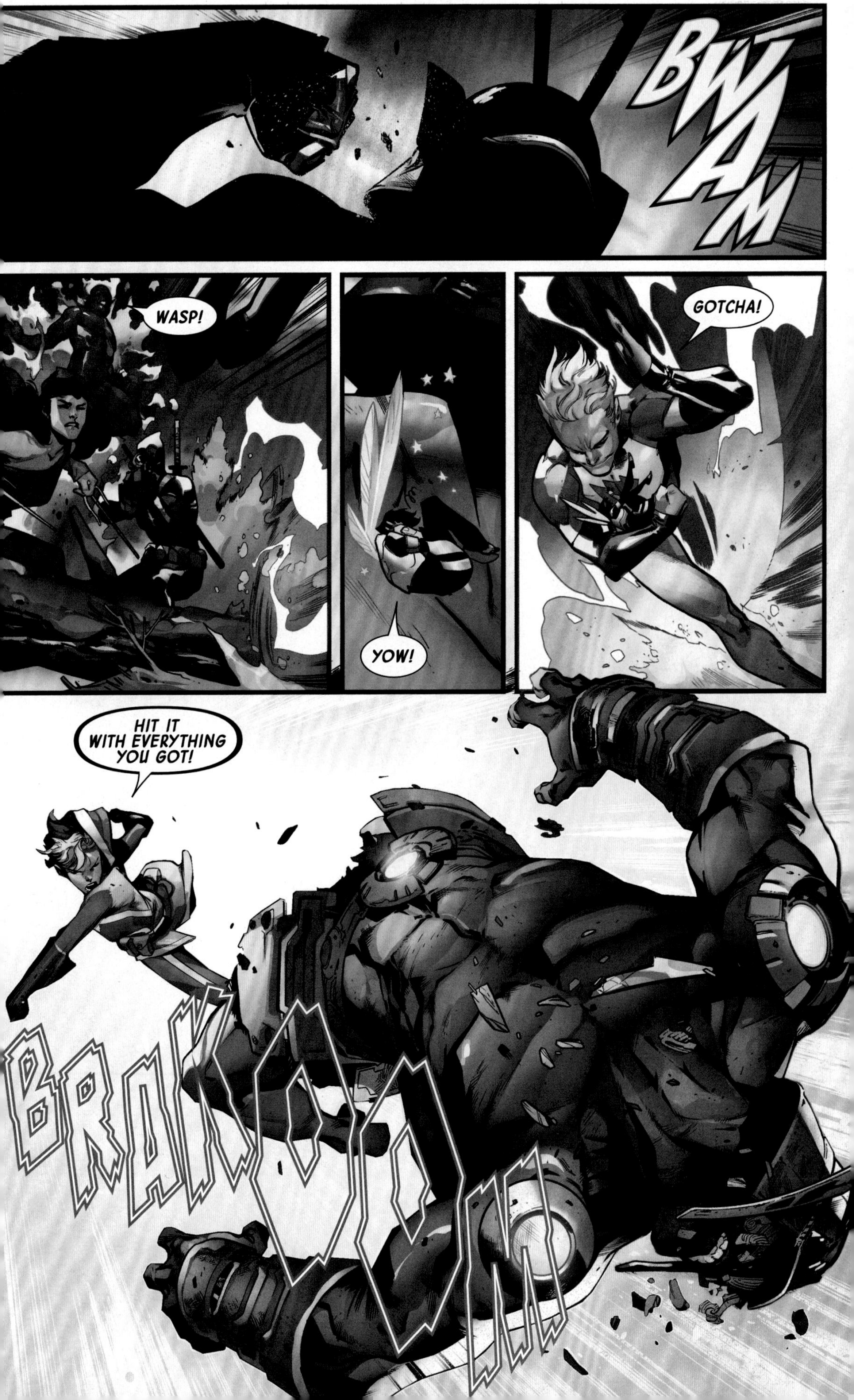

BWAM
WASP!
YOW!
GOTCHA!
HIT IT WITH EVERYTHING YOU GOT!
BRAKOOOM

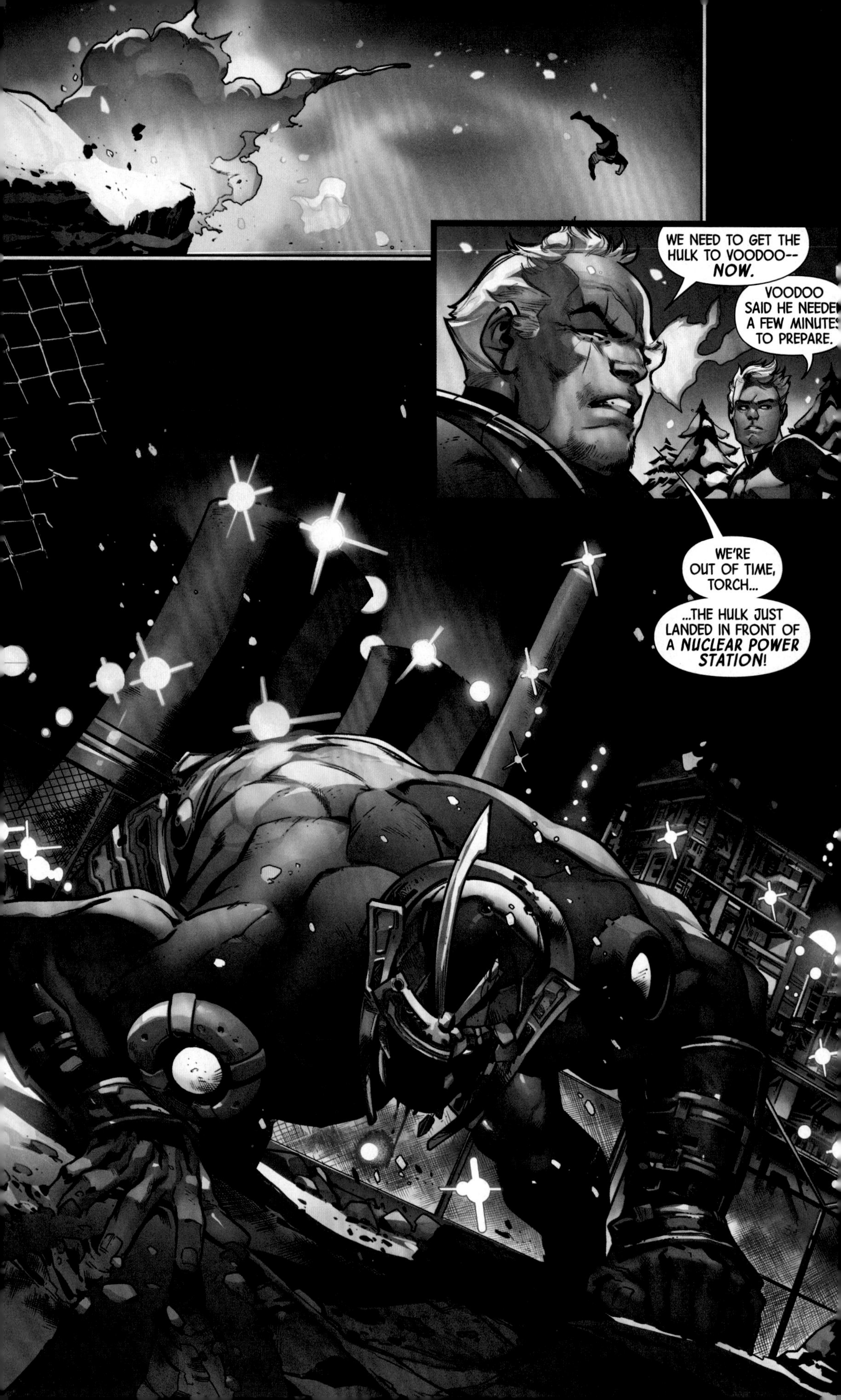
WE NEED TO GET THE HULK TO VOODOO-- NOW.
VOODOO SAID HE NEEDE A FEW MINUTE TO PREPARE.
WE'RE OUT OF TIME, TORCH...
...THE HULK JUST LANDED IN FRONT OF A NUCLEAR POWER STATION!

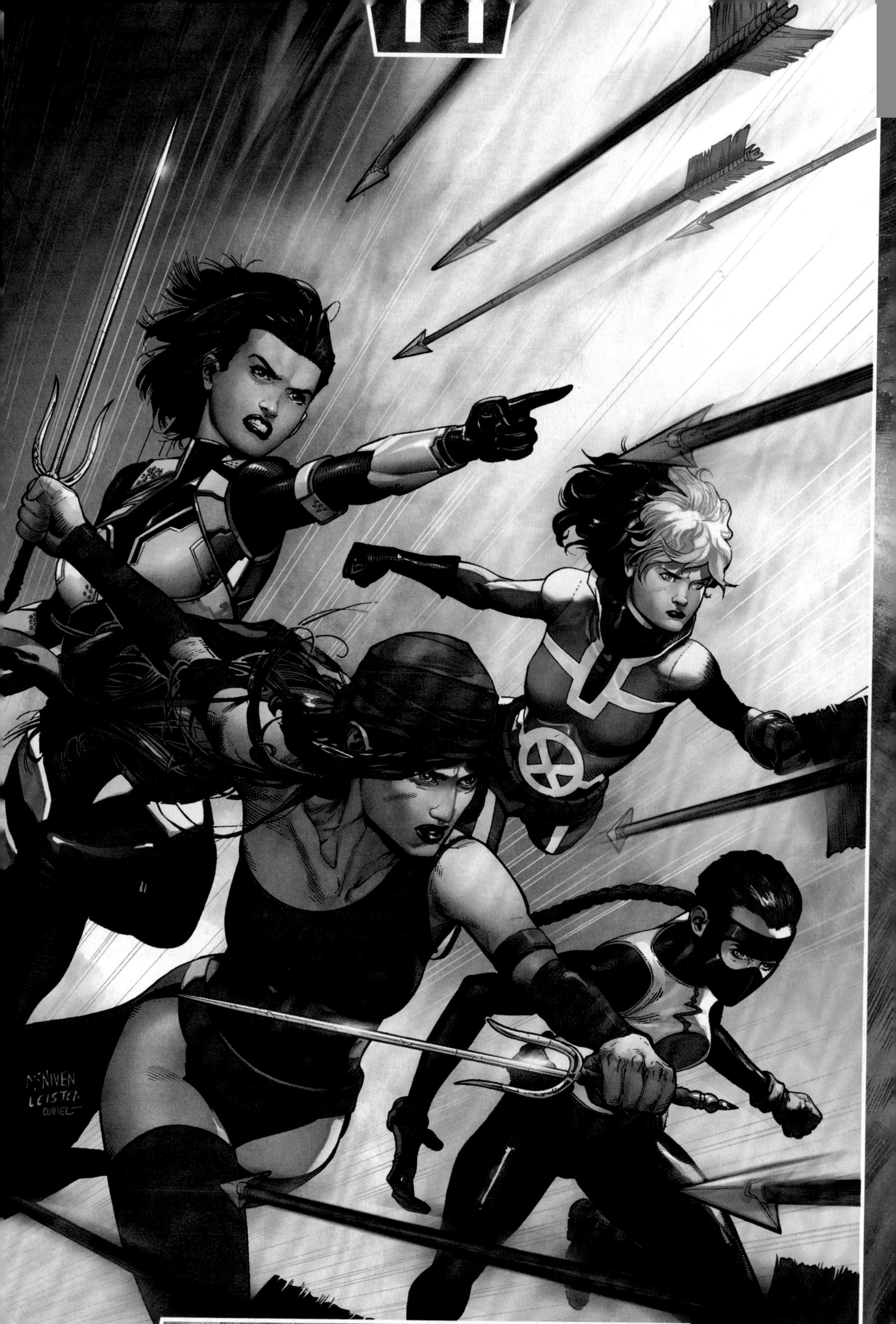
McNIVEN
LEISTEN
CURIEL

"NO REST FOR THE WEARY"

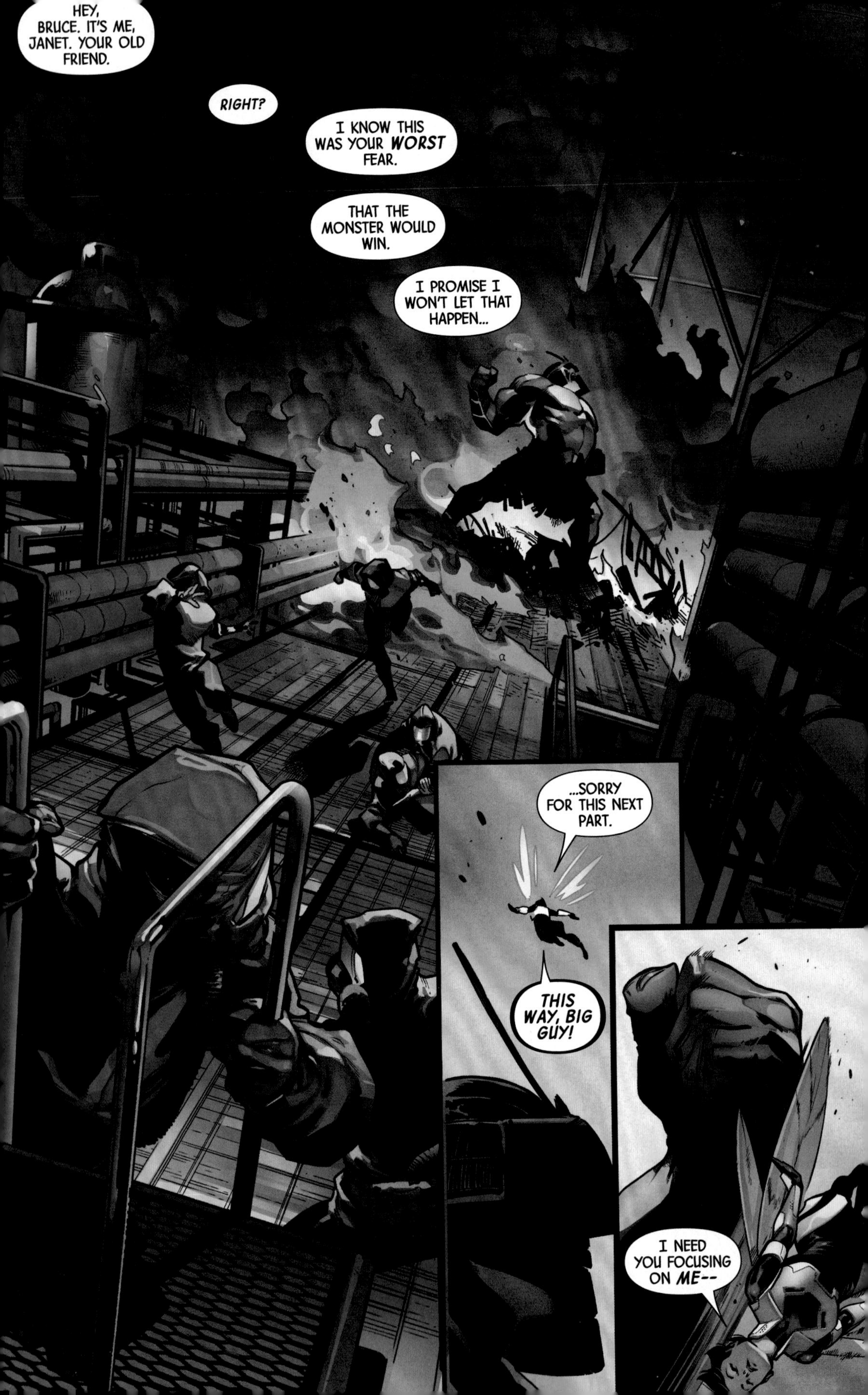
HEY, BRUCE. IT'S ME, JANET. YOUR OLD FRIEND.
RIGHT?
I KNOW THIS WAS YOUR WORST FEAR.
THAT THE MONSTER WOULD WIN.
I PROMISE I WON'T LET THAT HAPPEN...
...SORRY FOR THIS NEXT PART.
THIS WAY, BIG GUY!
I NEED YOU FOCUSING ON ME--

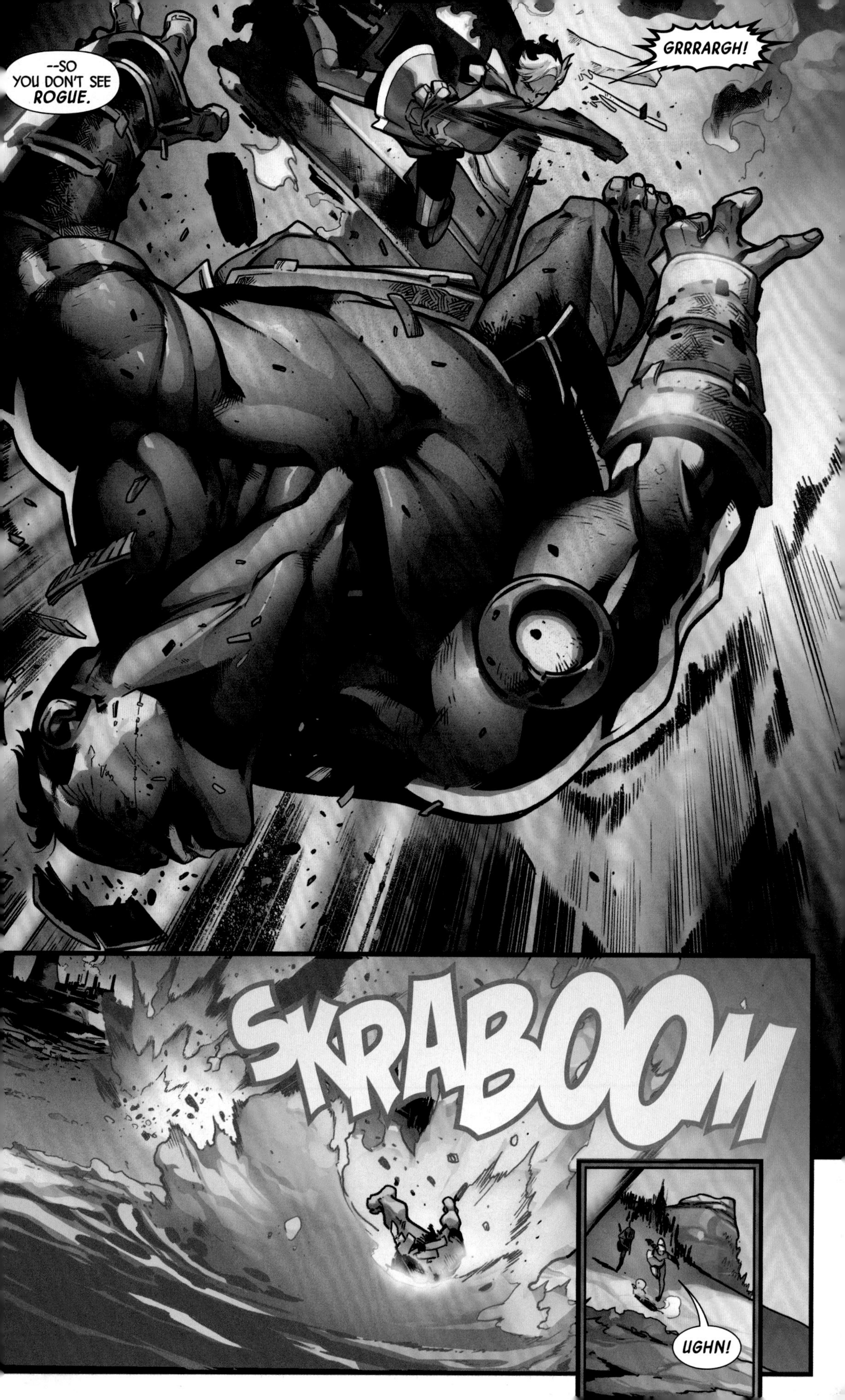
--SO YOU DON'T SEE ROGUE.
GRRRARGH!
SKRABOOM
UGHN!

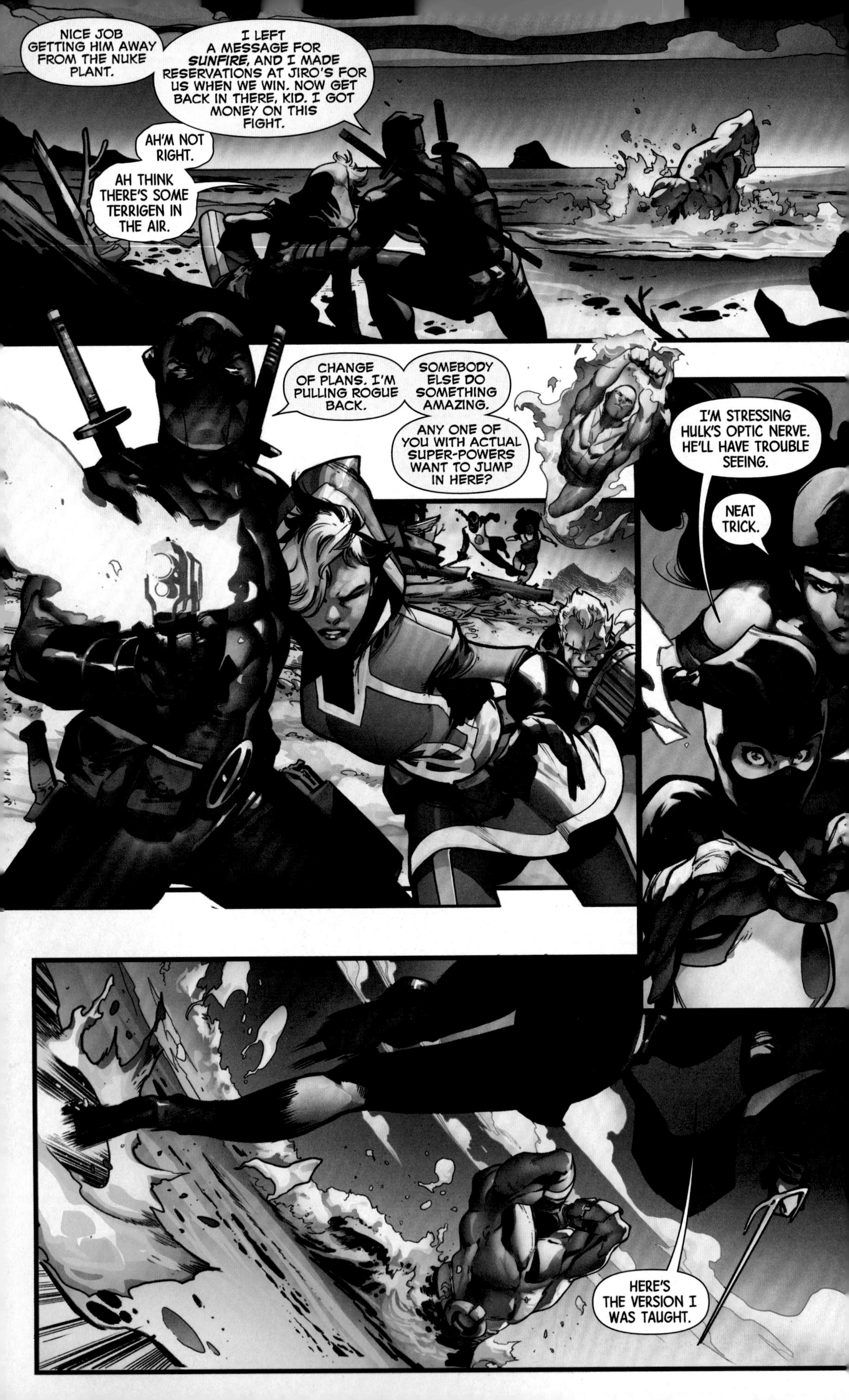
NICE JOB GETTING HIM AWAY FROM THE NUKE PLANT.
I LEFT A MESSAGE FOR SUNFIRE, AND I MADE RESERVATIONS AT JIRO'S FOR US WHEN WE WIN. NOW GET BACK IN THERE, KID. I GOT MONEY ON THIS FIGHT.
AH'M NOT RIGHT.
AH THINK THERE'S SOME TERRIGEN IN THE AIR.
CHANGE OF PLANS. I'M PULLING ROGUE BACK.
SOMEBODY ELSE DO SOMETHING AMAZING.
ANY ONE OF YOU WITH ACTUAL SUPER-POWERS WANT TO JUMP IN HERE?
I'M STRESSING HULK'S OPTIC NERVE. HE'LL HAVE TROUBLE SEEING.
NEAT TRICK.
HERE'S THE VERSION I WAS TAUGHT.

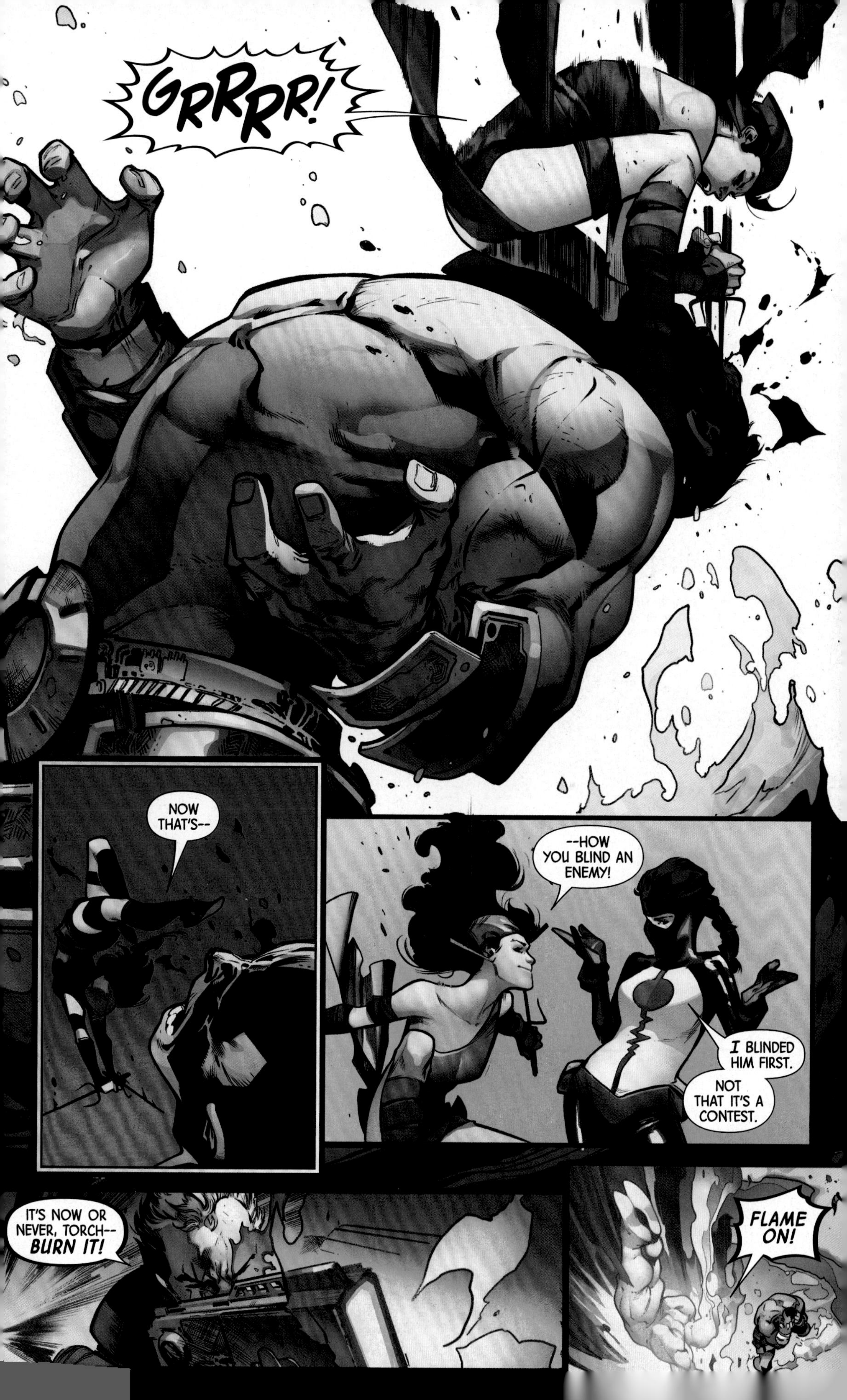
GRRRR!
NOW THAT'S--
--HOW YOU BLIND AN ENEMY!
I BLINDED HIM FIRST.
NOT THAT IT'S A CONTEST.
IT'S NOW OR NEVER, TORCH-- BURN IT!
FLAME ON!

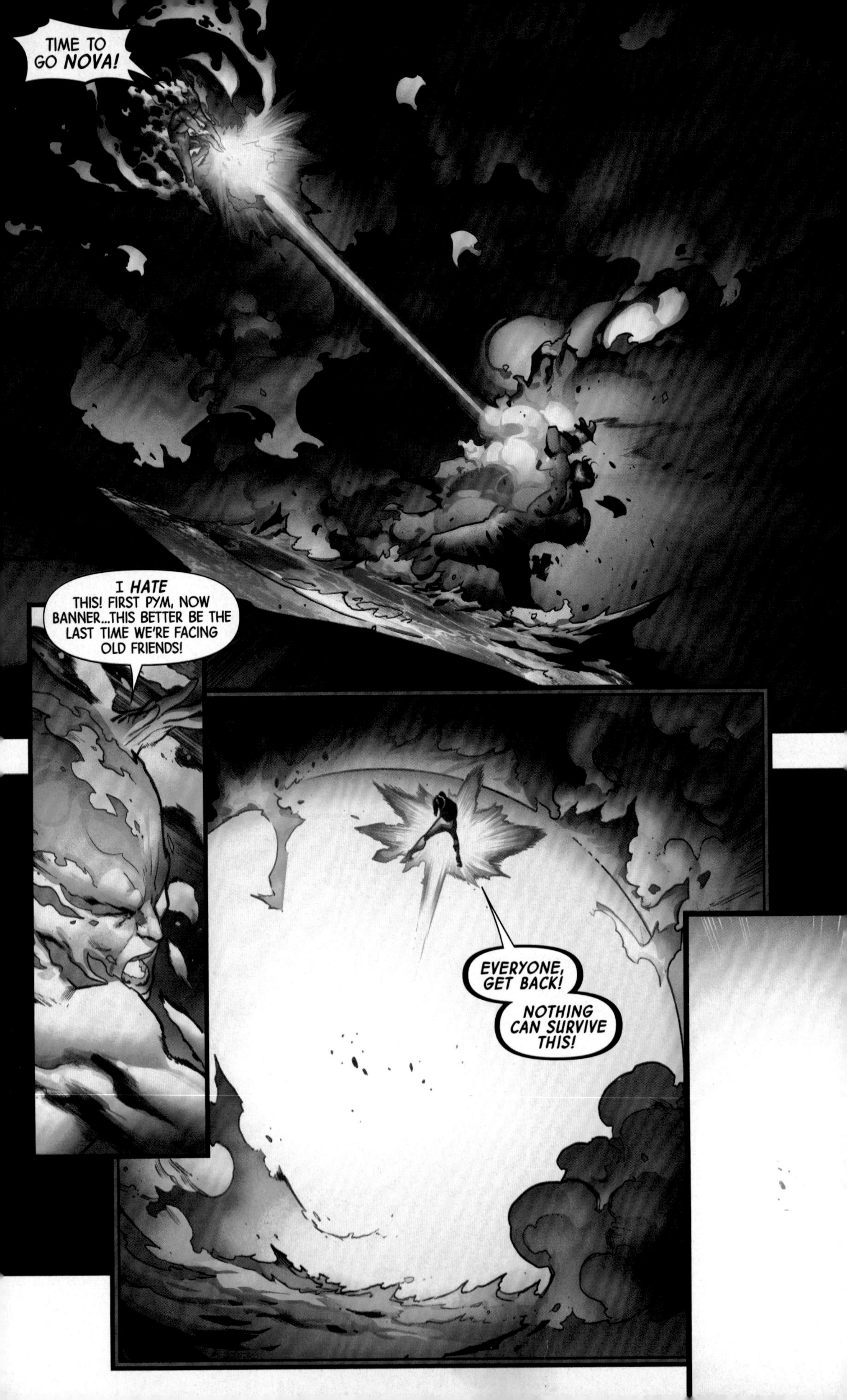
TIME TO GO NOVA!
I HATE THIS! FIRST PYM, NOW BANNER...THIS BETTER BE THE LAST TIME WE'RE FACING OLD FRIENDS!
EVERYONE, GET BACK!
NOTHING CAN SURVIVE THIS!

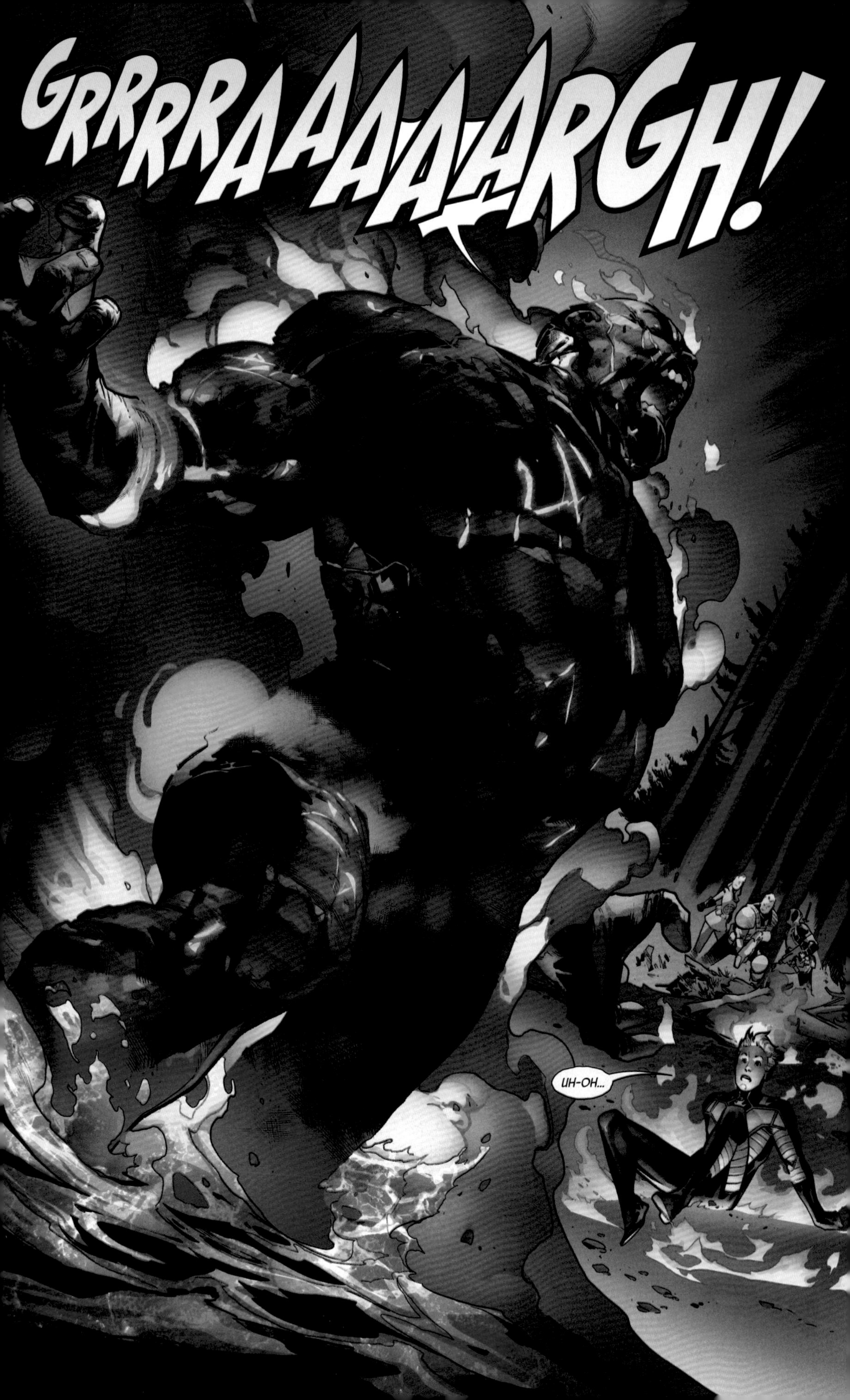
GRRRRAAAAAARGH!
UH-OH...

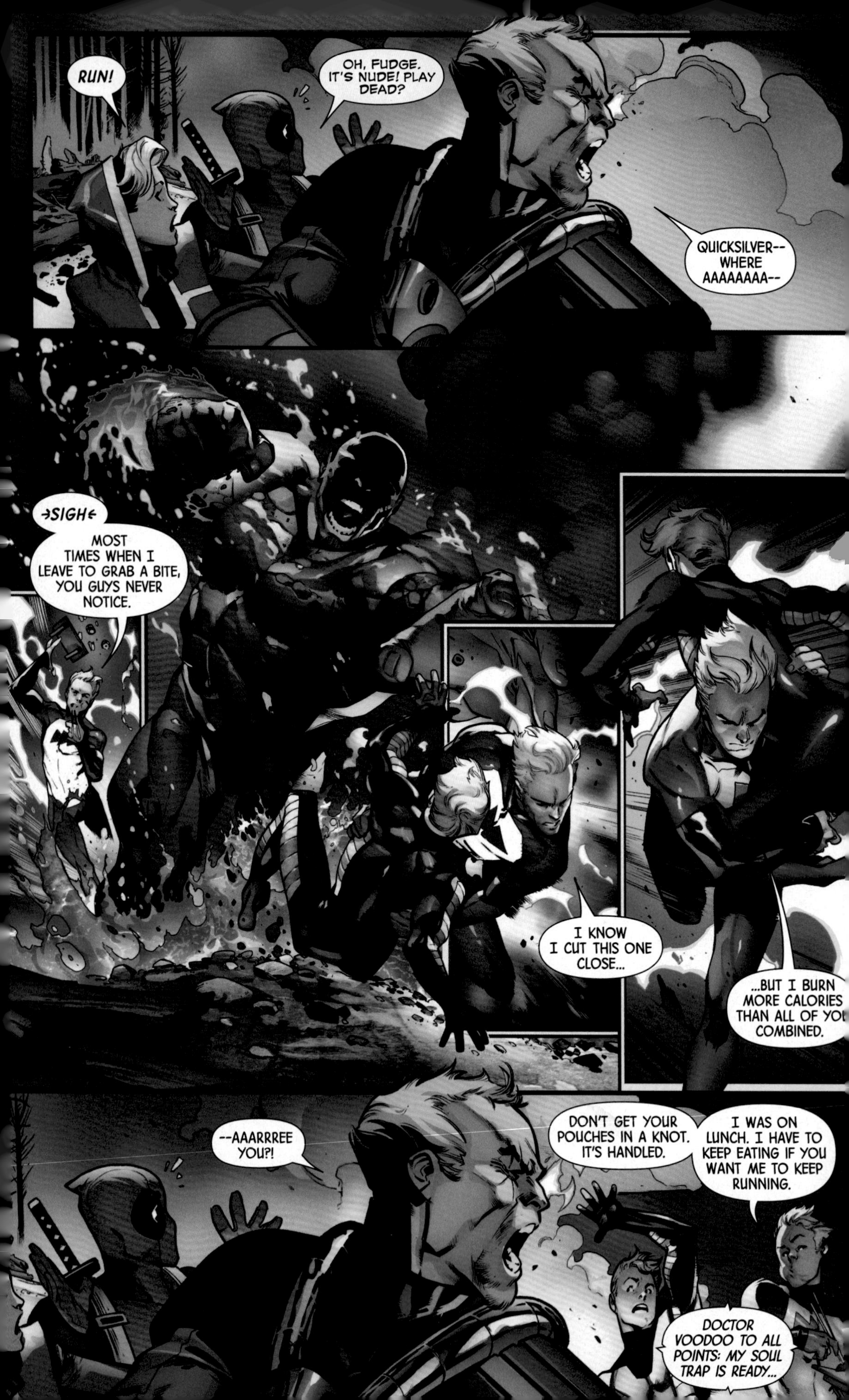
RUN!
OH, FUDGE. IT'S NUDE! PLAY DEAD?
QUICKSILVER-- WHERE AAAAAAAA--
→SIGH←
MOST TIMES WHEN I LEAVE TO GRAB A BITE, YOU GUYS NEVER NOTICE.
I KNOW I CUT THIS ONE CLOSE...
...BUT I BURN MORE CALORIES THAN ALL OF YOU COMBINED.
--AAARRREE YOU?!
DON'T GET YOUR POUCHES IN A KNOT. IT'S HANDLED.
I WAS ON LUNCH. I HAVE TO KEEP EATING IF YOU WANT ME TO KEEP RUNNING.
DOCTOR VOODOO TO ALL POINTS: MY SOUL TRAP IS READY...

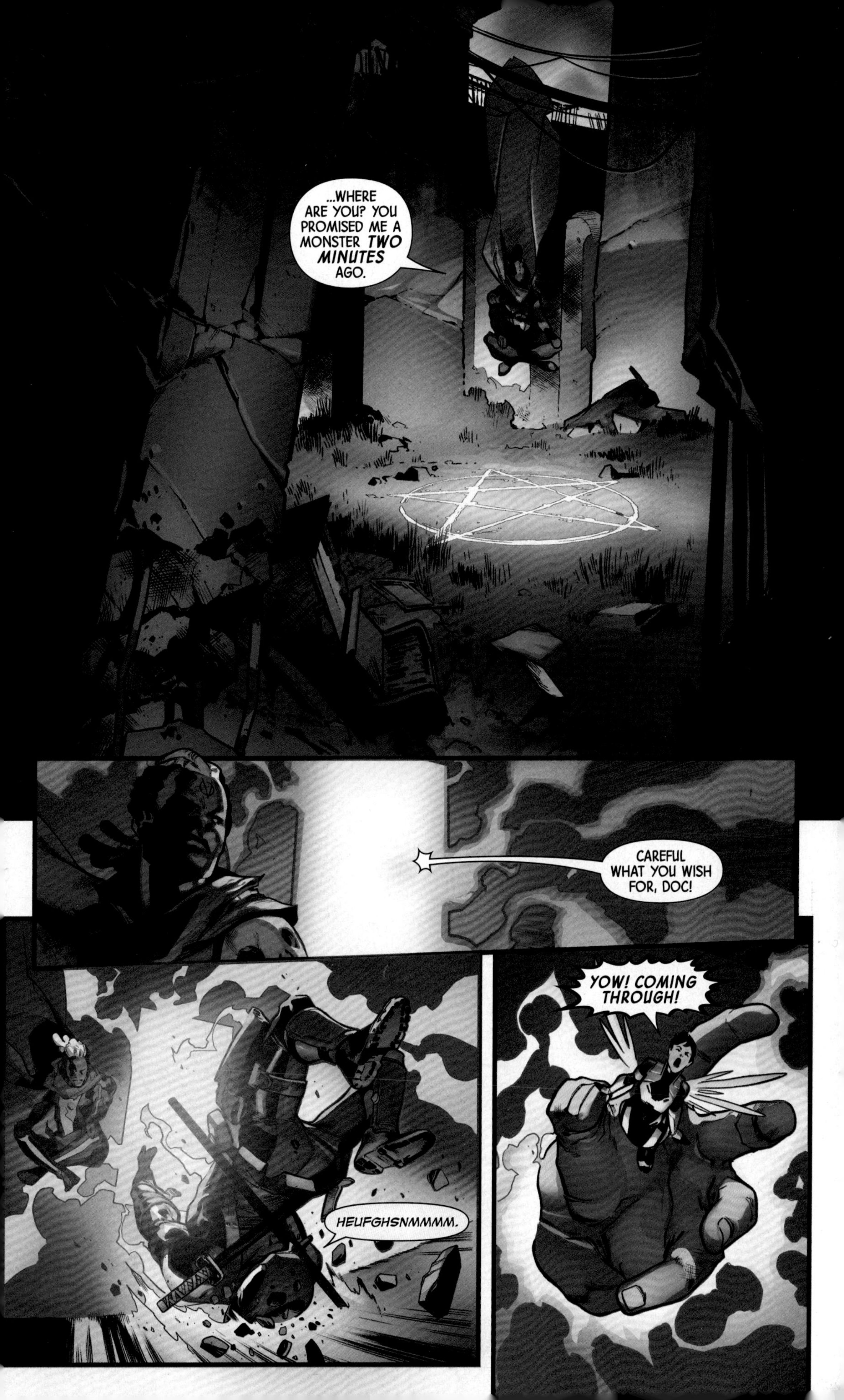
...WHERE ARE YOU? YOU PROMISED ME A MONSTER TWO MINUTES AGO.
CAREFUL WHAT YOU WISH FOR, DOC!
HEUFGHSNMMMM.
YOW! COMING THROUGH!

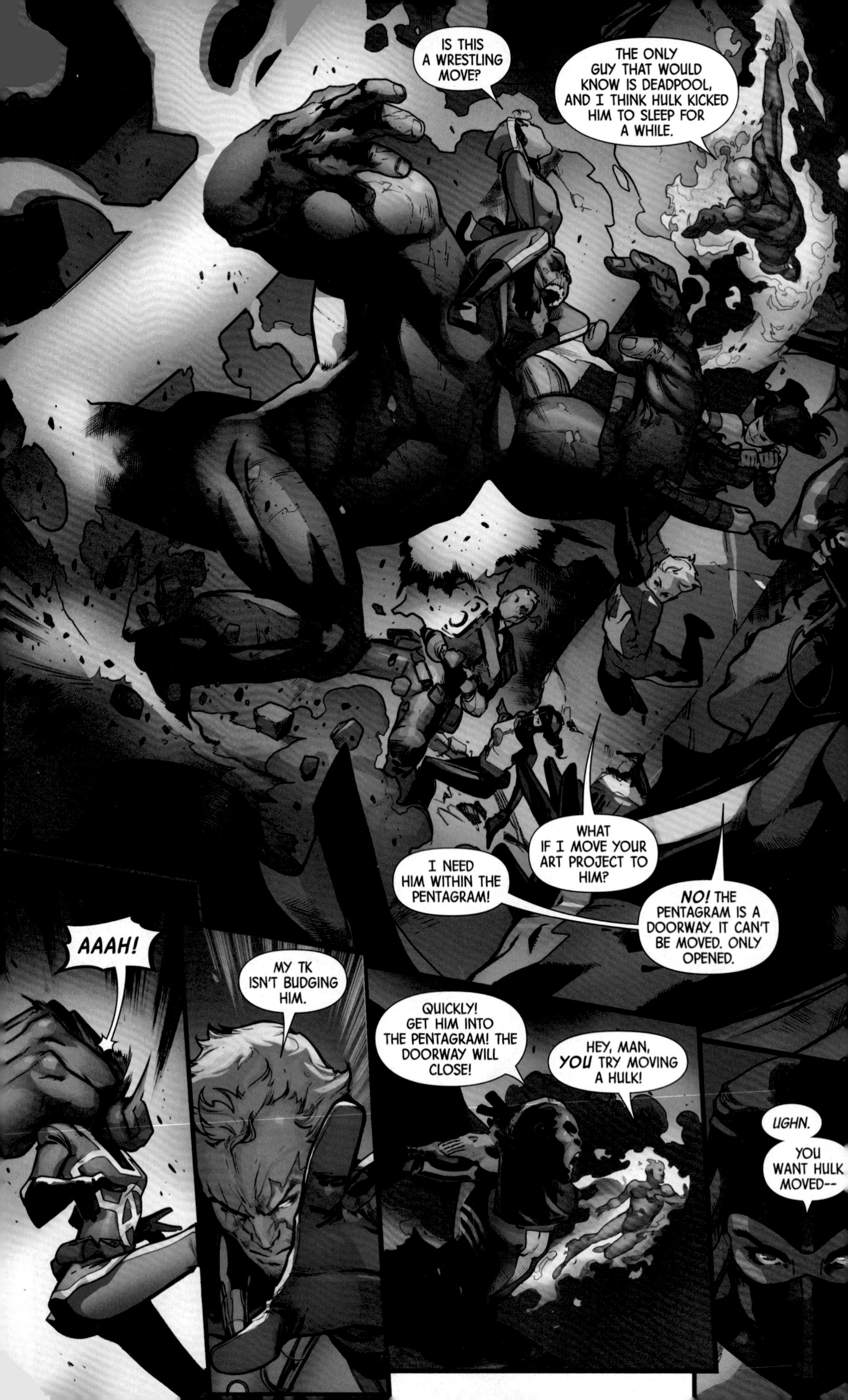
IS THIS A WRESTLING MOVE?
THE ONLY GUY THAT WOULD KNOW IS DEADPOOL, AND I THINK HULK KICKED HIM TO SLEEP FOR A WHILE.
I NEED HIM WITHIN THE PENTAGRAM!
WHAT IF I MOVE YOUR ART PROJECT TO HIM?
NO! THE PENTAGRAM IS A DOORWAY. IT CAN'T BE MOVED. ONLY OPENED.
AAAH!
MY TK ISN'T BUDGING HIM.
QUICKLY! GET HIM INTO THE PENTAGRAM! THE DOORWAY WILL CLOSE!
HEY, MAN, YOU TRY MOVING A HULK!
UGHN.
YOU WANT HULK MOVED--

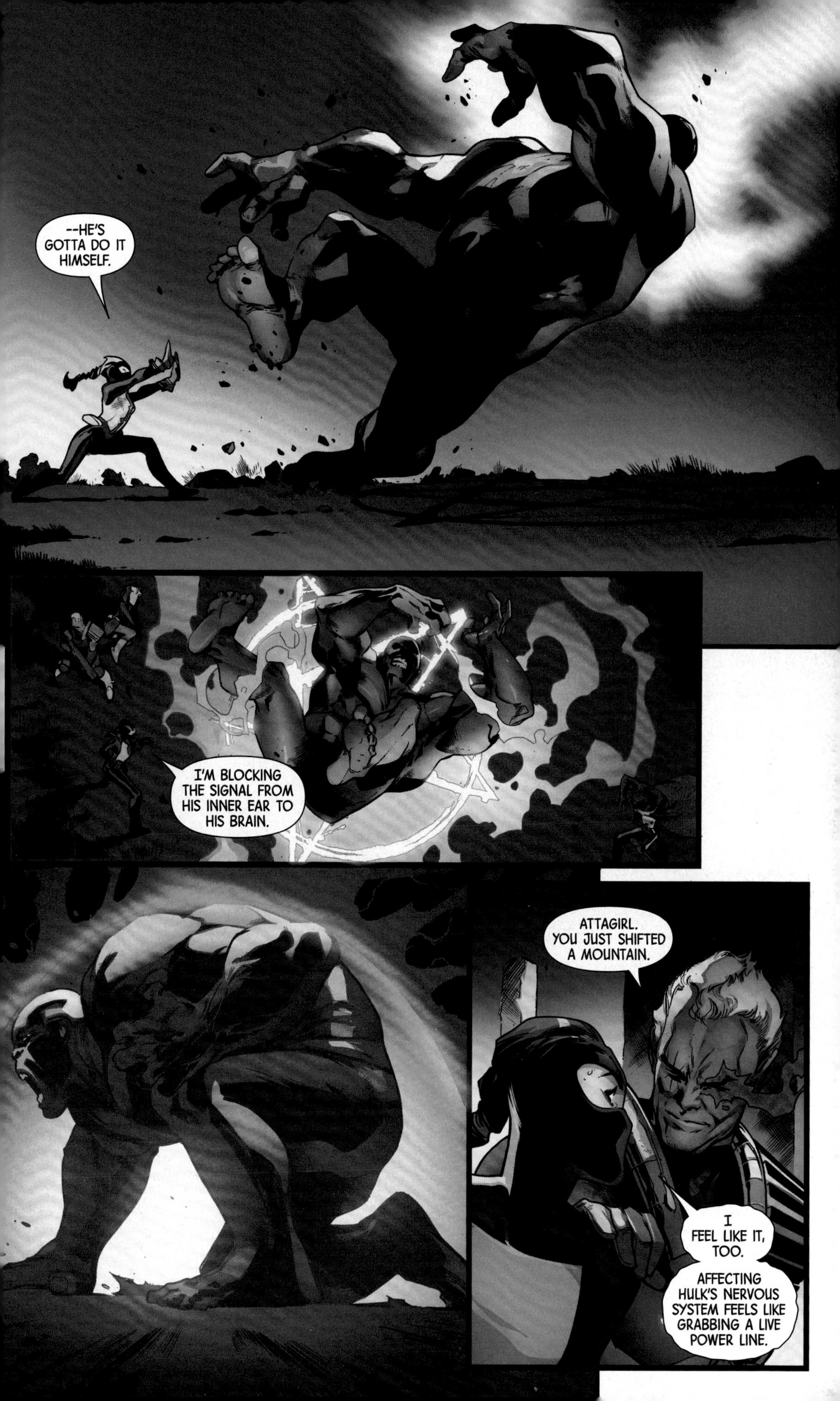
--HE'S GOTTA DO IT HIMSELF.
I'M BLOCKING THE SIGNAL FROM HIS INNER EAR TO HIS BRAIN.
ATTAGIRL. YOU JUST SHIFTED A MOUNTAIN.
I FEEL LIKE IT, TOO.
AFFECTING HULK'S NERVOUS SYSTEM FEELS LIKE GRABBING A LIVE POWER LINE.

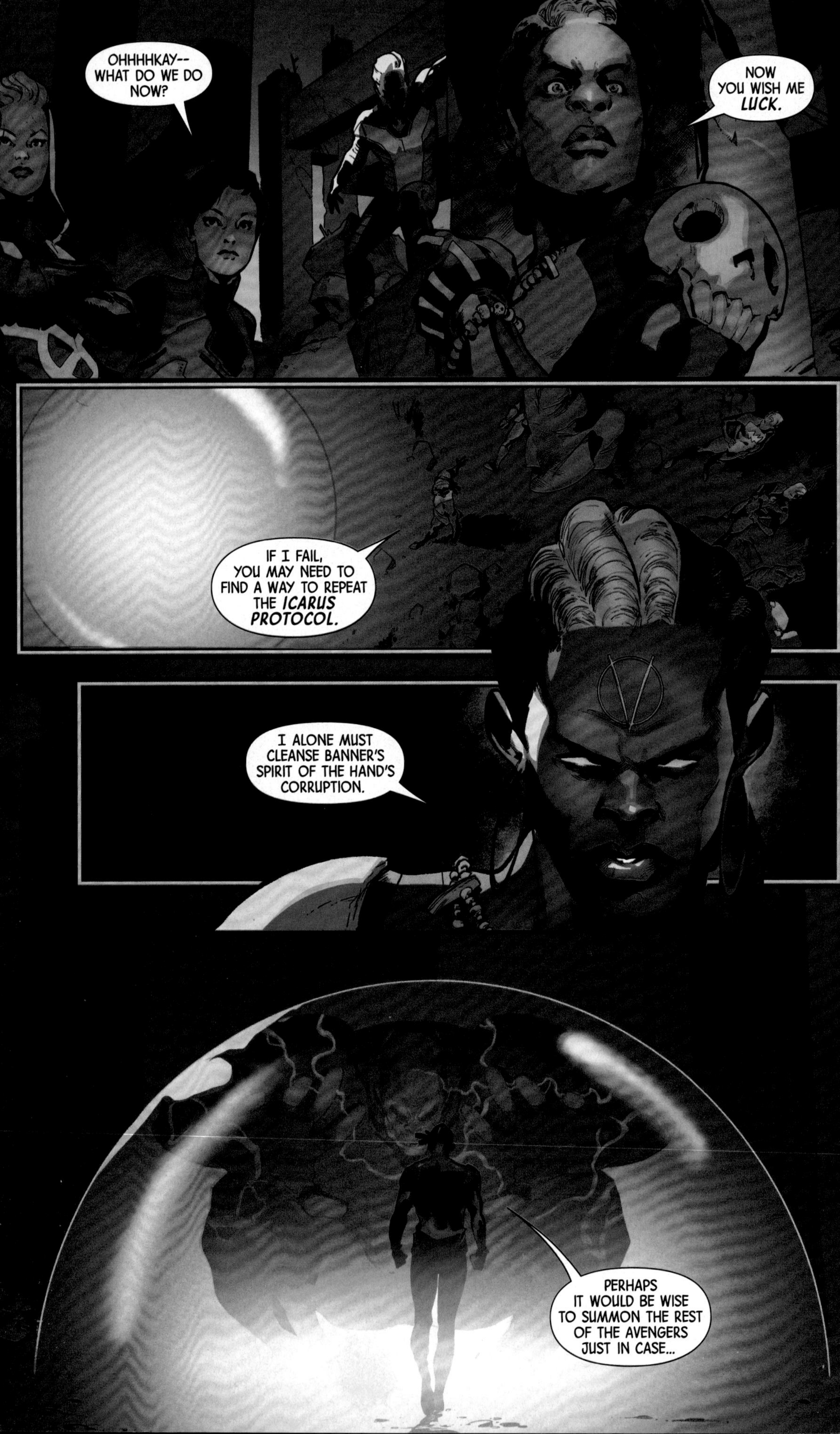
OHHHHKAY-- WHAT DO WE DO NOW?
NOW YOU WISH ME *LUCK.*
IF I FAIL, YOU MAY NEED TO FIND A WAY TO REPEAT THE *ICARUS PROTOCOL.*
I ALONE MUST CLEANSE BANNER'S SPIRIT OF THE HAND'S CORRUPTION.
PERHAPS IT WOULD BE WISE TO SUMMON THE REST OF THE AVENGERS JUST IN CASE...

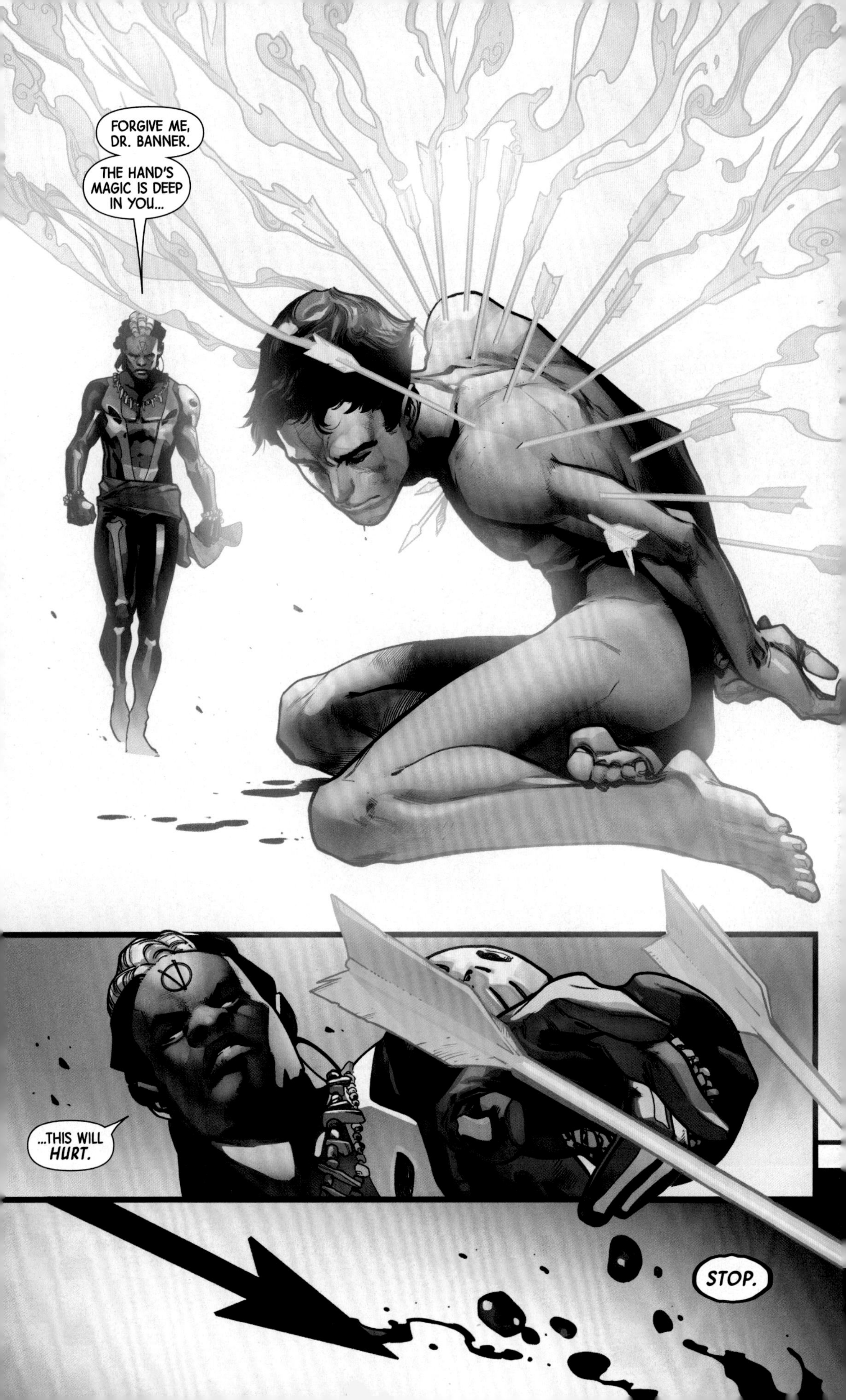
FORGIVE ME, DR. BANNER.
THE HAND'S MAGIC IS DEEP IN YOU...
...THIS WILL HURT.
STOP.

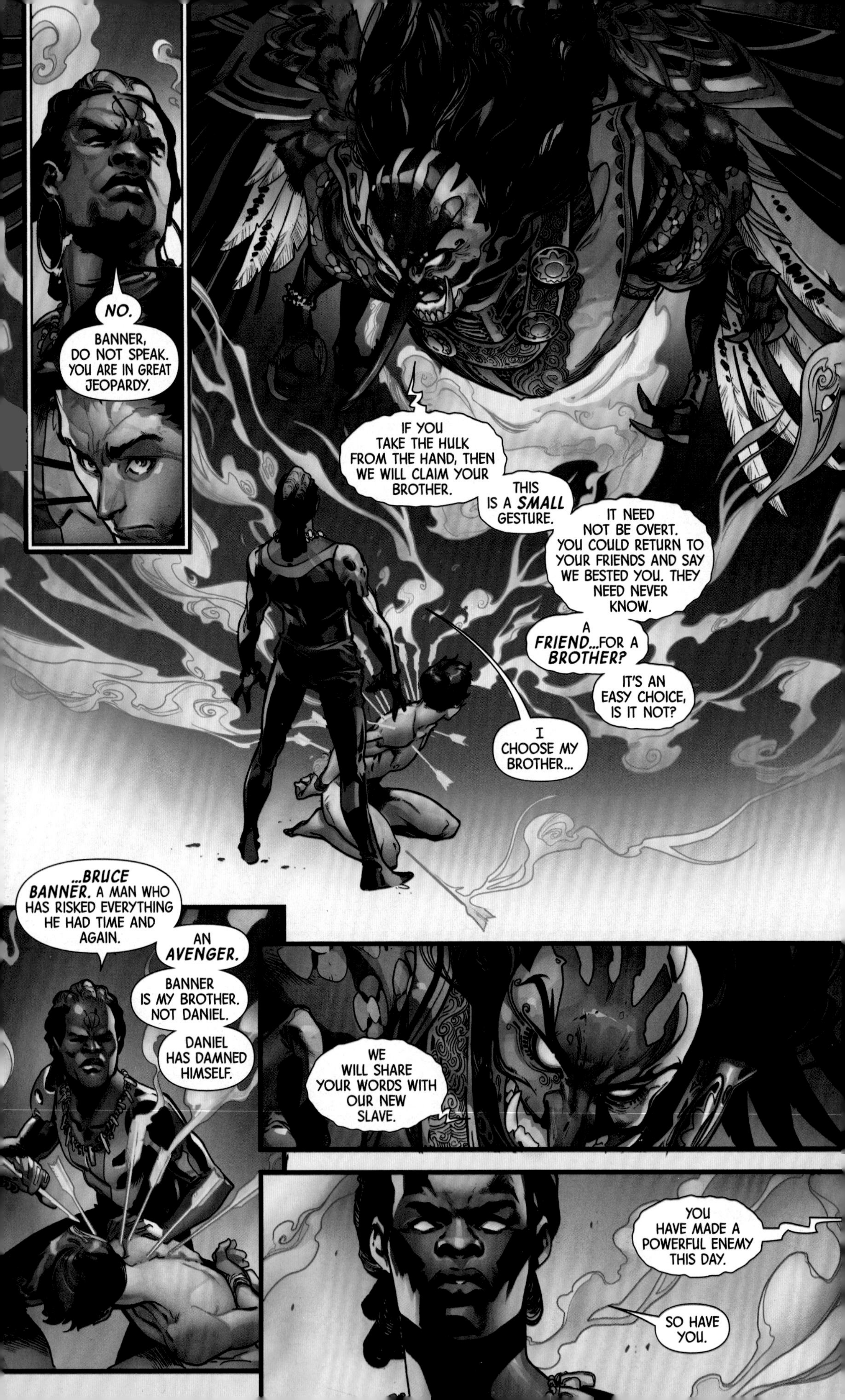
NO.
BANNER, DO NOT SPEAK. YOU ARE IN GREAT JEOPARDY.
IF YOU TAKE THE HULK FROM THE HAND, THEN WE WILL CLAIM YOUR BROTHER.
THIS IS A SMALL GESTURE.
IT NEED NOT BE OVERT. YOU COULD RETURN TO YOUR FRIENDS AND SAY WE BESTED YOU. THEY NEED NEVER KNOW.
A FRIEND...FOR A BROTHER?
IT'S AN EASY CHOICE, IS IT NOT?
I CHOOSE MY BROTHER...
...BRUCE BANNER. A MAN WHO HAS RISKED EVERYTHING HE HAD TIME AND AGAIN.
AN AVENGER.
BANNER IS MY BROTHER. NOT DANIEL.
DANIEL HAS DAMNED HIMSELF.
WE WILL SHARE YOUR WORDS WITH OUR NEW SLAVE.
YOU HAVE MADE A POWERFUL ENEMY THIS DAY.
SO HAVE YOU.

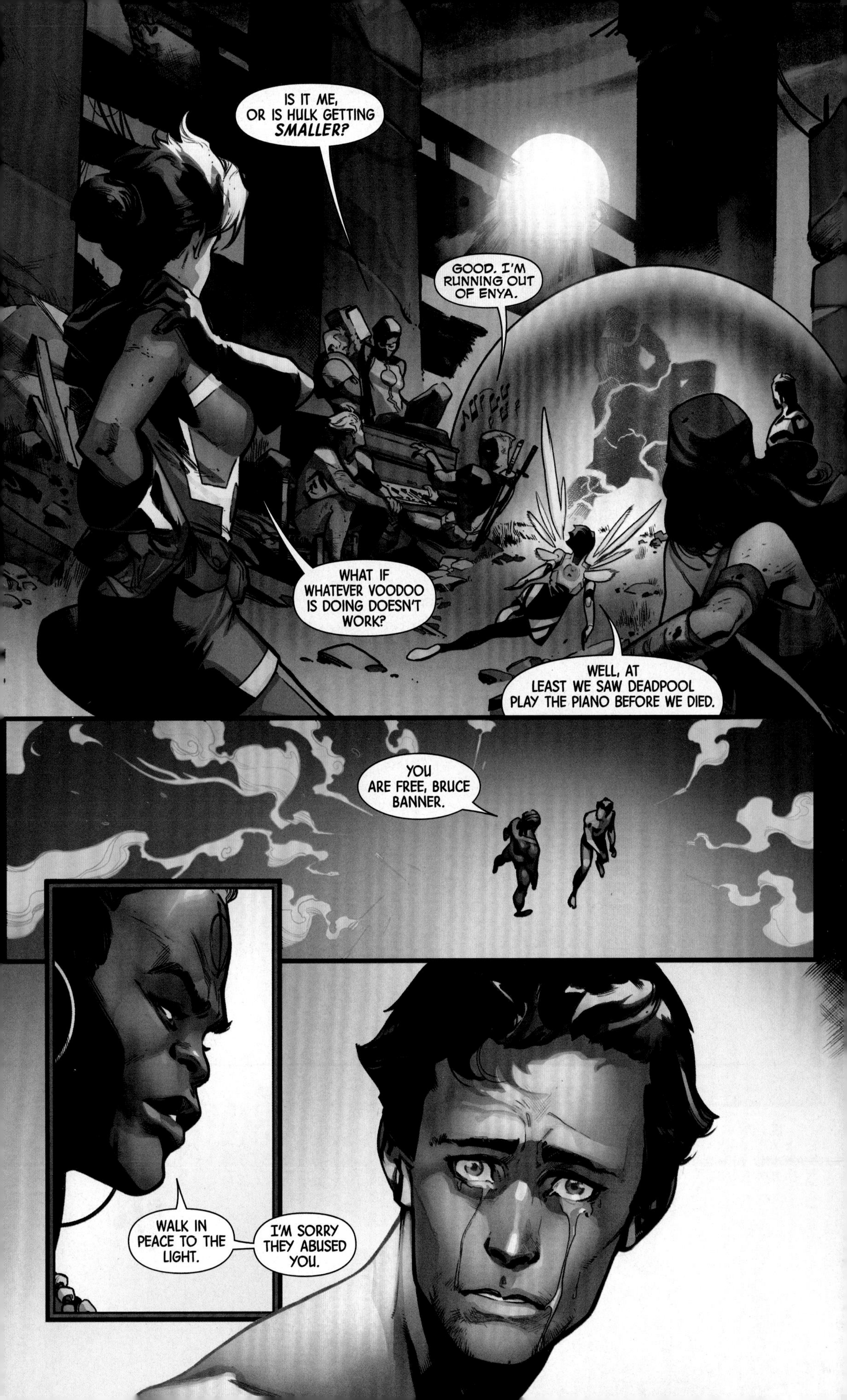
IS IT ME, OR IS HULK GETTING *SMALLER?*
GOOD. I'M RUNNING OUT OF ENYA.
WHAT IF WHATEVER VOODOO IS DOING DOESN'T WORK?
WELL, AT LEAST WE SAW DEADPOOL PLAY THE PIANO BEFORE WE DIED.
YOU ARE FREE, BRUCE BANNER.
WALK IN PEACE TO THE LIGHT.
I'M SORRY THEY ABUSED YOU.

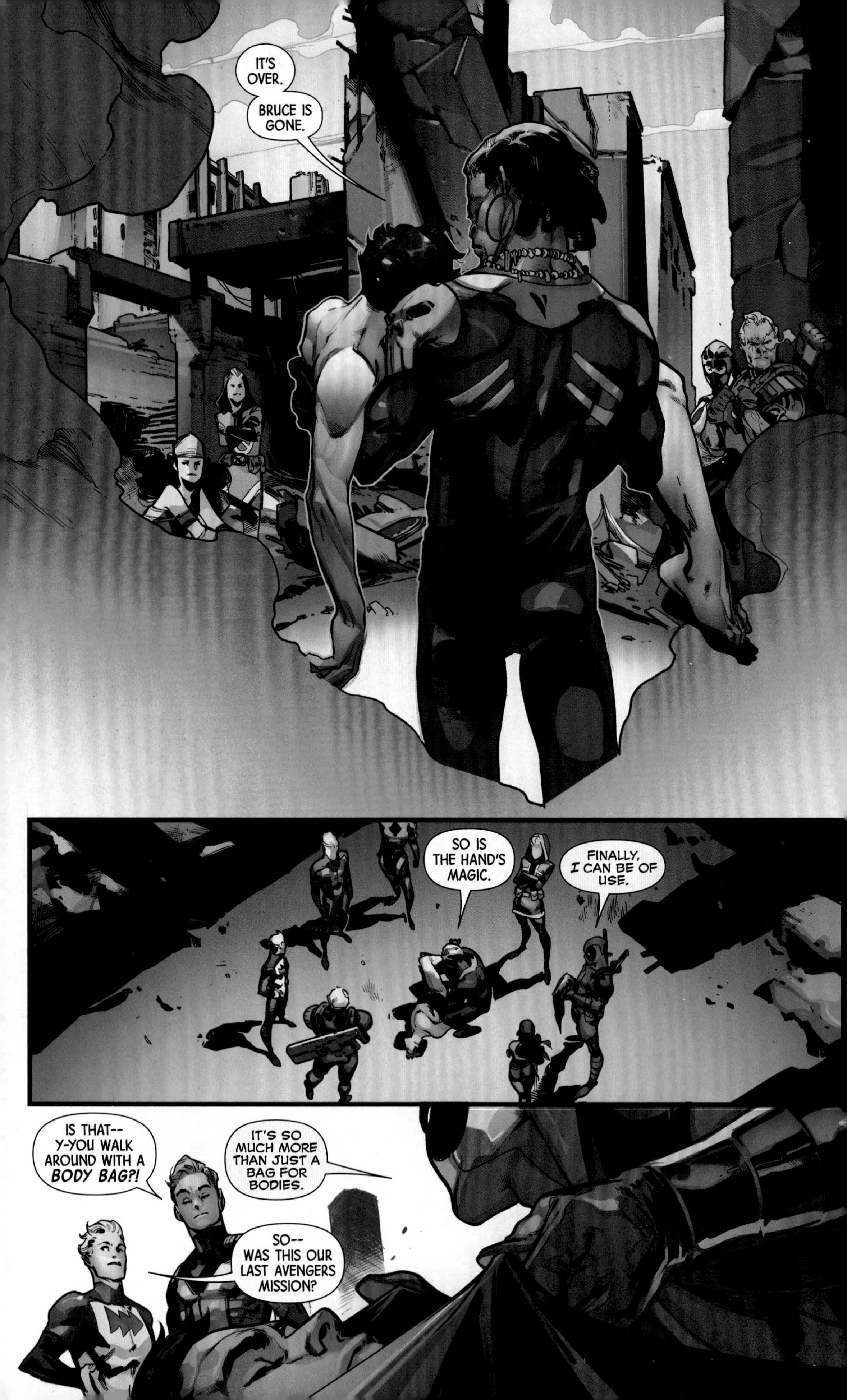
IT'S OVER.
BRUCE IS GONE.
SO IS THE HAND'S MAGIC.
FINALLY, I CAN BE OF USE.
IS THAT-- Y-YOU WALK AROUND WITH A BODY BAG?!
IT'S SO MUCH MORE THAN JUST A BAG FOR BODIES.
SO-- WAS THIS OUR LAST AVENGERS MISSION?

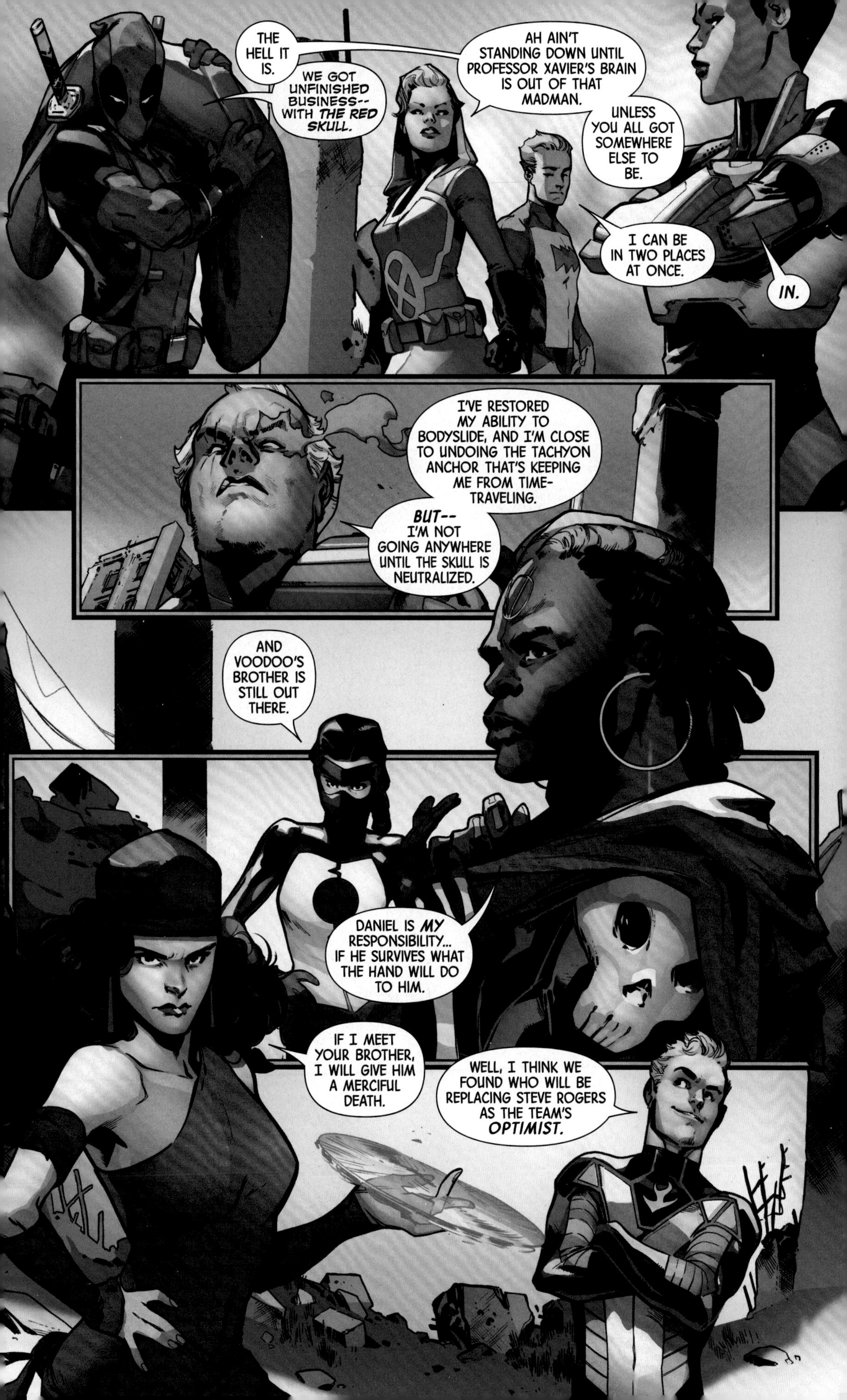

THE HELL IT IS.
WE GOT UNFINISHED BUSINESS-- WITH THE RED SKULL.
AH AIN'T STANDING DOWN UNTIL PROFESSOR XAVIER'S BRAIN IS OUT OF THAT MADMAN.
UNLESS YOU ALL GOT SOMEWHERE ELSE TO BE.
I CAN BE IN TWO PLACES AT ONCE.
IN.
I'VE RESTORED MY ABILITY TO BODYSLIDE, AND I'M CLOSE TO UNDOING THE TACHYON ANCHOR THAT'S KEEPING ME FROM TIME-TRAVELING.
BUT-- I'M NOT GOING ANYWHERE UNTIL THE SKULL IS NEUTRALIZED.
AND VOODOO'S BROTHER IS STILL OUT THERE.
DANIEL IS MY RESPONSIBILITY... IF HE SURVIVES WHAT THE HAND WILL DO TO HIM.
IF I MEET YOUR BROTHER, I WILL GIVE HIM A MERCIFUL DEATH.
WELL, I THINK WE FOUND WHO WILL BE REPLACING STEVE ROGERS AS THE TEAM'S OPTIMIST.

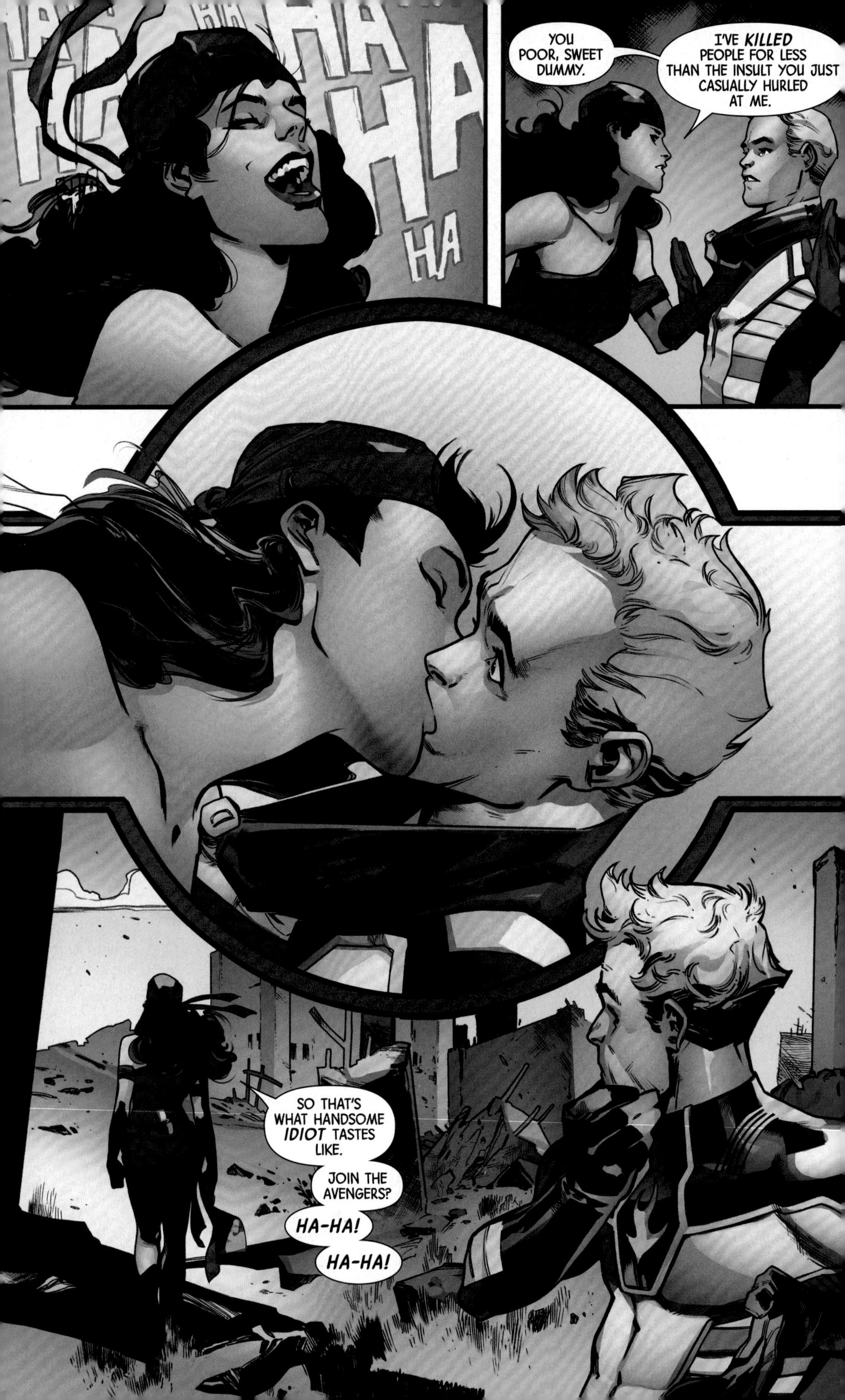
HA HA HA HA HA HA
HA
YOU POOR, SWEET DUMMY.
I'VE KILLED PEOPLE FOR LESS THAN THE INSULT YOU JUST CASUALLY HURLED AT ME.
SO THAT'S WHAT HANDSOME IDIOT TASTES LIKE.
JOIN THE AVENGERS?
HA-HA!
HA-HA!

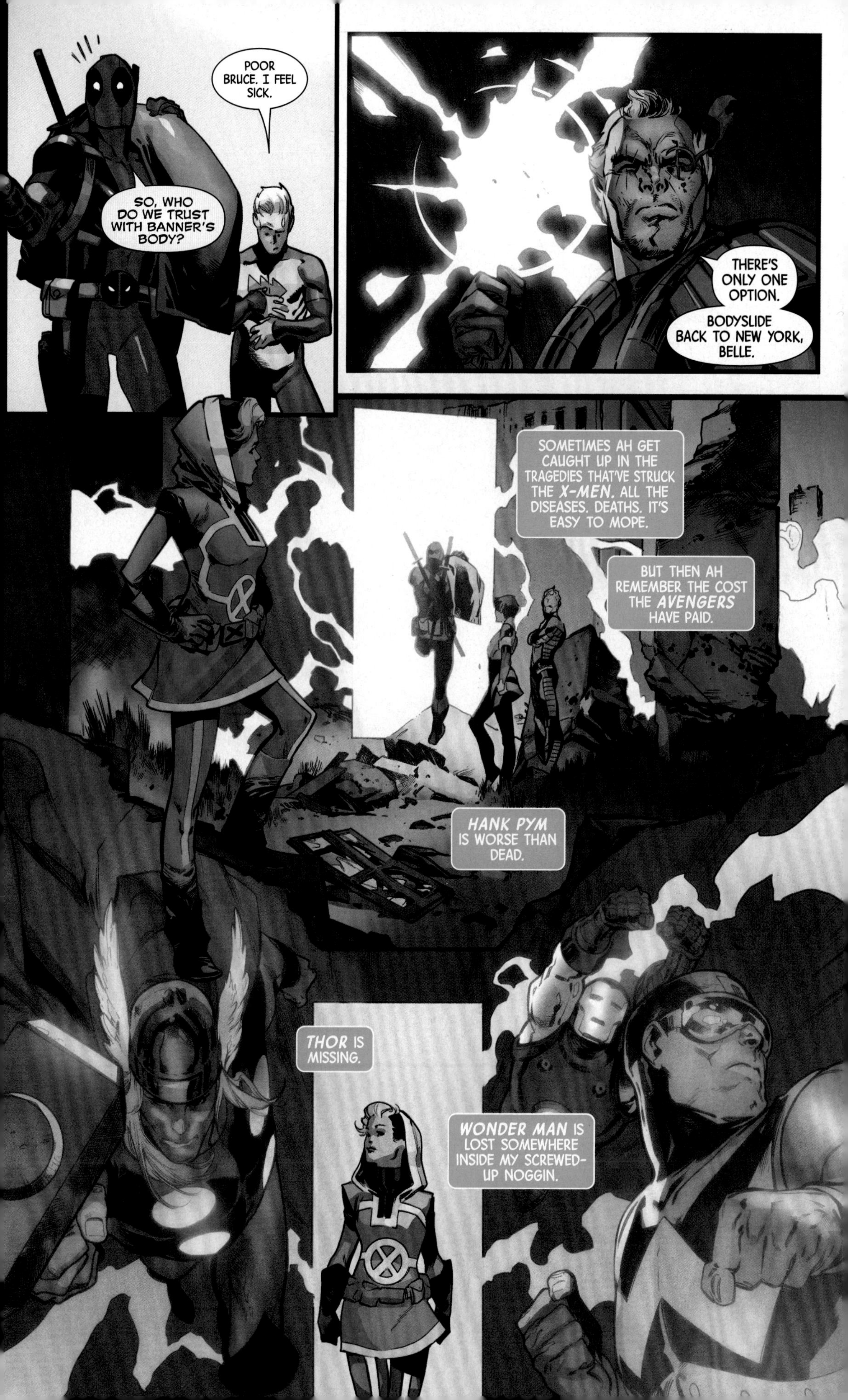
POOR BRUCE. I FEEL SICK.
SO, WHO DO WE TRUST WITH BANNER'S BODY?
THERE'S ONLY ONE OPTION.
BODYSLIDE BACK TO NEW YORK, BELLE.
SOMETIMES AH GET CAUGHT UP IN THE TRAGEDIES THAT'VE STRUCK THE X-MEN. ALL THE DISEASES. DEATHS. IT'S EASY TO MOPE.
BUT THEN AH REMEMBER THE COST THE AVENGERS HAVE PAID.
HANK PYM IS WORSE THAN DEAD.
THOR IS MISSING.
WONDER MAN IS LOST SOMEWHERE INSIDE MY SCREWED-UP NOGGIN.

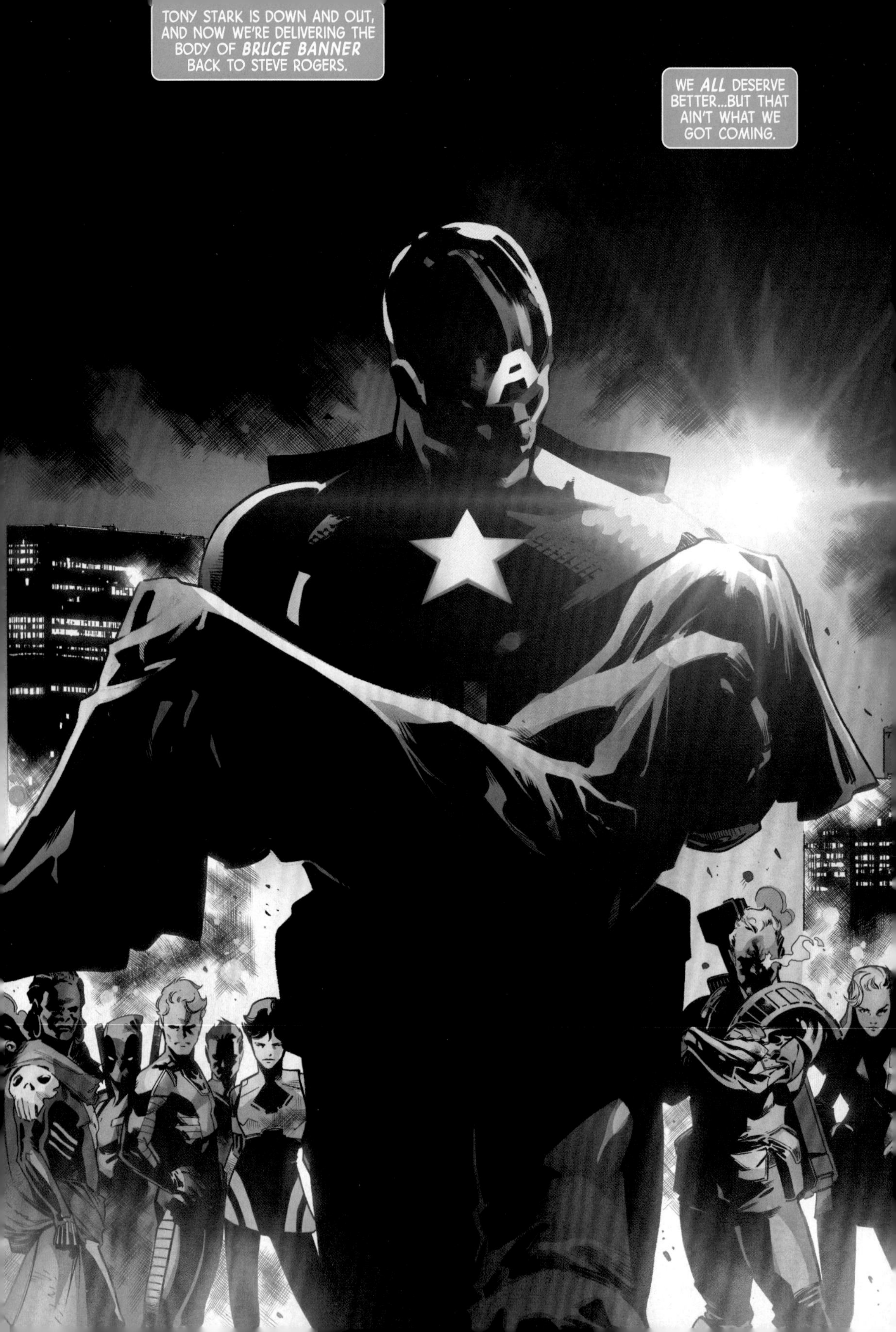
TONY STARK IS DOWN AND OUT, AND NOW WE'RE DELIVERING THE BODY OF BRUCE BANNER BACK TO STEVE ROGERS.
WE ALL DESERVE BETTER...BUT THAT AIN'T WHAT WE GOT COMING.

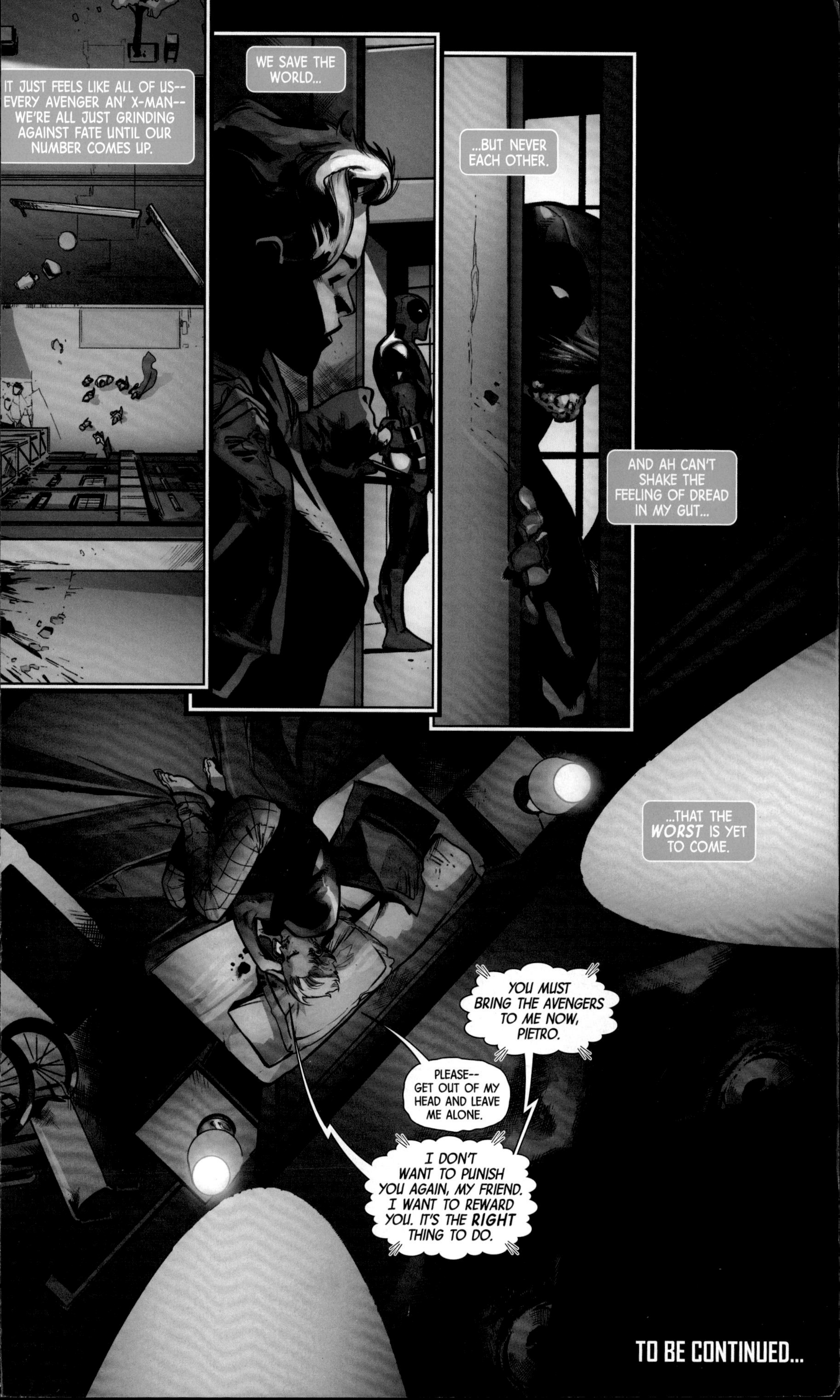

IT JUST FEELS LIKE ALL OF US-- EVERY AVENGER AN' X-MAN-- WE'RE ALL JUST GRINDING AGAINST FATE UNTIL OUR NUMBER COMES UP.
WE SAVE THE WORLD...
...BUT NEVER EACH OTHER.
AND AH CAN'T SHAKE THE FEELING OF DREAD IN MY GUT...
...THAT THE WORST IS YET TO COME.
YOU MUST BRING THE AVENGERS TO ME NOW, PIETRO.
PLEASE-- GET OUT OF MY HEAD AND LEAVE ME ALONE.
I DON'T WANT TO PUNISH YOU AGAIN, MY FRIEND. I WANT TO REWARD YOU. IT'S THE RIGHT THING TO DO.
TO BE CONTINUED...

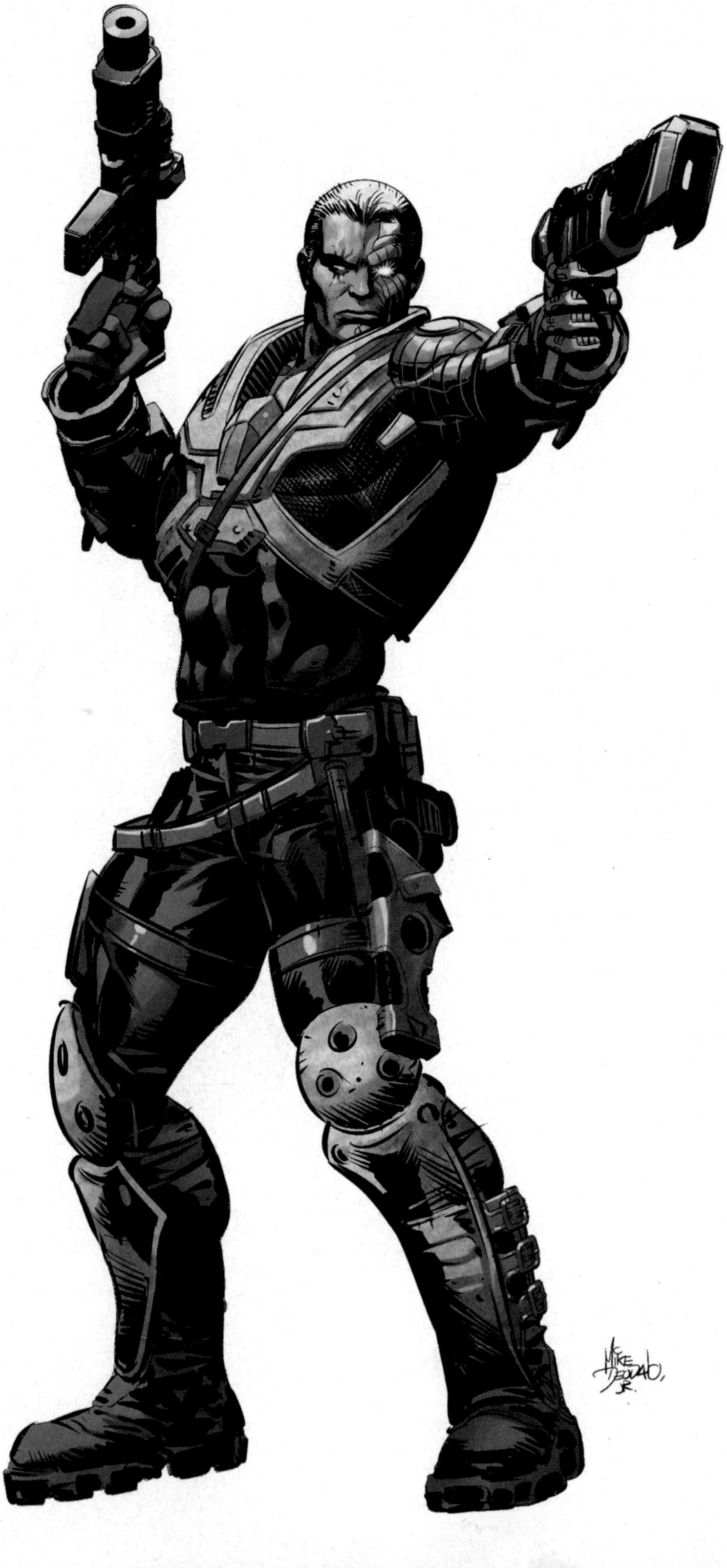

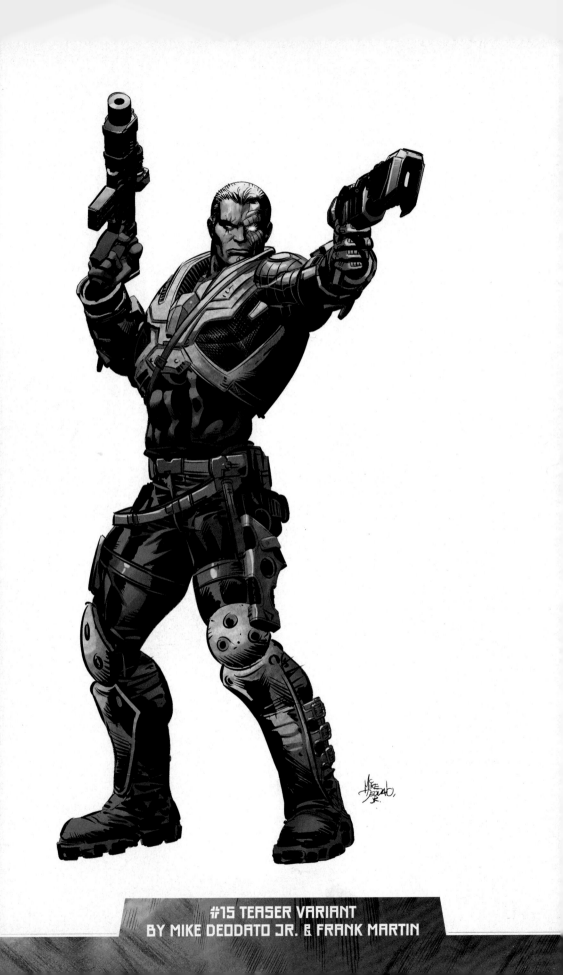

#15 TEASER VARIANT
BY MIKE DEODATO JR. & FRANK MARTIN

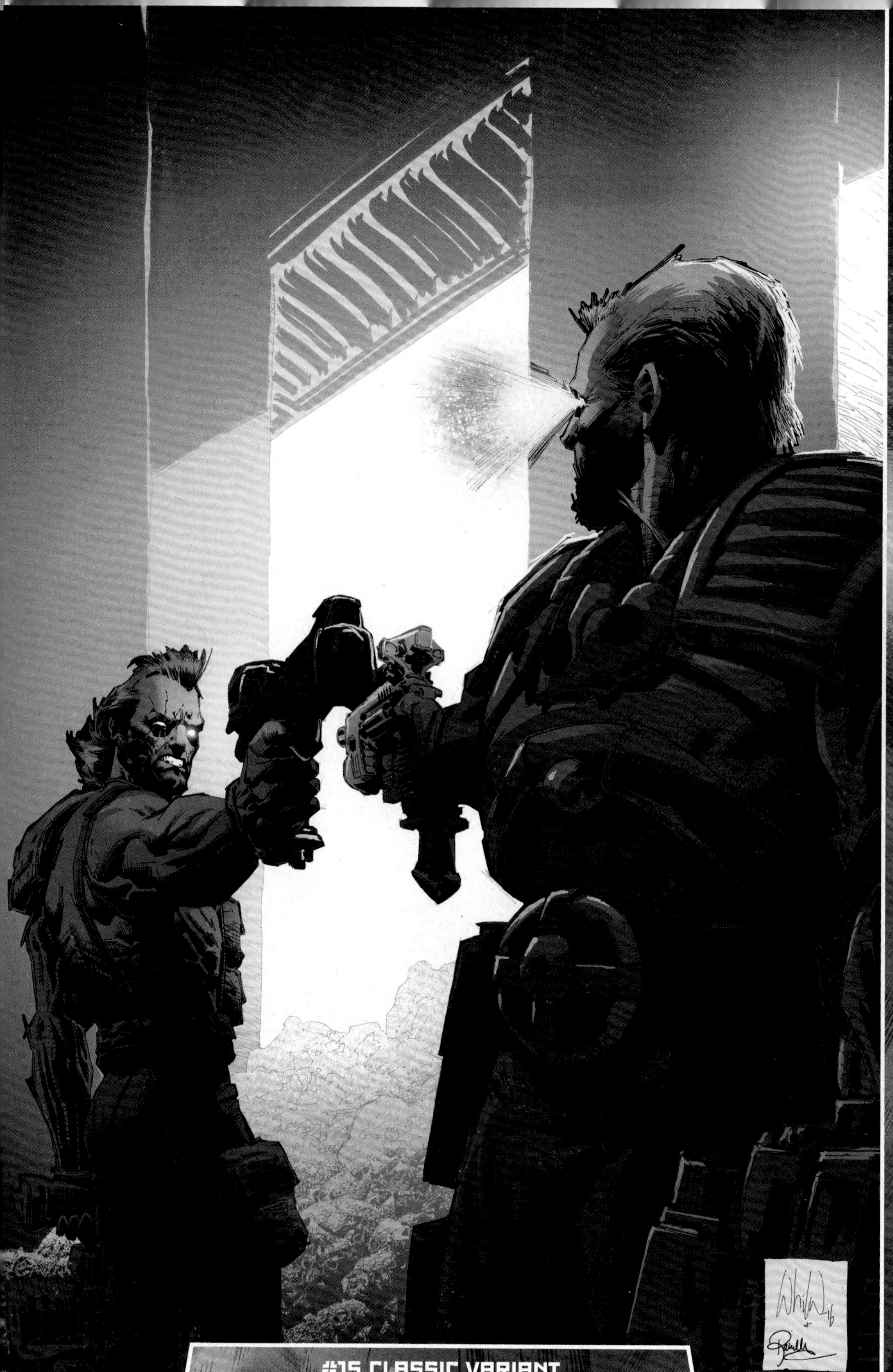

#15 CLASSIC VARIANT
BY WHILCE PORTACIO & CHRIS SOTOMAYOR